MW01578883

The Bishops of the American Church, Past and Present: Sketches, Biographical and Bibliographical, of the Bishops of the American Church, with a Preliminary Essay On the Historic Episcopate and Documentary Annals of the Introduction of the Anglican Line of

William Stevens Perry

The Bishops of the American Church Past and Present

Sketches, Biographical and Bibliographical, of the Bishops of the American Church, with a Preliminary Essay on the Historic Episcopate and Documentary Annals of the introduction of the Anglican line of succession into America

By

William Stevens Perry

Bishop of Iowa

and

Historiographer of the American Church

New York

The Christian Literature Co.

MDCCCXCVII

CONTENTS.

PAGE

ADVERTISEMENT vii
PREFACE ix
INTRODUCTION xi
BIOGRAPHIES:
Samuel Seabury 1
William White 5
Samuel Provoost 9
James Madison 11
Thomas John Claggett 13
Robert Smith 15
Edward Bass 17
Abraham Jarvis 19
Benjamin Moore 21
Samuel Parker 23
John Henry Hobart 25
Alexander Viets Griswold 29
Theodore Dehon 31
Richard Channing Moore 33
James Kemp 35
John Croes 37
Nathaniel Bowen 39
Philander Chase 41
Thomas Church Brownell 45
John Stark Ravenscroft 47
Henry Ustick Onderdonk 49
William Meade 51
William Murray Stone 53
Benjamin Tredwell Onderdonk 55
Levi Silliman Ives 57
John Henry Hopkins 59
Benjamin Bosworth Smith 63
Charles Pettit McIlvaine 65
George Washington Doane 67
James Hervey Otey 69
Jackson Kemper 71
Samuel Allen McCoskry 73
Leonidas Polk 75
William Heathcote De Lancey 77
Christopher Edwards Gadsden 79

PAGE
William Rollinson Whittingham 81
Stephen Elliott 83
Alfred Lee 85
John Johns 87
Manton Eastburn 89
John Prentiss Kewley Henshaw 91
Carlton Chase 93
Nicholas Hamner Cobbs 95
Cicero Stephens Hawks 97
William Jones Boone 99
George Washington Freeman 101
Horatio Southgate 103
Alonzo Potter 105
George Burgess 107
George Upfold 109
William Mercer Green 111
John Payne 113
Francis Huger Rutledge 115
John Williams 117
Henry John Whitehouse 119
Jonathan Mayhew Wainwright 121
Thomas Frederick Davis 123
Thomas Atkinson 125
William Ingraham Kip 127
Thomas Fielding Scott 129
Henry Washington Lee 131
Horatio Potter 133
Thomas March Clark 135
Samuel Bowman 137
Alexander Gregg 139
William Henry Odenheimer 141
Gregory Thurston Bedell 143
Henry Benjamin Whipple 145
Henry Champlin Lay 147
Joseph Cruikshank Talbot 149
William Bacon Stevens 151
Richard Hooker Wilmer 155
Thomas Hubbard Vail 157
Arthur Cleveland Coxe 159
Charles Todd Quintard 163
Robert Harper Clarkson 165
George Maxwell Randall 167
John Barrett Kerfoot 169
Channing Moore Williams 171
Joseph Pere Bell Wilmer 173
George David Cummins 175
William Edmond Armitage 177
Henry Adams Neely 179
Daniel Sylvester Tuttle 181

	PAGE
John Freeman Young	183
John Watrus Beckwith	185
Francis McNeece Whittle	187
William Henry Augustus Bissell	189
Charles Franklin Robertson	191
Benjamin Wistar Morris	193
Abram Newkirk Littlejohn	195
William Croswell Doane	197
Frederic Dan Huntington	199
Ozi William Whitaker	201
Henry Niles Pierce	203
William Woodruff Niles	205
William Pinkney	207
William Bell White Howe	209
Mark Antony De Wolfe Howe	211
William Hobart Hare	213
John Gottlieb Auer	215
Benjamin Henry Paddock	217
Theodore Benedict Lyman	219
John Franklin Spalding	221
Edward Randolph Welles	223
Robert Woodward Barnwell Elliott	225
John Henry Ducachet Wingfield	227
Alexander Charles Garrett	229
William Forbes Adams	231
Thomas Underwood Dudley	233
John Scarborough	235
George De Normandie Gillespie	237
Thomas Augustus Jaggar	239
William Edward McLaren	241
John Henry Hobart Brown	243
William Stevens Perry	245
Charles Clifton Penick	249
Samuel Isaac Joseph Schereschewsky	251
Alexander Burgess	253
George William Peterkin	255
George Franklin Seymour	257
Samuel Smith Harris	259
Thomas Alfred Starkey	261
John Nicholas Galleher	263
George Kelly Dunlop	265
Leigh Richmond Brewer	267
John Adams Paddock	269
Cortlandt Whitehead	271
Hugh Miller Thompson	273
David Buel Knickerbacker	275
Henry Codman Potter	277
Alfred Magill Randolph	279
William David Walker	281

PAGE
Alfred Augustin Watson 283
William Jones Boone 285
Nelson Somerville Rulison 287
William Paret 289
George Worthington 291
Samuel David Ferguson 293
Edwin Gardner Weed 295
Mahlon Norris Gilbert 297
Elisha Smith Thomas 299
Ethelbert Talbot 301
James Steptoe Johnston 303
Abiel Leonard 305
Leighton Coleman 307
John Mills Kendrick 309
Boyd Vincent 311
Cyrus Frederick Knight 313
Charles Chapman Grafton 315
William Andrew Leonard 317
Thomas Frederick Davies 319
Anson Rogers Graves 321
William Ford Nichols 323
Edward Robert Atwill 325
Henry Melville Jackson 327
Davis Sessums 329
Phillips Brooks 331
Isaac Lea Nicholson 335
Cleland Kinloch Nelson 337
Charles Reuben Hale 339
George Herbert Kinsolving 341
Lemuel Henry Wells 343
William Crane Gray 345
Francis Key Brooke 347
William Morris Barker 349
John McKim 351
Frederick Rogers Graves 353
Ellison Capers 355
Thomas Frank Gailor 357
William Lawrence 359
Joseph Blount Cheshire 361
Arthur Crawshay Alliston Hall 363
John Brockenbrough Newton 365
John Hazen White 367
Frank Rosebrook Millspaugh 369
Peter Trimble Rowe 371
Lewis William Burton 373
Joseph Horsfall Johnson 375
Henry Yates Satterlee 377
Gershom Mott Williams 379
James Dow Morrison 381
Chauncey Bunce Brewster 383
Robert Atkinson Gibson 385

ADVERTISEMENT.

THE interest surrounding the first complete collection of photographs of American bishops published warrants a brief recital of the difficulties involved in gathering them.

The aim to secure the best, as well as the latest, likeness had frequently to be limited to securing any likeness at all; for certain of the bishops never sat for portraits. It is generally believed, for example, that no portrait was ever made of Bishop Dehon, although a very rare silhouette exists. By diligent searching, however, a poor photograph was discovered, from which a pen-and-ink drawing was made, which is reproduced on page 30. Neither Mr. J. Pierpont Morgan's very full collection, nor any other that we know of, possesses a photograph of this prelate. Bishop Madison was never known to have sat for a portrait, and tradition says that the painting of that diocesan now in the possession of Mrs. S. M. Chamberlayne, of Richmond, Va. (through whose kind permission we secured a photograph from this painting), is in reality a portrait of his daughter, who strongly resembled him, taken after her father's death. Bishop Whittingham's portrait was not painted during his lifetime, although a daguerreotype was taken about 1845. Mrs. Rollinson Colburn, of Washington, D. C., a personal friend of Bishop Whittingham, made pencil-sketches of him in 1871, while he was visiting at her home, from which a large (copyright) portrait was painted after his death, in 1879. Huntington painted his portrait from the old daguerreotype; but as this represents the bishop in his younger days, it has been thought well to photograph the very excellent likeness by Mrs. Colburn, which she has generously allowed us to do. The painting was praised by Archbishop Trench and Bishop Pinkney, and is now reproduced for the first time, Brand, in his biography of Whittingham, having made use of Huntington's work.

We are also indebted to another member of this family—Miss Colburn—for our photographs of Bishops Green and Pinkney, taken from portraits painted by her, and truer in representation than hitherto published ones. Bishop C. M. Williams was one of those who would never sit for a portrait. His likeness appears in a group; but as the reproductions were unsatisfactory, a pen-and-ink sketch was made from the photograph.

Besides our portraits of Madison, Whittingham, Green, and Pinkney, taken from oil-paintings by photography, six others were produced in the same way, viz., those of Robert Smith, Jarvis, Kemp, H. U. Onderdonk, Stone, and Gadsden.

In cases where photographs are not known, or where they lack merit, we have, wherever it has been possible, made use of engravings. Twenty-nine of our portraits have been so taken. Of these the following were engraved by J. C. Buttre: White (from Sully's painting), Provoost, Claggett, Bass, Hobart, Griswold, R. C. Moore, Croes, Bowen, P. Chase, Brownell, Ravenscroft, McIlvaine, Otey, De Lancey, Henshaw, Freeman, Wainwright (from Brady's painting), and Cummins. The portrait of the senior Boone is from an engraving by Sartain, from Mooney's painting, and the likeness of Bishop Polk is also from an engraving by Sartain, and is used by permission of Dr. William H. Polk, of New York. The portraits of Bishops Meade and B. T. Onderdonk are from engravings by Neil and Ormsby respectively. The following are from engravings by unknown artists: Seabury, Benjamin Moore, Parker, Ives, Davis, and Hopkins.

All other illustrations are from photographs furnished by the bishops themselves, by members of their families, or by authorized photographers.

We are under obligations to the Rev. F. D. Jaudon, of Manston, Wis., and to the Rev. E. H. Porter, of Newport, R. I., for the loan of photographs and engravings from their collections, and to Mr. Rollinson Colburn, of Washington, D. C., for material assistance in many ways. Acknowledgments should also be made to the Rev. Samuel F. Jarvis, of Brooklyn, Conn., for the use of the large portrait of Bishop Jarvis, taken from the only painting of that prelate in existence; to Mr. D. E. Huger Smith, of Charleston, S. C., for a photograph of Bishop Smith, taken from the painting in possession of his brother, Mr. Robert Tilghman Smith; to the Rev. F. Chase, of Scarsdale, N. Y., for our likeness of Bishop Carlton Chase; and to the Rev. Montgomery Schuyler, of St. Louis, Mo., for that of Bishop Hawks.

PREFACE.

THE story of the introduction of the Anglican episcopate into America is full of incident. The lives of the men who have filled the office of bishop in the American Church are at once interesting and instructive. The contributions they have made to American literature, even in the midst of absorbing labors and constant cares, are both creditable and important. To tell the story of the struggle for the episcopate, to record briefly the lives of the bishops of the United States, and to furnish comprehensive lists of their literary works, is the object of this work. The dry skeleton of dates and facts has been clothed with such incidents and remarks as shall afford to the reader an understanding of their characters and the circumstances molding and influencing their lives. This has been attempted in the spirit of historical impartiality. The effort has been made to supply the means for correctly estimating both the men and the measures marking their official careers.

Besides the biographical sketches of the nearly two hundred priests who have been called to the office and administration of a bishop in the Church of God, we give, somewhat in detail, the story of the efforts, dating back to the early days of American discovery and settlement, made in this land and across the sea to secure for the colonial Church the completion of the three orders of the ministry, and the privilege and power of self-reproduction and self-rule. To this we add the documents which give the succession of the American bishops, connecting them through Aberdeen and Lambeth with the see of Canterbury, and back to the apostles and to the great Shepherd and Bishop of souls. An essay on "The Historic Episcopate" is added, embracing in simple statement and in the briefest possible compass the results of the latest scholarship respecting this question. The purpose of this paper is to give to those who are seeking a basis for Church unity an authoritative presentation of the Chicago-Lambeth propositions, and a defense of the position taken therein. There are papers on the episcopal succession in the Roman Catholic Church in the United States and on the Methodist "superintendency" of America, of which latter Thomas

Coke, LL.D., and Francis Asbury were the first appointments by the founder of Methodism, John Wesley.

The intelligent reader will find in these pages much to convince him that the episcopate in the United States, like that of other days and in other lands, has maintained the dignity of the order, and by labors, devotion, and consecrated lives has well and wisely ruled that portion of the Holy Catholic Church committed to its charge. Of these men of God it can truly be affirmed that their learning, their labors, their lives, will be found to have been freely, fully given *pro salute hominum et pro ecclesia Dei.*

BISHOP'S HOUSE, DAVENPORT, IA.,
Feast of the Ascension, A.D. 1895.

INTRODUCTION.

I.

THE HISTORIC EPISCOPATE.

THE critical examination of the New Testament writings for notices of the polity of the kingdom of heaven Christ set up when tabernacled in the flesh plainly indicates that the ultimate earthly authority there recognized was that exercised by the apostles, in the name of, and as representing, their Master, their Lord, their King, and that the means for the transmission of this authority was by the imposition of apostolic hands. The Church already existed. The kingdom of heaven had long had its rulers and its rules. In other words, the principle of individual overseership or episcopacy, exercised by the apostles first, and by apostolic delegates afterward, and gradually taking shape in most easily recognized and definite form, *is* found in the New Testament Scriptures as an existing fact, while we may search their pages in vain for any indication of the principle of presbyterian parity or of congregational democracy. Few and scattered as are the New Testament allusions to the polity of the Church in the days in which the apostles were still present on the earth, the trend of each and all of these passages is evident. The source of power in the Church was not from the people or of the people; it was from above; and in these scanty notices we see apostolic rule gradually merging into episcopal authority and power.

The exercise of the commission of their Master—"As the Father hath sent Me, even so send I you"—by the Twelve, chosen not by the company of believers, but by the Lord Himself; the solemn investiture of Matthias—not by the people, but by the Eleven acting under divine guidance—with the office from which Judas fell; the choice of the great apostle to the Gentiles by the Head of the Church Himself—"an apostle, not of men, neither by man, but by Jesus Christ, and God the Father";[1] the headship of the Church at Jerusalem, as well as the title of "apostle," so plainly accorded

[1] Galatians i. 1.

by St. Paul to "James, the Lord's brother," who was evidently not one of the Twelve; the absence of any hint that the apostolate was to be limited to the Twelve, and, on the other hand, the application of the title to Barnabas,[1] to Andronicus and Junia,[2] probably to Silvanus,[3] and to others by St. Paul; the condemnation of "false apostles"; the committal by St. Paul of the charge of the Churches he had founded to Timothy and Titus; the latest messages of the Head of the Church, not to the people, but to the rulers, the "angels," the individually responsible heads of the apocalyptic Churches—these are each and all parts of that vast network of scriptural testimony uniting with its countless meshes the Church's chief Shepherd and Bishop of souls with the threefold ministry and the polity of the kingdom of heaven which, ere the death of the last of the apostles, St. John, was universally established throughout the Church of Christ.

It is the judgment of Dr. Lightfoot, late bishop of Durham, that "history seems to show decisively that before the middle of the second century each church or organized Christian community had its three orders of ministers—its bishop, its presbyters, and its deacons. On this point there cannot reasonably be two opinions."[4] The same distinguished scholar, in commenting on the position occupied by St. James, the brother of the Lord, in the Church of Jerusalem, after expressing his conviction that "he was not one of the Twelve," asserts that "the episcopal office thus existed in the mother-church of Jerusalem from very early days, at least in a rudimentary form";[5] while the government of the Gentile churches,

[1] "The apostleship of Barnabas is beyond question. St. Luke records his consecration to the office as taking place at the same time with, and in the same manner as, St. Paul's (Acts xiii. 2, 3). In his account of their missionary labors he again names them together as 'apostles,' even mentioning Barnabas first (Acts xiv. 4, 14). St. Paul himself also in two different epistles uses similar language. In the Galatian letter he speaks of Barnabas as associated with himself in the apostleship of the Gentiles (ii. 9); in the first to the Corinthians he claims for his fellow-laborer all the privileges of an apostle, as one who, like himself, holds the office of an apostle and is doing the work of an apostle (ix. 5, 6). If, therefore, St. Paul has held a larger place than Barnabas in the gratitude and veneration of the Church of all ages, this is due, not to any superiority of rank or office, but to the ascendancy of his personal gifts, a more intense energy and self-devotion, wider and deeper sympathies, a firmer intellectual grasp, a larger measure of the spirit of Christ."—Bishop Lightfoot's "Epistle to the Galatians," pp. 96, 97.

[2] "On the most natural interpretation of a passage in the Epistle to the Romans (xvi. 7), Andronicus and Junia, two Christians otherwise unknown to us, are called distinguished members of the apostolate—language which indirectly implies a very considerable extension of the term."—*Ibid.*, p. 95.

[3] "In 1 Thessalonians ii. 6, again, where . . . he speaks of the disinterested labors of himself and his colleagues, adding, 'though *we* might have been burdensome to you, being apostles of Christ,' it is probable that under this term he includes Silvanus, who had labored with him in Thessalonica, and whose name appears in the superscription of the letter."—*Ibid.*

[4] Bishop Lightfoot's "Dissertation on the Christian Ministry," appended to his "Commentary on the Philippians," p. 184.

[5] *Ibid.*, p. 196.

though presenting no distinct traces of a similar organization, exhibits "stages of development tending in this direction."[1] Lightfoot, who discusses this subject with singular moderation and fairness, concedes that the position occupied by Timothy and Titus, whom he styles "apostolic delegates," "fairly represents the functions of the bishop early in the second century."[2] Even admitting with Lightfoot that "James, the Lord's brother, alone, within the period compassed by the apostolic writings, can claim to be regarded as a bishop in the later and more special sense of the term," and that "as late, therefore, as the year 70 no distinct signs of episcopal government have appeared in Gentile Christendom," still it must be acknowledged, in the language of the same authority, that "unless we have recourse to a sweeping condemnation of received documents, it seems vain to deny that early in the second century the episcopal office was firmly and widely established. Thus, during the last three decades of the first century, and consequently during the lifetime of the latest surviving apostle, this change must have been brought about."[3] Again and again does this great scholar refer to the fact of the early and general establishment of episcopacy "from the apostles' times." For example, he asserts that "the evidence for the early and wide extension of episcopacy throughout proconsular Asia, the scene of St. John's latest labors, may be considered irrefragable."[4] And again, "These notices, besides establishing the general prevalence of episcopacy, . . . establish this result clearly: that its maturer forms are seen first in those regions where the latest surviving apostles, more especially St. John, fixed their abode, and at a time when its prevalence cannot be dissociated from their influence or their sanction."[5]

And again, "It has been seen that the institution of an episcopate must be placed as far back as the closing years of the first century, and that it cannot, without violence to historical testimony, be dissevered from the name of St. John."[6] "It will appear," continues Lightfoot, "that the pressing needs of the Church were mainly instrumental in bringing about this result, and that this development of the episcopal office was a providential safeguard amid the confusion of speculative opinion, the distracting effects of persecution, and the growing anarchy of social life, which threatened not only the extension but the very existence of the Church of Christ."[7] With this cumulative presentation of the proofs of the historic episcopate from the writings of the leading scholar of the age, we may be prepared for the bishop's summing up of the whole matter among the closing words of his "Dissertation on the Christian Ministry": "If the preceding investigation is substantially cor-

[1] Lightfoot's "Christian Ministry," p. 196. [2] *Ibid.*, p. 197. [3] *Ibid.*, p. 199. [4] *Ibid.*, p. 212. [5] *Ibid.*, pp. 225, 226. [6] *Ibid.*, p. 232. [7] *Ibid.*

rect, the threefold ministry can be traced to apostolic direction; and short of an express statement we can possess no better assurance of a divine appointment, or at least a divine sanction."[1] In even stronger language, in his sermon before the Wolverhampton Church Congress, he asserts that the Church of England has "retained a from of church government which had been handed down in unbroken continuity from the apostles' times."

With these statements and these proofs the language of the Ordinal of the Book of Common Prayer is in strict accord: "It is evident unto all men diligently reading Holy Scripture and ancient authors that from the apostles' time there have been these three orders of ministers in Christ's Church—bishops, priests, and deacons." The full meaning of this statement appears in the fact that it is the requirement of the canon law of the Church, as well as of the Ordinal, that "no man shall be accounted or taken to be a lawful bishop, priest, or deacon, in this Church, or suffered to execute any of the said functions, except he be called, tried, examined, and admitted thereunto according to the form hereafter following, or hath had episcopal consecration or ordination." In the judgment of Lightfoot, as evidently in the intention of the Ordinal, the "historical episcopate" includes the apostolical succession—the threefold ministry communicated by the imposition of hands and continued "in unbroken continuity from the apostles' times."

To quote the language of Mr. Gladstone: "In the latter part of the second century of the Christian era the subject" of the apostolical succession "came into distinct and formal view; and from that time forward it seems to have been considered by the great writers of the Catholic body a fact too palpable to be doubted, and too simple to be misunderstood."[2]

We have thus far dealt merely with the proofs of the historic episcopate as indicated in the New Testament and as existing during the lifetime of St. John. We turn to the witness of history to the fact that our Lord instituted in His Church, by succession from the apostles, a threefold ministry, the highest order of these ministers alone having the authority and power to perpetuate this ministry by the laying on of hands.

The Church of Jerusalem, the mother of us all, as we have already seen, presents the earliest instance of a bishop in the sense in which the word was understood in post-apostolic times. The rule and official prominence of St. James, "the Lord's brother," is recognized both in the Epistles of St. Paul and in the Acts of the Apostles. That which is so plainly indicated in the canonical Scriptures is supported by the uniform tradition of the succeeding age.

[1] Lightfoot's "Christian Ministry," p. 265.
[2] Gladstone's "Church Principles Considered in their Results," p. 189.

On the death of St. James, which took place immediately before the war of Vespasian, Symeon succeeded to his place and rule. Hegesippus, who is our authority for this statement, and who represents Symeon as holding the same office with St. James, and with equal distinctness styles him a bishop, was doubtless born ere Symeon died. Eusebius gives us a list of Symeon's successors. In less than thirty years—such were the troubles and uncertainties of the times—there appear to have been thirty occupants of the see. On the building of Ælia Capitolina on the ruins of Jerusalem, Marcus presided over the Church in the holy city as its first Gentile bishop. Narcissus, who became bishop of Jerusalem in the year 190, is referred to by Alexander, in whose favor he resigned his see in the year 214, as still living at the age of one hundred and sixteen —thus in this single instance bridging over the period from the time when the Apostle John was still living to the date when, by universal consent, it is conceded that episcopacy was established in all quarters of the world.

Passing from the mother-church of Jerusalem to Antioch, where the disciples were first called Christians, and which may be regarded as the natural center of Gentile Christianity, we find from tradition that Antioch received its first bishop from St. Peter. We need not discuss the probabilities of this story, since there can be no doubt as to the name standing second on the list. Ignatius is mentioned as a bishop by the earliest authors. His own language is conclusive as to his own conviction on this point. He writes to one bishop, Polycarp. He refers by name to another, Onesimus. He contemplates the appointment of his successor at Antioch after his decease. The successor whose appointment Ignatius anticipated is said by Eusebius to have been Hero, and from his episcopate the list of Antiochian bishops is complete. If the authenticity of the entire catalogue is questionable, two bishops of Antioch at least, during the second century, Theophilus and Serapion, are confessedly historical personages. With reference to the epistles of Ignatius controversy has raged for centuries. Their outspoken testimony in favor of episcopacy has been regarded by the advocates of parity or of independency as a proof of their want of authenticity. But the discussion has been practically settled in our own day, and the judgment of Lightfoot, the latest and greatest commentator on these interesting remains of Christian antiquity, will be received without question by all whose opinion is worthy of consideration. He assigns these epistles to the earliest years of the second century, and he regards the testimony of Ignatius to the existence and universality of the threefold ministry at the period in which he lived and wrote as conclusive. The celebrated German critic and scholar, Dr. Harnack, who characterizes Lightfoot's work as "the most learned and careful patristic monograph of the century," accepts the conclusions of the bishop, and concedes that the genuineness of the Ignatian letters is rendered "certain." With such a witness, thus supported by scholars confessedly occupying the foremost place for learning and critical power, we may proceed to details.

In the Ignatian letters, the writer, the second bishop of Antioch, appears as a condemned prisoner traveling through Asia to his martyrdom at Rome. Though each step of his progress brought him nearer to death; though the severity of his guard—"a maniple of ten soldiers," whom he designates as "leopards"—makes his last days wretchedly uncomfortable, still his journey is a triumph. On his arrival at Smyrna representatives of the churches of Ephesus, Magnesia, and Tralles unite with the flock of Polycarp, the bishop of Smyrna, to do him honor. During his stay at Smyrna the aged bishop addresses four of his extant epistles to the Ephesians, to the Magnesians, to the Trallians, and to the Romans. The remaining three epistles, those to the Churches of Philadelphia and Smyrna, and to Polycarp, the bishop of the latter, were written from Troas, whither a deacon from Ephesus had borne him company. The saint proceeds from Neapolis to Philippi, where he is welcomed by the Church and escorted on his way, and thus he goes toward Rome. Though, in his modesty, choosing to speak of himself as "only now beginning to be a disciple," the nearness to the end evidently bringing to him new revelations of spiritual things and the life to come, he acts and writes as a man advanced in years. Doubtless he was near to man's estate when the great apostle wrote his epistles. He must have been in full maturity when Jerusalem was trodden underfoot of the Gentiles and the Church was driven from its cradle-home. He in whose life all this had transpired was now on his way to death. He fully realized that the end was near at hand. His days were numbered, and in his epistles he appears to have sought to crowd counsels of the highest moment, the dying legacy of one whose voice would soon be forever hushed in death. The points this aged saint chiefly dwells upon are two—the doctrine of the Incarnation as an historic fact, as perpetuated in sacraments, as a fundamental principle of the faith; and the threefold ministry, the divinely given rule for the Church, by which the Church itself would be recognized, and the religion of the Christ made known as something organic, real, lasting, disciplined.

In his statements of the prerogative of the threefold ministry Ignatius is emphatic: "It is meet, therefore, . . . that being perfectly joined together in one submission, submitting yourselves to your bishop and presbytery, ye may be sanctified in all things." [1]

[1] "Ad Eph.," 2. In our citations we avail ourselves of Bishop Lightfoot's translation.

"I was forward to exhort you, that ye run in harmony with the mind of God; for Jesus Christ also, our inseparable life, is the mind of the Father, even as the bishops that are settled in the farthest parts of the earth are in the mind of Jesus Christ. So then it becometh you to run in harmony with the mind of the bishop, which thing also ye do. For your honorable presbytery, which is worthy of God, is attuned to the bishop, even as its strings to a lyre."[1]

"Let no man be deceived. If any one be not within the precinct of the altar, he lacketh the bread [of God]. For, if the prayer of one and another hath so great force, how much more that of the bishop and of the whole Church! . . . Let us therefore be careful not to resist the bishop, that by our submission we may give ourselves to God. And in proportion as a man seeth that his bishop is silent, let him fear him the more. For every one whom the Master of the household sendeth to be steward over His own house we ought so to receive as Him that sent him. Plainly, therefore, we ought to regard the bishop as the Lord Himself."[2]

"Assemble yourselves together, . . . to the end that ye may obey the bishop and the presbytery without distraction of mind; breaking one bread, which is the medicine of immortality and the antidote that we should not die."[3]

"Forasmuch, then, as I was permitted to see you in the person of your godly bishop, Damas, and your worthy presbyters, Bassus and Apollonius, and my fellow-servant the deacon, Sotion, of whom I would fain have joy, for that he is subject to the bishop as unto the grace of God, and to the presbytery as unto the law of Jesus Christ. Yea, and it becometh you also not to presume upon the youth of your bishop, but according to the power of God the Father to render unto him all reverence; . . . yet not to him, but to the Father of Jesus Christ, even to the Bishop of all. . . . For a man does not so much deceive this bishop, who is seen, as cheat that other who is invisible."[4]

"Be ye zealous to do all things in godly accord, the bishop presiding after the likeness of God, and the presbyters after the likeness of the council of the apostles, with the deacons also who are most dear to me, having been intrusted with the diaconate of Jesus Christ."[5]

"When ye are obedient to the bishop as to Jesus Christ, it is evident to me that ye are living, not after men, but after Jesus Christ. . . . It is therefore necessary, even as your wont is, that you should do nothing without the bishop; but be ye obedient also to the presbytery, as to the apostles. . . . And those likewise who are deacons of the mysteries of Jesus Christ must please all men in all ways. . . . In like manner let all men respect the deacons as

[1] "Ad Eph.," 3, 4. [2] *Ibid.*, 5, 6. [3] *Ibid.*, 20.
[4] "Ad Magn.," 2, 3. [5] *Ibid.*, 6.

Jesus Christ, even as they should respect the bishop as being a type of the Father, and the presbyters as the council of God and as the college of apostles. Apart from these there is not even the name of a Church."[1]

"For as many as are of God and of Jesus Christ, they are with the bishop; and as many as shall repent and enter into the unity of the Church, these also shall be of God. . . . Be ye careful, therefore, to observe one eucharist, for there is one flesh of our Lord Jesus Christ and one cup unto union in His blood; there is one altar, as there is one bishop, together with the presbytery and the deacons, my fellow-servants."[2]

"Shun divisions as the beginning of evils. Do ye all follow your bishop as Jesus Christ followed the Father, and the presbytery as the apostles; and to the deacons pay respect, as to God's commandment. Let no man do aught of things pertaining to the Church apart from the bishop. Let that be held a valid eucharist which is under the bishop, or one to whom he shall have committed it. Wheresoever the bishop shall appear, there let the people be; even as where Jesus may be, there is the universal Church. It is not lawful apart from the bishop either to baptize or to hold a love-feast, but whatever he shall approve; this is well pleasing also to God, that everything which ye do may be sure and valid."[3]

"It is good to recognize God and the bishop. He that honoreth the bishop is honored of God. He that doeth aught without the knowledge of the bishop rendereth service to the devil."[4]

There can be no question that the writer of these extracts held clear and well-defined views both as to the existence of a visible, organized Church of Christ, and a threefold, divinely authorized ministry ruling that Church. This he deems to be the "mind of God"; this is the "commandment"; and so fully does he hold this view that in his dying counsels he emphasized the idea that he who would keep the "commandment" and run in accord with the divine mind must lose sight of his very individuality in the fellowship of the Church, and unhesitatingly and without reserve submit himself in action, word, or purpose to the divinely appointed rule and order of the Church. Nor is this all. He regards the threefold ministry as essential to the very being of the Church; for, to quote his own words, as rendered by Lightfoot, "without these three orders no church has a title to the name."[5] This hierarchy, this monarchical episcopate, this established and divinely authorized rule in the kingdom of God, the aged bishop of Antioch regards as "firmly rooted," as "beyond dispute," and as coextensive with the Church. He speaks of bishops as established in "the farthest parts of the earth,"[6]

1 "Ad Trall.," 2, 3.
2 "Ad Philad.," 3, 4.
3 "Ad Smyrn.," 8.
4 *Ibid.*, 9.
5 "Ad Trall.," 3.
6 "Ad Eph.," 3.

and it is evident from his language that, in his judgment, the episcopate is not an evolution from the presbyterate, but is from above, the ordering of God Himself.

We cannot, in the space at our command, give all of the many and convincing citations from these epistles, which, as translated by Lightfoot, afford the fullest proof of our position. In the language of Canon MacColl, which has the approval of Bishop Lightfoot himself:[1] "The Ignatian epistles place at least two facts plainly beyond dispute, namely, first, that diocesan episcopacy was then the universal and undisputed form of church government; secondly, that the diocese, under the administration of its bishops, presbyters, and deacons, was the unit of the Church. The bishop stood at the summit of the ecclesiastical hierarchy. In him the Church was summed up. From him it could be reproduced."

In reply to the notion that during the last three decades of the first century, and consequently during the lifetime of St. John, a change had been brought about from a presbyterate governed by apostles to diocesan episcopacy, Canon MacColl interprets Bishop Lightfoot's contention as follows: "If episcopacy 'was firmly and widely established' during the lifetime of the latest surviving apostle, it can hardly be disputed that it is the form of church government which is according to the mind of Christ. 'The latest surviving apostle'—'the disciple whom Jesus loved'—must have learned, during the forty days' intercourse with the risen Saviour before the ascension, the mind of his Master on so vital a question, and it is simply inconceivable that he should have sanctioned any ecclesiastical polity which was not in full harmony with his Lord's instruction while 'speaking of the things pertaining to the kingdom of God.'"[2]

From the words of Ignatius, so clear, so strong, so abundant, we turn to the testimony of Irenæus, who was born not later than A.D. 130. He asserts that in his youth he "sat at the feet of Polycarp, who had been appointed by the apostles a bishop for Asia in the Church of Smyrna," and that he had listened to the discourses in public and private of this venerable man, whose very looks and ways, he assures us, were indelibly impressed upon his mind. Irenæus further claims that he had opportunities of instruction from Asiatic "elders," some of whom, he tells us, had been disciples of the apostles. With these means of learning the traditions of the Church in Asia Minor, as shaped by no less an authority than St. John himself, the latest living of the apostolic band, Irenæus, while yet a young man, and probably prior to Polycarp's martyrdom (*circa* A.D. 155), removed from Asia to Rome. At the latest, in the year 177, when persecution visited the churches of southern Gaul,

[1] "Christianity in Relation to Science and Morals," third edition, 1890, pp. xxv., 258.
[2] Acts i. 3.

Irenæus was a presbyter of Lyons, and was elevated to the see of the martyred bishop Pothinus. There is record of his visiting Rome prior to his entrance upon the episcopal office, as well as afterward, his object in each case being to promote the peace of the Church. Thus fitted by circumstances as well as by his character to know and maintain the "traditions of the elders," we find in his writings, to quote the language of the latest authority on this subject, the Rev. Charles Gore, in his work on "The Ministry of the Christian Church," "the picture of the universal Church, spread all over the world, handing down in unbroken succession the apostolic truth; and the bond of unity, the link to connect the generations in the Church, is the episcopal succession."[1]

The language of Irenæus is clear and determinate with reference to the succession of the bishops to the authority and rule exercised by the apostles in the Church; and "because it would be tedious . . . to enumerate the succession of all the churches," he gives that of the Church of Rome, and records the committal of the episcopate by the apostles St. Peter and St. Paul to Linus (A.D. 68), and then the succession from him of Anencletus (A.D. 80), Clement (A.D. 92), Evarestus (A.D. 100), Alexander (A.D. 109), Xystus (A.D. 119), Telesphorus the Martyr (A.D. 128), Hyginus (A.D. 139), Pius (A.D. 142), Anicetus (A.D. 157), Soter (A.D. 168), and at length, in his own day, of Eleutherus (A.D. 177).[2] Certain discrepancies which confessedly exist in the various lists of Roman bishops which have come down to us may be explained by assuming the existence in the very first ages of two distinct Churches, one Jewish and one Gentile, at Rome. Lightfoot, while claiming that "no more can safely be assumed of Linus and Anencletus than that they held some prominent position in the Romish Church,"[3] adds that "the reason for supposing Clement to have been a bishop is as strong as the universal tradition of the next ages can make it." It in no way detracts from this admission with respect to Clement that Lightfoot regards him rather as "the chief of the presbyters than the chief over presbyters," and consequently not in the position of irresponsible authority occupied by his successors, Eleutherus (A.D. 177) and Victor (A.D. 189), or even by his contemporaries, Ignatius of Antioch and Polycarp of Smyrna.

With Victor, apparently the first Latin prelate who held the bishopric of Rome, a new era begins. The line of ecclesiastical descent is now clearly defined, and by the participation in each consecration of three or more of the episcopal order, required by the early can-

[1] [illegible]

[2] [illegible] the see of [illegible]

[3] [illegible]

ons and continued with scrupulous exactness till the modern view of episcopacy as held by the papacy permitted at times the substitution of the papal authority for the presence of more than a single consecrator, there have been knitted together the meshes of that vast network which in its comprehensiveness includes the Church's chief rulers from the very first, and by the multitude of interlacing lines of succession makes any serious defect in the direct connection with the apostles of any individual bishop well-nigh impossible. The succession of bishops from the apostles' times is not to be regarded as a chain of single links, the whole being of no greater strength than its weakest part, but as a network or web of interwoven strands, now innumerable, which would hold together even if, to venture an impossible supposition, nine tenths of these lines could be proved defective and therefore invalid. In other words, a possible defect in one or in a hundred of the different lines of succession would in no way affect the consecration of any bishop of our day, so infinite in number are the interlacing strands of the great network uniting one who has been set apart for this office and administration in the Church of God with the apostles, and through the apostles with Christ, the great Shepherd and Bishop of souls.

AUTHORITIES.—In addition to the late bishop of Durham's "Dissertation on the Christian Ministry," appended to his "Commentary on the Philippians," and the many special treatises on the apostolical succession by Perceval, Haddon, Elrington, Morse, and others, the latest and most conclusive work on the general subject is that of Gore, "The Ministry of the Christian Church" (Rivingtons, London, 1889). A compact treatise by the Rev. Prof. J. H. Barbour, of the Berkeley Divinity School, Middletown, Conn., is admirably arranged and deserves general reading. Its title is "The Beginnings of the Historic Episcopate Exhibited in the Words of Holy Scripture and Ancient Authors" (New York, E. & J. B. Young & Co., 1887). Canon Liddon, in his sermon entitled "A Father in Christ" (Rivingtons, 1875), effectually disposes of the arguments of the late Dr. Hatch, in his Bampton Lectures on "The Organization of Early Christian Churches," as well as those of a later paper in the "Contemporary Review" from the same source. A scholarly and conclusive volume, written in Latin, of upward of six hundred pages octavo, gives in detail, and with sufficient critical apparatus, both the arguments for the apostolical succession and the lists of bishops from the apostles' time to our own day. The title of this work is as follows: "De Successione Apostolica necnon Missione et Jurisdictione Hierarchiæ Anglicanæ et Catholicæ, unacum appendicibus et indicibus: auctore Venerabili Doctore Jacobo Clark, Archidiacono Antiguensi, Sacellano Exam. Dno. Antiguensi Epo Rectore Par. S. Philippi in Antigua. Georgiopoli in Guiana Britannica: MDCCCXC." The third edition of a clever compendium of the argument, by the Rev. Andrew Gray, a priest of the diocese of Massachusetts, has been published in Boston. It is entitled "Apostolical Succession in the English, Scottish, and American Church, from St. John the Apostle to the Present Time, in the Line of Consecrators, Taken from Authentic Records." A learned work by the present bishop of Oxford, the eminent historian Dr. William Stubbs, gives the succession in the Church of England. The title of this work is "Registrum Sacrum Anglicanum: An Attempt to Exhibit the Course of Episcopal Succession in England from the Records and Chronicles of the Church" (Oxford, University Press, 1858).

II.

THE INTRODUCTION OF THE EPISCOPATE INTO THE UNITED STATES.

THE American branch of the Holy Catholic Church recognizes the order of bishops as existing from the apostles' time. She has not defined the functions pertaining to this order of the sacred ministry, or expressly marked out the limitations of its powers. She refers to Scripture and ancient authors for the fact of the existence "from the apostles' time" of this order and office. In other words, the episcopate, sought for and at length secured by our fathers, was the historic episcopate; and in the absence of any definition, in constitution, canons, liturgy, or symbols, of the nature of this office and administration, it may be inferred that whatever the bishop was, in the judgment and acknowledged practice of the Church, the American bishop was to be; so that all rights, powers, and privileges inhering in this office or appertaining to the same were sought for and secured in obtaining the episcopate.

In the efforts made for the episcopate we see at the outset, and throughout the struggle, even to the moment of success, the hand and head of him who, as his distinguished successor[1] rightly claimed, "will be recognized as the founder and wise master builder of a system of ecclesiastical polity which, though not faultless, is as perfect as the condition of things then admitted, and of which the essential excellence is likely to be demonstrated by the progress of events."

In "The Case of the Episcopal Churches Considered" William White had argued that "it may fairly be inferred that Episcopalians on this continent will wish to institute among themselves an

[1] Bishop Alonzo Potter.

episcopal government as soon as it shall appear practicable, and that this government will not be attended with the danger of tyranny, either temporal or spiritual." The proposition "to include in the proposed frame of government a general approbation of episcopacy, and a declaration of an intention to procure the succession as soon as conveniently may be, but in the meantime to carry the plan into effect without waiting for the succession," was happily rendered unnecessary, and the writer of this pamphlet became most actively concerned in securing this "succession" for the Church of which he was already a leading spirit. At the meeting of clergy and laity convened in Philadelphia on the 24th of May, 1784, at which Dr. White was chosen chairman, the fourth of the "instructions or fundamental principles" adopted provided "that the succession of the ministry be agreeable to the usage which requireth the three orders of bishops, priests, and deacons; that the rights and powers of the same, respectively, be ascertained; and that they be exercised according to reasonable laws, to be duly made." In this provision it is easy to recognize the hand of White. Out of the meeting of May, 1784, there grew, under the fostering care of White, the organization or "association" of the "Protestant Episcopal Church in the State of Pennsylvania," which was effected on the 24th of May, 1785. The important document relating to this named as the objects had in view by the clergy and congregations in this "act of association" the following: "For maintaining uniformity in divine worship, *for procuring the powers of ordination*, and for establishing and maintaining a system of ecclesiastical government." [1]

In the active correspondence kept up by White with the leading Churchmen North and South we find evidence of his purposes concerning the "succession." In a letter addressed, in 1784, to the Rev. Samuel Parker, of Trinity Church, Boston, the exact date of which is unfortunately lost, Dr. White thus expresses his views on this important matter:

> "On the subject of procuring the succession, I shall only observe that if any private measures said to have been undertaken for this end should prove successful, I think the whole Church should gladly avail itself of the acquisition.[2] If not, an application to our Mother-Church from representatives of the Episcopal Church generally will be, surely, too respectable to be slighted; and such an application might be easily framed by correspondence among ourselves." [3]

Writing again on the 10th of August, 1784, to the same correspondent, White observes:

> "The Fundamental Principles which you have seen were merely meant as instructions to a committee in their consultations with our brethren in the other States for the form-

[1] Perry's "Historical Notes and Documents," p. 40.

[2] This evidently refers to the election of Seabury by the Connecticut clergy and the efforts already made abroad to secure his consecration.

[3] Perry's "Historical Notes and Documents," p. 60.

ing a general constitution for the continent, which we think should be attempted before we venture to form a constitution for this State in particular. . . . The independence asserted is intended in the most unlimited sense; but we do not think this precludes us from procuring a bishop from England, he becoming on his arrival a citizen of the United States. Proper measures for procuring an episcopate we wish to see taken at the ensuing meeting in New York; but as to his support, I know no source for it but a parochial living."[1]

The clergy of Massachusetts and Rhode Island, under the guidance of Parker, adopted the Pennsylvania Fundamental Principles with slight additions, the first of these expressing "the opinion of the Convention that this independence be not construed or taken in so rigorous a sense as to exclude the churches in America, separately or collectively, from applying for and obtaining from some regular episcopal foreign power an American episcopate."[2]

In the letter accompanying the minutes of this Convention, which, though signed by the moderator, the Rev. J. Graves, is in the handwriting and is evidently the composition of Parker, the position respecting the episcopate expressed in the resolution is further emphasized:

"As to the mode of obtaining what we stand in such need of, we wish above all things to procure it in the most regular manner, and particularly from our mother-church in England. Whether any of the bishops in England or Ireland would consecrate a person chosen among ourselves and sent there for that purpose, without a mandate from the king of England or the authority of her Parliament, we are at a loss to determine; but we have no doubt that a regular application made by a representative body of the Episcopal churches in America would easily obtain a consecrated head, and in order to do this we earnestly wish a mode of applying in some such way as may be immediately adopted by the American churches.

"We are of the opinion that we ought to leave no means untried to procure a regular succession of the episcopacy before we think of obtaining it in an irregular manner. To accomplish this we have chosen a committee of our body to correspond with you upon this, and adopt such measures for the same as may be expedient or necessary."[3]

The letter from the Massachusetts and Rhode Island clergy expressed the sentiments prevailing in Connecticut, and which seem to have been current throughout New England. The conservative elements in the North were alarmed, not only at the proposition, in "The Case of the Episcopal Churches Considered," for "a temporary departure from episcopacy," but by the radical measures adopted at the southward, where, in Virginia, anticipatory canons were enacted defining and circumscribing the exercise of the episcopal office, and making the bishop not only amenable to trial by the Convention, but even liable to "suspension or dismission" from office at its will; while in South Carolina it was stipulated that bishops should not be introduced at all.

Prior to the meeting of the Convention of the churches in the Middle and Southern States in 1785, the efforts of the Connecticut clergy to secure an episcopal head had resulted in success. On the

[1] Perry's "Historical Notes and Documents," p. 61.
[2] *Ibid.*, p. 63. [3] *Ibid.*, pp. 65, 66.

In Dei Nomine Amen.

Omnibus ubique Catholicis per Praesentes pateat, Nos Robertum Kilgour Miseratione Divina Episcopum Aberdonien. Arthurum Petrie Episcopum Rossen et Moravien. et Joannem Skinner Episcopum Coadjutorem, Mysteria Sacra Domini nostri Jesu Christi in Oratorio supradicti Joannis Skinner apud Aberdoniam celebrantes, Divini Numinis Praesidio fretos (praesentibus tam e Clero, quam e Populo Testibus idoneis) Samuelem Seabury Doctorem Divinitatis, sacro Presbyteratus Ordine jam decoratum, ac Nobis pro Vitae integritate Morum probitate, et Orthodoxia commendatum, et ad docendum et regendum aptum et idoneum, ad sacrum et sublimem Episcopatus Ordinem promovisse, et rite ac canonice, secundum Morem et Ritus Ecclesiae Scoticanae, Consecrasse, Die Novembris Decimo Quarto, Anno Aerae Christianae Millesimo septingentesimo octagesimo quarto. In cujus rei Testimonium, Instrumento huic (Chirographis nostris primo munito) Sigilla nostra apponi mandavimus

Robertus Kilgour Episcopus et Primus

Arthurus Petrie Episcopus.

Joannes Skinner Episcopus.

14th of November, 1784, at Aberdeen, the Rev. Samuel Seabury, D.D. Oxon., was consecrated the first American bishop by the bishops of the Catholic remainder of the Church in Scotland. Entering into a concordat with the Church from which he received his episcopal character, Seabury lost no time in beginning his work, and was joyfully received by his clergy, the formal welcome being extended in Convocation in Middletown, August, 1785. At this Convocation in Middletown the churches in Massachusetts and Rhode Island were represented by the Rev. Samuel Parker, while the conservative element in New York was represented by the Rev. Benjamin Moore. Both of these gentlemen were friends and correspondents of White, and each had taken part in the preliminary measures and meetings of 1784, which had prepared the way for the Convention in Philadelphia in September, 1785. To this meeting Bishop Seabury and his clergy were invited; but as there was no provision in the Fundamental Principles adopted in New York at the preliminary meeting of 1784 for the proper recognition of his office, Seabury courteously declined the invitation, as the clergy at the southward did his suggestion that they should attend the meeting at Middletown.

It is in evidence that had there been the provision that one of the episcopal order, if present, should preside, as was originally intended by White, Bishop Seabury would have gone to Philadelphia in 1785, as he did later, in 1789; but there can be little doubt that such a step would have been premature, and might have absolutely prevented, in place of furthering, the unity so greatly desired by both White and himself. There was no little to be done by the statesmanship and wise, conciliatory measures of White ere the conflicting elements in the Church could be calmed, and order arise out of chaos.

Prior to the meeting in Philadelphia, letters from Bishop Seabury to Drs. William White and William Smith, the leading spirits in the Convention, frankly communicated information respecting the rejection of the Connecticut application in England, and offered the bishop's services for the ordination of candidates until a bishop was secured at the southward. At the same time the bishop objected to the policy which had obtained in the Conventions at the South of encumbering their plans for organization by establishing so many and such precise fundamental rules. He claimed that the powers of the bishop were too much circumscribed, since "government as essentially pertains to bishops as ordination." He denied that "the laity can with any propriety be admitted to sit in judgment on bishops and presbyters, especially when deposition may be the event; because they cannot take away a character which they cannot confer." The bishop was careful to state that he did not think it requisite that the churches at the southward should be modeled on the Church in Connecticut; but he earnestly urged that, "in so essential a matter as church government is, no alterations should be made that affect its foundations." The bishop professed himself ready "to assist in procuring bishops in America" so far as he could do this consistently. His desire is stated as follows: "I do most earnestly wish to have our Church in all the States so settled that it may be one Church, united in government, doctrine, and discipline; that there may be no divisions among us, no opposition of interests, no clashing of opinions."[1]

The objections raised by the bishop of Connecticut, and repeated by the venerable Thomas Bradbury Chandler, of New Jersey, were answered by the indefatigable William White. On the very eve of the meeting in Philadelphia, Parker wrote to his correspondent, in reply to a letter which indicates that the fatal defect of withholding the presidency of the Convention from the episcopal order was adopted in opposition to the wish of the far-seeing White. "I am sorry," White writes to Parker, "to find that those measures have been so construed by some of our friends in England as if we had refused to the episcopal order the right of precedency in our Conventions. Probably you will recollect that in the original draft it was provided the senior bishop present should preside; and that this was erased, not from the idea that any other than a bishop ought to be president, but from an observation of Dr. S[mith] that to restrain it to the senior bishop might be sometimes inconvenient. I wish that the clause had stood."

Parker's letter throws further light on this unfortunate action: "I am, with you, equally sensible that the fifth of the Fundamental Principles in the paper printed at New York has operated much to the disadvantage of that Convention. Had it stood as I proposed, that a bishop (if one in any State) should be president, I make no doubt there would have been one present. You will be at no loss to conclude that I mean Dr. Seabury, who, you must ere this have heard, is arrived and entered upon the exercise of his office in Connecticut. Being present in Convocation at Middletown the 4th of August last, I much urged his attending the Convention at Philadelphia this month; but that very article discouraged him so much that no arguments I could use were sufficient to prevail with him. Had that article stood as proposed, the gentleman who moved the amendment would not have suffered by it, nor the Convention been stigmatized as anti-Episcopalian."[2]

The opening pages of the "Journal" of the Convention at Philadelphia in 1785 bring to our notice a proposed "Plan for Obtaining the Consecration of Bishops, together with an Address to the Most

1 Perry's "Historical Notes and Documents," pp. 76–82. 2 *Ibid.*, pp. 89, 90.

In the Name of the holy and undivided Trinity, Father, Son, and Holy Ghost, One God blessed for ever Amen —

The wise and gracious Providence of this merciful God having put it into the hearts of the Christians of the Episcopal persuasion in Connecticut in North America, to desire that the Blessings of a free, valid and purely Ecclesiastical Episcopacy might be communicated to them, and a Church regularly formed in that part of the western World upon the most antient and primitive Model. And application having been made for this purpose, by the Reverend Dr. Samuel Seabury Presbyter in Connecticut, to the Right Reverend the Bishops of the Church in Scotland. The said Bishops having taken this proposal into their serious Consideration, most heartily concurred to promote and encourage the same, as far as lay in their power, and accordingly began the pious and good Work recommended to them, by complying with the request of the Clergy in Connecticut, and advancing the said Dr. Samuel Seabury to the high Order of the Episcopate, at the same time earnestly praying that this Work of the Lord thus happily begun might prosper in his hands, till it should please the great and glorious Head of the Church, to increase the number of Bishops in America, and send forth more such Labourers into that part of his Harvest. — Animated with this pious hope, and earnestly desirous to establish a Bond of Peace, and holy Communion, between the two Churches, the Bishops of the Church in Scotland, whose Names are underwritten, having had full and free Conference with Bishop Seabury, after his Consecration and Advancement as aforesaid, agreed with him on the following Articles, which are to serve as a Concordate, or Bond of Union, between the Catholic remainder of the antient Church of Scotland, and the now rising Church in the State of Connecticut ——

Art. I.st They agree in thankfully receiving, and humbly and heartily embracing the whole Doctrine of the Gospel, as revealed and set forth in the holy Scriptures: And it is their earnest and united Desire to maintain the Analogy of the common Faith once delivered to the Saints, and happily preserved in the Church of Christ, thro his divine power and protection, who promised that the Gates of Hell should never prevail against it. —

Art II.d They agree in believing this Church to be the mystical Body of Christ, of which he alone is the Head, and supreme Governour, and that under him, the chief Ministers or Managers of the Affairs of this spiritual Society, are those called Bishops, whose Exercise of their sacred Office being independent on all Lay powers, it follows of consequence, that their spiritual Authority and Jurisdiction cannot be affected by any Lay-Deprivation

Art III. They agree in declaring that the Episcopal Church in Connecticut is to be in full Communion with the Episcopal Church in Scotland; it being their sincere Resolution to put matters on such a footing as that the Members of both Churches may with freedom and safety communicate with either when their Occasions call them from the one Country to the other. Only taking care when in Scotland not to hold Communion in sacred Offices with those persons, who under pretence of Ordination by an English or Irish Bishop, do or shall take upon them to officiate as [illegible] Church of Scotland and whom the Scottish Bishops cannot help looking upon, as schismatical Intruders, designed only to answer worldly purposes, [illegible]

... clergymen in any part of the [illegible] ...

and [illegible] Distributors of the poor Remains of that once flourishing Church, which both their predecessors and they have under many Difficulties laboured to preserve pure and uncorrupted to future Ages. —

Art. IV. With a view to the salutary purpose mentioned in the preceding Article, they agree in desiring that there may be as near a Conformity in Worship and Discipline established between the two Churches, as is consistent with the different Circumstances and Customs of Nations. And in order to avoid any bad Effects that might otherwise arise from political Differences, they hereby express their earnest Wish and firm Intention to observe such prudent Generality in their public Prayers with respect to these points, as shall appear most agreeable to Apostolic Rules and the practice of the primitive Church. —

Art. V. As the Celebration of the holy Eucharist, or the Administration of the Sacrament of the Body and Blood of Christ, is the principal Bond of Union among Christians, as well as the most solemn Act of Worship in the Christian Church, the Bishops aforesaid agree in desiring that there may be as little Variance here as possible. And tho the Scottish Bishops are very far from prescribing to their Brethren in this matter, they cannot help ardently wishing that Bishop Seabury would endeavour all he can consistently with peace and prudence, to make the Celebration of this venerable Mystery conformable to the most primitive Doctrine and practice in that respect: Which is the pattern the Church of Scotland has copied after in her Communion Office, and which it has been the Wish of some of the most eminent Divines of the Church of England, that she also had more closely followed, than she seems to have done since she gave up her first reformed Liturgy used in the Reign of King Edward VI, between which and the form used in the Church of Scotland there is no Difference in any point which the primitive Church reckoned essential to the right Ministration of the holy Eucharist. — In this capital Article therefore of the Eucharistic Service, in which the Scottish Bishops so earnestly wish for as much Unity as possible, Bishop Seabury also agrees to take a serious View of the Communion Office recommended by them, and if found agreeable to the genuine Standards of Antiquity, to give his Sanction to it, and by gentle Methods of Argument and persuasion, to endeavour, as they have done, to introduce it by degrees into practice without the Compulsion of Authority on the one side, or the prejudice of former Custom on the other.

Art. VI. It is also hereby agreed and resolved upon for the better answering the purposes of this Concordate, that a brotherly fellowship be henceforth maintained between the Episcopal Churches in Scotland and Connecticut, and such a mutual Intercourse of Ecclesiastical Correspondence carried on, when Opportunity offers, or Necessity requires, as may tend to the Support and Edification of both Churches. —

Art. VII. The Bishops aforesaid do hereby jointly declare, in the most solemn manner, that in the whole of this Transaction they have nothing else in view but the Glory of God, and the Good of his Church. And being thus pure and upright in their Intentions, they cannot but hope, that all whom it may concern, will put the most fair and candid Construction on their Conduct, and take no Offence at their feeble but sincere Endeavours to promote what they believe to be the Cause of Truth, and of the common Salvation. —

In Testimony of their Love to which, and in mutual good Faith and Confidence, they have for themselves, and their Successors in Office cheerfully put their Names and Seals to these presents at Aberdeen this fifteenth day of November, in the year of our Lord, one thousand, seven hundred and eighty four.

Robert Kilgour Bishop & Primus

Arthur Petrie Bishop.

John Skinner Bishop.

Samuel Seabury Bishop.

Ordered, that the Plan for obtaining con-secration ~~[illegible]~~ ~~[illegible]~~ be again read, which having discussed & amended was agreed to, & is as follows

1.st That this Convention address the Arch-Bishops and Bishops of the Church of Engd and requesting them to confer the Episcopal Character on such Persons as shall be chosen and recommended to them for that Purpose from the Conventions of this Church in the respective States.

2. That it be recommended to the said Conventions, That they elect Persons for this Purpose.

3. That it be further recommended to the different Conventions, at their next respective Sessions, to appoint Committees with Powers to correspond with the English Bishops for the carrying these Resolutions into Effect; and that, until such Committees shall be appointed, they be requested to direct any Communications which they may be pleased to make on this Subject, to the Committee consisting of the Revd Doct. White, the Revd Doct. Smith, Revd Mr. Provoost, Hon. James Duane, Samuel Powell & Richard Peters Esqrs.

4. That it be further recommended to the different Conventions, that they pay a special Attention to the making

it appear to their Lordships, that the Persons who shall be sent by them for Consecration are desired in the Character of Bishops, as well by the Laity as by the Clergy of this Church, in the said States respectively; and that they will be received by them in that Character on their Return.

5. And, in Order to shew their Lordships of the Legality of the present proposed Application, That the Deputies, now assembled, be desired to make a respectful Request to the Civil Rulers of the States, in which they respectively reside, to certify That the said Application is not contrary to the Constitutions and Laws of the same.

6. And whereas the Bishops of this Church will not be entitled to any of such temporal Honors as are due to the Arch-Bishops and Bishops of the Parent Church in Quality of Lords of Parliament; and whereas the Reputation and Usefulness of our Bishops will considerably depend on their assuming no higher Title or Stile than will be due to their spiritual Employments; That it be recommended to this Church, in the States here represented, to provide that each of their respective Bishops may be [illegible] called the Right Reverend, and as Bishop, may have no other Title; and may not use any such Stile as is usually descriptive of temporal Power and Precedency.

Done in Philadelphia Christ Church in Convention of the Clerical & lay Deputies of the protestant Episcopal Church in the States under mentioned this 5th day of October 1785 —

William White. President. D.D. Rector of Christ Church & St Peters. Philadelphia —

Saml Provoost Rector of Trinity Church and Clerical Deputy
Jas Duane Lay Deputy
} for New York

Abraham Beach
Rector of Christ Church
[redacted]nswick, Clerical
Deputy. —
Uzal Ogden,
Rector of Christ's Church
in Sussex County, Cleri-
cal Deputy
Patrick Dennis Lay Depy
} for New Jersey

Sam. Magaw Rect. of St Pauls Phila

Robt Blackwell Asst Minr of Christ Church & St Peters Phila
Joseph Hutchins, Rector of St James's Church, Lancaster

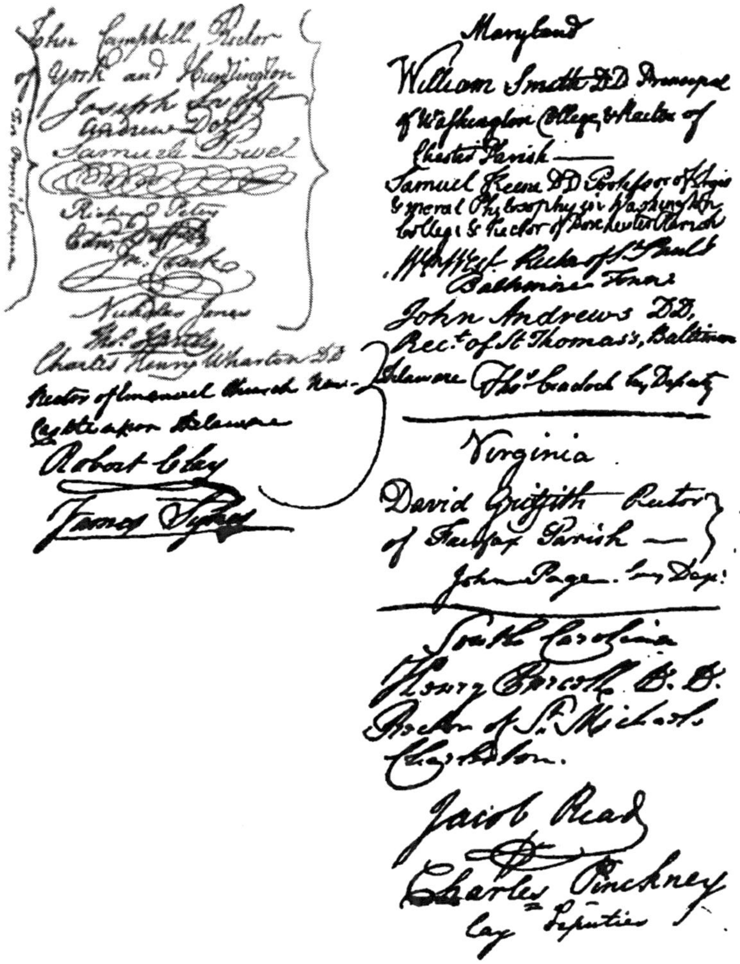
John Campbell Rector of York and Huntingdon
Joseph Swift
Andrew Doz
Samuel Powel
[illegible]
Richard Peters
[illegible]
[illegible]
[illegible]
Nicholas Jones
[illegible]
Charles Henry Wharton D.D. Rector of Immanuel Church New-Castle upon Delaware
Robert Clay
James Sykes
Delaware

Maryland
William Smith D.D. Principal of Washington College & Rector of Chester Parish
Samuel Keene D.D. Professor of Ethics & general Philosophy in Washington College & Rector of Dorchester Parish
Wm West Rector of St Pauls Baltimore Town
John Andrews D.D. Rec.t of St Thomas's, Baltimore
Thos Cradock Lay Deputy

Virginia
David Griffith Rector of Fairfax Parish
John Page Lay Dep.

South Carolina
Henry Purcell D.D. Rector of St Michaels Charleston
Jacob Read
Charles Pinckney
Lay Deputies

Reverend the Archbishops and the Right Reverend the Bishops of the Church of England, for that purpose." [1]

The Plan and the Address attest the wide-spread desire of the Churchmen represented in this Convention for the episcopate as a necessary bond of union. They further prove the preference of the churches of the Middle and Southern States for the succession in the English line. Recognizing as the acknowledged hindrance to the success of Dr. Seabury's application to the English prelates the lack of evidence of the concurrence of the civil authorities and the coöperation of the laity in the effort for the succession, they directed the attention of the State Conventions to measures for the removal of this obstacle. Proofs of the desire of the laity for the introduction of the episcopate were to be provided, and documents certifying the concurrence of the State authorities in the proposed measures, or at least attesting the absence of any constitutional or legislative bar to the introduction of episcopacy, were to be obtained from the various civil rulers. In true republican simplicity, and for the removal of popular prejudices, the framers of the Plan sought to prevent, in the concluding paragraph, the assumption on the part of future bishops of the lordly titles of the English prelates—a proposition not infrequently, though erroneously, quoted as of authority at the present day.

The Address to the English prelates was manly and dignified. Bishop White informs us [2] that this paper and the Plan itself, "as they stand on the 'Journals,'" were his own composition, "with the exception of a few verbal alterations." It expressed the "earnest desire and resolution" of "the members of our communion" "to retain the venerable form of episcopal government, handed down to them, as they conceived, from the time of the apostles; and endeared to them by the remembrance of the holy bishops of the primitive Church, of the blessed martyrs who reformed the Church of England, and of the many great and pious prelates who have adorned that Church in every succeeding age." Its plea was summed up in these words: "The petition which we offer to your venerable body is that, from a tender regard to the religious interests of thousands in this rising empire, professing the same religious principles with the Church of England, you will be pleased to confer the episcopal character on such persons as shall be recommended by this Church in the several States here represented; full satisfaction being given of the sufficiency of the persons recommended, and of its being the intention of the general body of the Episcopalians in the said States, respectively, to receive them in the quality of bishops."

1 Perry's "Reprinted Journals," i., 19.
2 "Memoirs of the Church," second edition, p. 101.

Reference is felicitously made to the possibility of obstacles arising from political complications; and stress is laid on the fact that in view of the separation of Church and State the civil rulers of the United States cannot unite officially in the application for the episcopal succession. The Address closes with a graceful as well as grateful acknowledgment of the kind offices rendered by the English hierarchy and the Society for the Propagation of the Gospel to the American Church, to which, under God, its "prosperity is in an eminent degree to be ascribed."

It was in this Address that, as Bishop White asserts, "a foundation was thus laid for the procuring of the present episcopacy." "To have abandoned the episcopal succession," writes Bishop White in his "Memoirs of the Church," "would have been in opposition to primitive order and ancient habits, and, besides, would at least have divided the Church. To have had recourse to Scotland, independently of the objections entertained against the political principles of the nonjurors of that country, would not have been proper, without previous disappointment on a request made to the mother-church. Another resource remained, in foreign ordination; which had been made the easier by the act of the British Parliament, passed in the preceding year, to enable the bishop of London to ordain citizens or subjects of foreign countries without exacting the usual oaths. But besides that this would have kept the Church under the same hardships which had heretofore existed, and had been so long complained of, dependence on a foreign country in spirituals, when there had taken place independence in temporals, is what no prudent person would have pleaded for."

The reply of the English prelates was courteous but cautious, and, in fact, non-committal. It was prepared by the archbishop of Canterbury, and was signed by the two archbishops and the bishops of London, Chichester, Bath and Wells, St. Asaph, Salisbury, Peterborough, Ely, Rochester, Worcester, Oxford, Exeter, Lincoln, Bangor, Lichfield and Coventry, Gloucester, St. David's, and Bristol. The letter expresses the wish of the English prelates to promote the spiritual welfare of their "Episcopal brethren in America," and their desire to be instrumental in procuring for them "the complete exercise of our holy religion, and the enjoyment of that ecclesiastical constitution" which they believed "to be truly apostolical," and for which the letter of request expressed "so unreserved a veneration." The archbishop did not conceal his satisfaction that "this pious design" was "not likely to receive any discountenance from the civil powers" in America, and promised "the best endeavors" of the English prelates "to acquire a legal capacity of complying with the prayer" of the American Address. At the same time, and with every allowance for the difficulties of the situation, the fear is expressed that in the proceedings of the Convention "some alterations may have been adopted or intended which those difficulties do not seem to justify." In view of the fact that these alterations are not mentioned in the Address, and that the knowledge of their nature possessed by the bishops in England had reached them "through private and less certain channels," the bishops thought it but just to "wait for an explanation." "Anxious to give every proof," not only of "brotherly affection," but also of facility in forwarding the wishes of their American brethren, they felt that they could not "but be extremely cautious lest" they "should be the instruments of establishing an ecclesiastical system" which "could be called a branch of the Church of England, but afterward" might "possibly appear to have departed from it essentially, either in doctrine or discipline."

The correspondence between the Philadelphia Convention and the primate had been carried on through the kindly intervention of the celebrated John Adams, the American minister at the court of St. James. Mr. Adams, although connected with the Congregational body of Massachusetts, and coming from a State where the opposition to the introduction of episcopacy into America had been more decided than elsewhere—the aversion to the measure being occasioned by religious as well as political prejudices—undertook this office of furthering the object—which the celebrated Samuel Adams had declared to be a moving cause of the war for independence—with an alacrity and enthusiasm most honorable to the man and to his freedom from religious or political prejudices. He delivered the Address to the archbishop in person, and by his personal efforts in public and private greatly facilitated the progress of the measure. It was through Mr. Adams that the reply of the archbishops and bishops was transmitted to Dr. White. That the office thus kindly undertaken was one liable to misconception, and that the prejudices against the introduction of the episcopate were not wholly allayed, making the service rendered by the American minister the more valuable and effective, may be inferred from the language used by Mr. Adams nearly thirty years afterward, when referring to his share in the successful effort for securing the episcopate for America. "There is no part of my life," writes ex-President Adams to Bishop White, under date of October 29, 1814, "on which I look back and reflect with more satisfaction than the part I took, bold, daring, and hazardous as it was to myself and mine, in the introduction of the episcopacy into America."

There had been an active correspondence kept up by William White and prominent English friends from the very moment of the cessation of hostilities between Great Britain and the independent States of America. The letters which passed between Dr. Inglis, formerly of Trinity, New York, and later the first British colonial bishop, the celebrated Philadelphia refugee clergyman, the Rev. Jacob Duché, together with the Rev. Dr. Alexander Murray, who had, for a time, been the missionary of the Venerable Society at Reading, in Pennsylvania, and Dr. White, the leading spirit in the measures now rife for the organization and perpetuation of the American Church, are full of interest and throw no little light on the inner workings of the plan to secure the episcopate. Beginning with the appearance of "The Case of the Episcopal Churches Considered," the letters from these English correspondents became most important in acquainting White, informally and often confidentially, with difficulties arising from misapprehensions of the steps taken in America, or from fears entertained of the doctrinal unsoundness or moral unfitness of some who were known, or supposed, to be candidates for the office of bishop in the American Church.

The loyalist clergy in London, who were naturally in the confidence of the archbishop and the leading dignitaries of the Establishment, were soon able to assure their correspondent in Philadelphia that a proper application for the episcopate would be favorably regarded. The passage of the act of Parliament authorizing the dispensing with the usual oaths in the case of American candidates for orders gave further assurance of a kindly interest in the rising American Church. The needs of the Church in the United States became a matter of interest and discussion in the public press. Pamphlets were published on the subject by leading men, such as the celebrated philanthropist, Granville Sharp, Esq., a grandson of a former archbishop of York. The offices not alone of Mr. Adams, the American minister, but also of the celebrated Benjamin Franklin, then in Paris, were invoked. The proper foundation of the independent American Church, and its completion, by the gift of the succession, seem to have occupied the thoughts, the labors, and the prayers of the leading men in Church and State at this critical period.

At length the correspondents of William White were able to write definitely as well as encouragingly. Murray begins his communication of the 11th of March, 1786, with the prophetic words: "I would fain hope the day is not far distant when I shall have the honor of addressing you as *Right Reverend*." He proceeds: "Mr. Adams has finally obviated all political objections to your application, and reconciled the king, the members, and the whole bench of bishops to it." It was a relief to find that the alterations in the Prayer-book, comprising what is now known as the Proposed Book, were "not yet approved, but only proposed and recommended." As Bishop White informs us, it was "the omission of Christ's descent into hell, in the Apostles' Creed," as given in the

Proposed Book, that was specially distasteful to the English prelates, though this objection was urged only by the bishop of Bath and Wells, Dr. Moss. The failure of the archbishops and bishops to receive the advance sheets of the Proposed Book (which, though sent to them from time to time as the work was hurried through the press, failed, through some mischance, to reach their destination) occasioned the "caution" which Bishop White notices as characterizing the English prelates' reply. Even in the United States there was a lack of unanimity in this effort to remove the reference to the descent into hell from the Apostles' Creed. Both at the North and the South it was felt that such radical changes were likely to prejudice the success of the application in England for the episcopate, and also imperil the unity of the Church in the United States. A very large number of Churchmen sympathized with the bishop of Connecticut and the conservative element in New England, New York, and New Jersey. All these deprecated any liturgical changes from the English book, or doctrinal departure from the standards of the mother-church. This was deemed, to quote the language of Parker, of Boston, addressed to Dr. White, "in direct violation of the fourth Fundamental Principle agreed on by the Convention in New York" in 1784. This principle provided that the American Church should maintain the doctrines of the Church of England, and adhere to the liturgy of that Church so far as consistent with the American Revolution and the constitutions of the respective States.

A confidential letter from the Rev. Dr. Inglis, to whom alone the archbishop's letter had been communicated, to Dr. White, under date of June 6, 1786, expressed the satisfaction of the English bishops at finding, on the receipt of the Proposed Book, "that the great essential doctrines of Christianity" were "preserved; particularly the doctrine of the holy Trinity and our Saviour's atonement." The archbishop of Canterbury had now "taken up the business with greater zeal," and was about to apply for an act of Parliament authorizing the consecration of bishops for America. The conditions required by the archbishops and bishops, as stated by Dr. Inglis, were these: "(1) A restoration of the article which has been expunged out of the Apostles' Creed. (2) A restoration of the Nicene and Athanasian creeds, so far, at least, as to leave the use of them discretional. (3) Securing to the future bishops that just and permanent authority which is not only necessary for the right discharge of their duty and the benefit of the Church, but which is warranted by Holy Scripture and the practice of the Christian Church in every period of its existence. And (4) proper testimonials, such as the peculiarity of the case demands, of the competency in point of learning, the unblemished moral character, and the soundness in the faith, of those who may be sent over for consecration." [1] Proceeding to discuss these conditions, Dr. Inglis gives us some light on the action taken in New York, to which, as we have seen, Dr. Parker, of Boston, so strenuously excepted:

"With regard to your future bishop's permanent authority, I consider it as absolutely necessary to the peace, order, and good government of your churches. When I first saw the regulation made on this head I was astonished how any people professing themselves members of an Episcopal church could think of degrading their bishop in such a manner. No episcopal power whatever is reserved for him but that of *ordination*, and perhaps confirmation. He is only a *member, ex officio*, of the Convention where he resides, but is not to take the chair, or preside, unless he is asked; whereas such *presidency* is as essential to his character as *ordination*. St. Paul's bishop was to receive and judge of accusations brought against presbyters, as hath been the case of bishops ever since; but your bishop has nothing to do with such matters—the Convention, consisting mostly of laymen, are to receive and judge of accusations against him. In short, his barber may shave him in the morning, and in the afternoon vote him out of his office.

"I was astonished, I say, at this regulation, and could not account for the clergy's agreeing to it; but my astonishment ceased when I was assured by a letter from America that all the clergy except *one* opposed it, but were outvoted, or overawed into a compliance, by the laity. This accounted for the matter: it is only one of the evils which I foresaw would attend the introduction of so many laymen into Conventions; and be assured it will be followed by many others."

The Convention of the Episcopal churches of the Middle and Southern States met in Philadelphia in June, 1786. It assembled, Bishop White informs us, "under circumstances which bore strong appearances of a dissolution of the union in this stage of it." There contributed to this state of affairs several circumstances. The "interfering instructions from the churches in the different States"—each of these churches being independent of the others and each cherishing its own notions as to the organization and perpetuation of the Church—afforded one source of danger. The "embarrassment which had arisen from the rejection of the Proposed Book in some of the States and the use of it in others," together with the almost universal disposition to revise still further this revision and amend its proposed amendments, afforded another source of apprehension. There had grown up in the minds of some, notably through the influence of the patriot Provoost, the Whig rector of Trinity, New York, a spirit of opposition to the bishop of Connecticut, and a disposition to discredit the source whence he had received the episcopate; and the warmth of feeling thus engendered threatened the lasting separation of the Churchmen in America. The unwillingness of the Church in South Carolina to receive a bishop at all, and the growing indifference in Virginia to the adoption of measures for securing the succession, indicated a lack of Churchly sentiment and an indifference to religion itself most discouraging. The attempts of the able but erratic Dr. William Smith, of Maryland, to obtain the episcopate of the Church in that State, and the attitude

[1] Perry's "Historical Notes and Documents," p. 302.

of Provoost, of New York, toward those of his brethren who were in sympathy with Seabury and the New England Churchmen, were elements of weakness in the union of the churches of the Middle and Southern States. Remonstrances from the conservative Churchmen of New Jersey had been addressed to the Convention, deprecating the radical measures already taken. It was evident that there was no prospect of securing any coöperation from New England in their further efforts for organization. Parker, of Boston, had expressed his conviction that the Scotch succession was less likely to excite prejudice than that of England, at this time. "In these Northern States," he wrote to Dr. White, "I much doubt whether a bishop from England would be received, so great is the jealousy still existing of the British nation. Of a Scotch bishop there can be no suspicions, because, wholly unconnected with the civil powers themselves, they could introduce none into these States. Were it not for these reasons I frankly confess I should rather have the succession from the English Church, to which we have always been accustomed to look as children to a parent." [1]

Besides these unpromising circumstances, the caution so evident in the letter of the English prelates, and the question whether the conditions they laid down would be granted by the Convention, added to the difficulties of the situation. One man alone in the midst of these complications pursued the even tenor of his way. William White never lost heart; never remitted his exertions in the interest of the Church of which he was now confessedly the leading spirit. Correcting misapprehensions, overcoming opposition, removing prejudices, he labored with one single end and aim in view. It was for the Church of God that he worked untiringly, and we may well bless God for his patient toil and well-deserved success.

The conflicting instructions to the deputies accredited to the Convention of June, 1786, from their respective constituencies, were skilfully gotten over by their reference "to the first Convention which should meet, fully authorized to determine on a Book of Common Prayer." This adroit use of a rule of parliamentary procedure was the suggestion of William White. It was through this expedient that, as White expressed it, "the instructions, far from proving injurious, had the contrary effect, by showing as well the necessity of a duly constituted ecclesiastical body as the futility of taking measures to be reviewed and authoritatively judged of in the bodies of which we were the deputies. Such a system appeared so evidently fruitful of discord and disunion that it was abandoned from this time." [2] The same judicious delay of definite action with respect to the Proposed Book removed the embarrassment threat-

[1] Perry's "Historical Notes and Documents," p. 309.
[2] White's "Memoirs of the Church," De Costa's edition, p. 131.

ened by the acceptance in some quarters, and the rejection in others, of this crude and hasty compilation. In the settlement of the question of the Scotch succession, which was only indirectly attacked, the conservatism and Christian courtesy of William White were specially apparent. The opposition to the Scottish episcopate was, so far as the clerical deputies were concerned, confined to the Rev. Samuel Provoost, afterward first bishop of New York, and the Rev. Robert Smith, afterward first bishop of South Carolina. Personal and political prejudices seem to have had their influence in this attempt to throw discredit on the source whence Seabury had obtained the episcopate. The Convention was barely organized when the Rev. Robert Smith introduced a resolution "That the clergy present produce their letters of orders, or declare by whom they were ordained." This motion was aimed at the Rev. Joseph Pilmore, a convert from the Methodists, who had received orders from Seabury, and the Rev. William Smith,[1] of Stepney parish, Md., and afterward of Newport, R. I., and Norwalk, Conn., who had been ordained in Scotland by a bishop of the Church from which Seabury had received consecration. The judicious application of the "previous question" prevented the discussion which it was anticipated would grow out of this motion, and the resolution itself was lost.

Provoost, not satisfied with this expression of the temper of the Convention, offered the following resolution: "That this Convention will resolve to do no act that shall imply the validity of ordinations made by Dr. Seabury." Again the "previous question" cut off discussion, and the motion itself was determined in the negative. So determined was the feeling of opposition to Dr. Seabury indicated by these motions that action of some kind could not be avoided, and consequently a compromise resolution offered by Dr. White was unanimously adopted. This motion provided "That it be recommended to this Church, in the States here represented, not to receive to the pastoral charge, within their respective limits, clergymen professing canonical subjection to any bishop in any State or country other than those bishops who may be duly settled in the States represented in this Convention." This resolution, as explained by Dr. White himself, was pressed with a view of meeting the charge, made on the floor of Convention, that clergymen ordained under the Scotch succession were under canonical subjection to the bishop who ordained them, even though they might reside outside of the limits of his see. The Rev. Mr. Pilmore, the only one of the deputies who had received orders from the bishop of Connecticut, "denied that any such thing had been exacted of him," and the resolution (for which, as Bishop White is careful to state, there was

[1] The compiler of the Institution Office, originally known as the Induction Office.

never "any ground" other than "in the apprehension which has been expressed") was adopted without opposition.

On the following day the Rev. Robert Smith returned to the subject and offered the following resolution, which, evidently regarded by the Convention, as Bishop White informs us, as a "temperate guarding" against a possible difficulty, was unanimously adopted:

> "*Resolved*, That it be recommended to the Conventions of the Church represented in its General Convention, not to admit any person as a minister, within their respective limits, who shall receive ordination from any bishop residing in America during the application now pending to the English bishops for episcopal consecration."

This matter disposed of, the Convention proceeded to the consideration of the letter from the English bishops. Resolutions expressing the "grateful sense of the Christian affection and condescension manifested in this letter" were adopted, and with this acknowledgment of the kindness of the English prelates the application for the succession was renewed, coupled with fresh assurances of attachment to the system of the Church of England. The reply to the archbishops and bishops was originally drafted by Dr. William Smith, but this paper being deemed "too full of compliment," it was, on the motion of the Hon. John Jay, considerably modified in tone and language. As finally adopted, it expressed a grateful appreciation of the fatherly sentiments contained in this letter of the English prelates; it reiterated the assurance that there was no purpose in America "of departing from the constituent principles of the Church of England"; it claimed that no alterations or omissions had been made in the Book of Common Prayer but such as were necessary to make it consistent with the civil constitutions, or "such as were calculated to remove objections" on the part of the people of the United States. The "proposed ecclesiastical constitution and Book of Common Prayer" accompanied this renewed request for the succession, and the alterations and modifications of the former made this second application more acceptable. As Bishop White observes, referring particularly to the development of a more conservative and Churchly spirit, as seen in the fuller recognition of episcopal character and dignity by this Convention: "In the preceding year the points alluded to were determined on with too much warmth, and without investigation proportioned to the importance of the subjects. The decisions of that day were now reversed, not to say without a division, but without even an opposition." It should not be forgotten that these constitutional changes in the direction of conservative Churchmanship were introduced by Dr. White and carried through his influence. These alterations gave to the bishop, if present, the presidency of the Convention, and required the bishop's presence at all ecclesiastical trials, giving to him the sole right of pronouncing the "sentence of deposition or degradation on any clergyman, whether bishop or presbyter or deacon."

Bishop White, who gives us in his "Memoirs of the Church" the unwritten history of this period, specifies as among the chief means of securing the moderation in tone and temper for which this Convention was noticeable the presentation of a memorial from the Convention of New Jersey, drawn up, as was "afterward learned with certainty," by the learned and devout Dr. Thomas Bradbury Chandler, of Elizabethtown, and couched in language both conservative and conclusive. This memorial urged the General Convention to revise the proceedings of the meeting of 1785, and to "remove every cause that may have excited any jealousy or fear that the Episcopal Church in the United States of America have any intention or desire essentially to depart, either in doctrine or discipline, from the Church of England." Bishop White regards this letter as "among the causes which prevented the disorganizing of" "the American Church," since its arguments must have convinced the deputies "that the result of considerable changes would have been the disunion of the Church."

Shortly after the rising of the Convention there came into the hands of Dr. White a communication from the archbishops of Canterbury and York, which was followed by a letter from the archbishop of Canterbury alone, inclosing a recent act of Parliament authorizing the consecration of bishops for America. On the receipt of these letters the committee appointed for this purpose convened the Convention at Wilmington, Del., on the 10th of October.

The archbishops prefaced their words with an earnest deprecation. It is "impossible," write the prelates, "not to observe with concern that if the essential doctrines of our common faith were retained, less respect, however, was paid to our liturgy than its own excellence, and your declared attachment to it, had led us to expect. Not to mention a variety of verbal alterations, of the necessity or propriety of which we are by no means satisfied, we saw with grief that two of the confessions of our Christian faith, respectable for their antiquity, have been entirely laid aside; and that even in that called the Apostles' Creed an article is omitted which was thought necessary to be inserted, with a view to a particular heresy, in a very early age of the Church, and has ever since had the venerable sanction of universal reception." The letter announced the application of the bishops for the passage of an act of Parliament authorizing the consecrations desired. This step was taken in the expectation that their representations would secure the modification of the radical action of the American Convention. Great stress was laid upon the necessity of affording "the most decisive proofs of the qualifications" of those recommended for consecration. The bishops called

To the Committee of the general Convention at Philadelphia, the Revd Dr White President, the Revd Dr Smith, the Revd Mr Provost, the Honble James Duane, Samuel Powell and Richard Peters Esqrs

Mr President and Gentlemen

Influenced by the same Sentiments of fraternal Regard expressed by the Archbishops and Bishops in their Answer to your Address, We desire you to be persuaded that if We have not yet been able to comply with your Request, the Delay has proceeded from no Tardiness on our part. The only Cause of it has been the Uncertainty in which We were left by receiving your Address unaccompanied by those Communications with regard to your Liturgy, Articles and Ecclesiastical Constitution, without the Knowledge of which we could not presume to apply to the Legislature for such Powers as were necessary to the Completion of your Wishes. The Journal of the Convention, and the first part of your Liturgy, did not reach us till more than two Months after our Receipt of your Address; and We were not in possession of the remaining part of it, and of your Articles, till the last day of April. The whole of your Communications was then, with as little Delay as possible, taken into Consideration at a Meeting of the Archbishops and Fifteen of the Bishops, being all who were then in London and able to attend; and it was impossible not to observe with Concern, that if the essential Doctrines of our Common Faith were retained, less Respect however was paid to our Liturgy than its own Excellence and your declared Attachment to it, had led us to expect. Not to mention a Variety of verbal Alterations, of the Necessity or propriety of which We are by no means satisfied, We saw with Grief, that Two of the Confessions of our Christian Faith, respectable for their Antiquity, have been entirely laid aside; and that even in That which is called the Apostles Creed, an Article is omitted, which was thought necessary to be inserted, with a View to a particular Heresy, in a very early Age of the Church, and has ever since had the venerable Sanction of universal Reception. Nevertheless as a Proof of the sincere Desire which We feel to continue in spiritual Communion with the Members of your Church in America, and to complete the Orders of your Ministry, and trusting that the Communications which We shall make to you, on the Subject of these and some other Alterations, will have their desired Effect. We have, even under these Circumstances, prepared a Bill for conveying to Us the Powers necessary for this purpose. It will in a few Days be presented to Parliament, and We have the best Reasons to hope that it will receive the Assent of the Legislature. This Bill will enable the Archbishops and Bishops to give Episcopal Consecration to the persons who

shall

shall be recommended, without requiring from them any Oaths or Subscriptions inconsistent with the Situation in which the late Revolution has placed them; upon Condition that the full Satisfaction of the Sufficiency of the Persons recommended, which you offer to Us in your Address, be given to the Archbishops and Bishops. You will doubtless receive it as a Mark both of our friendly Disposition towards you and of our Desire to avoid all Delay on this Occasion, that We have taken this earliest Opportunity of conveying to you this Intelligence, and that We proceed (as supposing ourselves invested with that Power which for your sakes We have requested) to state to you particularly the several Heads, upon which that Satisfaction which you offer, will be accepted, and the Mode in which it may be given. The Anxiety which is shown by the Church of England to prevent the Intrusion of unqualified Persons into even the Inferior Offices of our Ministry, confirms our own Sentiments, and points it out to be our Duty, very earnestly to require the most decisive Proofs of the Qualifications of those who may be offered for Admission to that Order, to which the Superintendence of those Offices is committed. At our several Ordinations of a Deacon and a Priest, the Candidate submits himself to the Examination of the Bishop as to his Proficiency in Learning; He gives the proper Security of his Soundness in the Faith by the Subscriptions which are made previously necessary; He is required to bring Testimonials of his virtuous Conversation during the Three preceding Years; and that no Mode of Inquiry may be omitted, publick Notice of his offering himself to be ordained is given in the Parish Church where he resides or ministers, and the People are solemnly called upon to declare, if they know any Impediment for the which he ought not to be admitted. At the Time of Ordination too the same solemn Call is made on the Congregation then present.

Examination, Subscription and Testimonials are not indeed repeated at the Consecration of an English Bishop, because the Person to be consecrated has added to the Securities given at his former Ordinations that Sanction, which arises from his having constantly lived and exercised his Ministry under the Eyes and Observation of his Country. But the Objects of our present Consideration are very differently circumstanced: Their Sufficiency in Learning, the Soundness of their Faith and the Purity of their Manners, are not Matters of Notoriety here. Means therefore must be found to satisfy the Archbishops who consecrate, and the Bishops who present them; that, in the Words of our Church, "They be apt and meet for their "Learning and godly Conversation, to exercise their Ministry duly to the Honour of "God, and the edifying of his Church, and to be wholesome Examples and Patterns "to the Flock of Christ."

With Regard to the first Qualification, Sufficiency in good Learning, We apprehend that the subjecting a Person, who is to be admitted to the Office of a Bishop in the Church, to that Examination which is required previous to the

Ordination

Ordination of Priests and Deacons, might lessen that reverend Estimation, which
ought never to be separated from the Episcopal Character: We therefore do not require any
farther Satisfaction on this point than will be given to Us by the Forms of
Testimonials in the annexed paper; fully trusting that those who sign them
will be well aware, how greatly Incompetence in this Respect must lessen the
Weight and Authority of the Bishop and affect the Credit of the Episcopal Church.

Under the second Head, that of Subscription, our Desire is to require that
Subscription only to be repeated, which you have already been called upon to make by
the Tenth Article of your Ecclesiastical Constitution: but We should forget the Duty
which We owe to our own Church, and act inconsistently with that sincere Regard which
We bear to yours, if We were not explicit in declaring, that, after the Disposition
We have shown to comply with the Prayer of your Address, We think it now
incumbent upon you to use your utmost Exertions also for the Removal of any
stumbling block of Offence, which may possibly prove an Obstacle to the Success of
it. We therefore most earnestly exhort you, that previously to the Time of your making
such Subscription, you restore to its Integrity the Apostles' Creed, in which you have
omitted an Article merely, as it seems, from Misapprehension of the Sense in which it
is understood by our Church. Nor can We help adding, that We hope you will think
it but a decent proof of the Attachment which you profess to the Services of our
Liturgy, to give to the other two Creeds a place in your Book of Common Prayer,
even tho' the Use of them should be left discretional. We should be inexcusable too
if at the Time when you are requesting the Establishment of Bishops in your
Church, We did not strongly represent to you that the Eighth Article of your
Ecclesiastical Constitution appears to Us to be a Degradation of the Clerical
and still more of the Episcopal Character. We persuade ourselves that in your
ensuing Convention some Alteration will be thought necessary in this Article
before this reaches you: or, if not, that due Attention will be given to it in Consequence
of our Representation.

On the Third and last Head, which respects Purity of Manners,
the Reputation of the Church, both in England and America, and the Interest of
our common Christianity, is so deeply ~~interested~~ concerned in it, that We feel it our indispensible
Duty to provide on this Subject the most effectual Securities. It is presumed that
the same previous public Notice of the Intention of the Person to be consecrated
will be given in the Church where he resides in America, for the same Reasons, and
therefore nearly in the same Form, with that used in England [before our Ordinations]. The Call upon the
Persons present at the Time of Consecration, must be deemed of little Use before a
Congregation composed of those to whom the person to be consecrated is unknown.
The Testimonials signed by Persons living in England admit of Reference and
Examination, and the Characters of those who give them are subject to Scrutiny; and
in Case of criminal Deceit, to Punishment. In Proportion as these Grounds, hence
and

are less applicable to Testimonials from America: these Testimonials must be more explicit, and supported by a greater Number of Signatures. We therefore think it necessary that the several Persons Candidates for Episcopal Consecration should bring to us both a Testimonial from the general Convention of the Episcopal Church, with as many Signatures as can be obtained, and a more particular one, from the respective Conventions in those States which recommend them. It will appear from the Tenor of the Letters Testimonial used in England a Form of which is annexed that the Ministers who sign them bear Testimony to the Qualifications of the Candidates on their own personal Knowledge. Such a Testimony is not to be expected from the Members of the General Convention of the Episcopal Church in America on this Occasion. We think it sufficient therefore that they declare they know no Impediment but believe the Person to be consecrated is of a virtuous Life and sound Faith. We have sent you such a Form as appears to us proper to be used for that purpose. More specific Declarations must be made by the Members of the Convention in each State from which the Persons offered for Consecration are respectively recommended, their personal Knowledge of them there can be no Doubt of. We trust therefore they will have no Objection to the Adoption of the Form of a Testimonial which is annexed and drawn upon the same Principles and containing the same Attestations of personal Knowledge with that abovementioned as required previously to our Ordinations. We trust We shall receive these Testimonials signed by such a Majority in each Convention that recommend as to leave no Doubt of the Fitness of the Candidates upon the Minds of those whose Consciences are concerned in the Consecration of them.

Thus much We have thought it right to communicate to you without Reserve at present, intending to give you further Information as soon as We are able. In the mean Time We pray God to direct your Counsels in this very weighty Matter and are Mr. President and Gentlemen

Your affectionate Brethren

J. Cantuar:

W. Ebor

ANNO REGNI

GEORGII III.

REGIS

Magnæ Britanniæ, Franciæ, & Hiberniæ,

VICESIMO SEXTO.

At the Parliament begun and holden at *Westminster*, the Eighteenth Day of *May*, *Anno Domini* 1784, in the Twenty-fourth Year of the Reign of our Sovereign Lord GEORGE the Third, by the Grace of God, of *Great Britain*, *France*, and *Ireland*, King, Defender of the Faith, *&c.*

And from thence continued, by several Prorogations, to the Twenty-fourth Day of *January*, 1786; being the Third Session of the Sixteenth Parliament of *Great Britain*.

LONDON:
Printed by C. Eyre and the Executors of W. Strahan, Printers to the King's most Excellent Majesty. 1786.

ANNO VICESIMO SEXTO

Georgii III. Regis.

CAP. LXXXIV.

An Act to empower the Archbishop of *Canterbury*, or the Archbishop of *York*, for the Time being, to consecrate to the Office of a Bishop, Persons being Subjects or Citizens of Countries out of His Majesty's Dominions.

WHEREAS, by the Laws of this Realm, no Person can be consecrated to the Office of a Bishop without the King's Licence for his Election to that Office, and the Royal Mandate under the Great Seal for his Confirmation and Consecration: And whereas every Person who shall be consecrated to the said Office is required to take the Oaths of Allegiance and Supremacy, and also the Oath of due Obedience to the Archbishop: And whereas there are divers Persons, Subjects or Citizens of Countries out of His Majesty's Dominions, and inhabiting and residing within the said Countries, who profess the Publick Worship of Almighty God, according to the Principles of the Church of England, and who, in order to provide a regular Succession of Ministers for the Service of their Church, are desirous of having certain of the Subjects or Citizens of those Countries consecrated Bishops, according to the Form of Consecration in the Church of England: Be it enacted by the King's most Excellent Majesty, by and with the Advice and Consent of the Lords Spiritual and Temporal, and Commons, in this present Parliament assembled, and by Preamble

The Archbishop of Canterbury or York, with such other Bishops as they shall think fit to assist, may consecrate Subjects of foreign States Bishops, without the King's Licence for the Election, or requiring them to take the usual Oaths;

the Authority of the same, That, from and after the passing of this Act, it shall and may be lawful to and for the Archbishop of Canterbury, or the Archbishop of York, for the Time being, together with such other Bishops as they shall call to their Assistance, to consecrate Persons, being Subjects or Citizens of Countries out of His Majesty's Dominions, Bishops, for the Purposes aforesaid, without the King's Licence for their Election, or the Royal Mandate, under the Great Seal, for their Confirmation and Consecration, and without requiring them to take the Oaths of Allegiance and Supremacy, and the Oath of due Obedience to the Archbishop for the Time being.

but not without first obtaining His Majesty's Royal Licence for performing the Consecration, &c.

II. Provided always, That no Persons shall be consecrated Bishops in the Manner herein provided, until the Archbishop of Canterbury, or the Archbishop of York, for the Time being, shall have first applied for and obtained His Majesty's Licence, by Warrant under His Royal Signet and Sign Manual, authorising and empowering him to perform such Consecration, and expressing the Name or Names of the Persons so to be consecrated, nor until the said Archbishop has been fully ascertained of their sufficiency in good Learning, of the Soundness of their Faith, and of the Purity of their Manners.

No Persons so consecrated, &c. thereby enabled to exercise their Offices in His Majesty's Dominions.

III. Provided also, and be it hereby declared, That no Person or Persons consecrated to the Office of a Bishop in the Manner aforesaid, nor any Person or Persons deriving their Consecration from or under any Bishop so consecrated, nor any Person or Persons admitted to the Order of Deacon or Priest by any Bishop or Bishops so consecrated, or by the Successor or Successors of any Bishop or Bishops so consecrated, shall be thereby enabled to exercise his or their respective Office or Offices within His Majesty's Dominions.

Certificate of Consecration to be given by the Archbishop, &c.

IV. Provided always, and be it further enacted, That a Certificate of such Consecration shall be given under the Hand and Seal of the Archbishop who consecrates, containing the Name of the Person so consecrated, with the Addition, as well of the Country whereof he is a Subject or Citizen, as of the Church in which he is appointed Bishop, and the further Description of his not having taken the said Oaths, being exempted from the Obligation of so doing by virtue of this Act.

9 FINIS.

upon the Convention, before the bishops elect should make the subscription required by the tenth article of the proposed ecclesiastical constitution, to "restore to its integrity the Apostles' Creed"; to "give to the other two creeds a place" in the Prayer-book, "even though the use of them should be left discretional;" and to make some alteration in the eighth article of the ecclesiastical constitution, removing what appeared to the bishops "to be a degradation of the clerical, and still more of the episcopal character."

The solicitude of the bishops respecting the "purity of manners" of those recommended for consecration led them to require "the most effectual securities"; and forms of testimonial, to be signed by the General and State Conventions, accompanied the letter, which have been ever since, and are still, in use in the American Church. These testimonials, Bishop White assures us, gave "general satisfaction." "The General Convention," continues Bishop White, "had not been without apprehensions that some unsuitable character, as to morals, might be elected; and yet for them to have assumed a control might have been an improper interference with the churches in the individual States."

It is at this point, and evidently calling to mind the grave issues depending on the proper action at this critical moment, that Bishop White, in his "Memoirs of the Church," interrupts the narrative with the paragraph we quote:

"The question to be determined on at the present session was, Whether the American Church would avail herself of the opportunity of obtaining the episcopacy, which had been so earnestly desired ever since the settlement of the colonies, the want of which had been so long complained of, and which was now held out in offer. When the author considers how much, besides the preference due to episcopal government, the continuance or the restoration of divine worship in the almost deserted churches, their very existence as a society, and, of course, the interests of religion and virtue, were concerned in the issue, he looks back with a remnant of uneasy sensation at the hazard which this question run, and at the probability which then threatened that the determination might be contrary to what took place."[1]

On the assembling of the adjourned Convention at Wilmington, Del., the papers from England were referred to a committee of which Dr. White was evidently the leading member. This committee, we are told by Bishop White, "sat up the whole of the succeeding night digesting the determinations in the form in which they appear on the 'Journal.'" These conclusions were comprised in a paper entitled "An Act of the General Convention of Clerical and Lay Deputies of the Protestant Episcopal Church, in the States of New York, New Jersey, Pennsylvania, Delaware, and South Carolina, held at Wilmington, in the State of Delaware, on Wednesday, the 11th of October, 1786." This act, after reciting the precedent circumstances of the organization and conventional action of the American Church, proceeds to "determine and declare":

[1] White's "Memoirs of the Church," De Costa's edition, p. 138.

"First, That in the creed commonly called the Apostles' Creed these words, 'He descended into hell,' shall be and continue a part of that creed.

"Secondly, That the Nicene Creed shall also be inserted in the said Book of Common Prayer, immediately after the Apostles' Creed, prefaced with the rubric [*or this*].

"And whereas, in consequence of the objections expressed by their lordships to the alterations in the Book of Common Prayer last mentioned, the Conventions in some of the States represented in this General Convention have suspended the ratification and use of the said Book of Common Prayer, by reason whereof it will be improper that persons to be consecrated or ordained as bishops, priests, or deacons, respectively, should subscribe the declaration contained in the tenth article of the general ecclesiastical constitution, without some modification;

"Therefore it is hereby determined and declared, Thirdly, That the second clause so to be subscribed by a bishop, priest, or deacon of this Church in any of the States which have not already ratified or used the last-mentioned Book of Common Prayer, shall be in the words following:

"'And I do solemnly engage to conform to the doctrine and worship of the Protestant Episcopal Church, according to the use of the Church of England, as the same is altered by the General Convention, in a certain instrument of writing passed by their authority, entitled "Alterations in the Liturgy of the Protestant Episcopal Church in the United States of America, in order to render the same conformable to the American Revolution and the constitutions of the respective States," until the new Book of Common Prayer, recommended by the General Convention, shall be ratified or used in the State in which I am (bishop, priest, or deacon, as the case may be), by the authority of the Convention thereof. And I do further solemnly engage that when the said new Book of Common Prayer shall be ratified or used by the authority of the Convention in the State for which I am consecrated a bishop (or ordained a priest or deacon) I will conform to the doctrines and worship of the Protestant Episcopal Church, as settled and determined in the last-mentioned Book of Common Prayer and Administration of the Sacraments, set forth by the General Convention of the Protestant Episcopal Church in the United States.'

"And it is hereby further determined and declared:

"That these words in the Preface to the new proposed Book of Common Prayer—viz., 'in the creed commonly called the Apostles' Creed one clause is omitted as being of uncertain meaning, and'—together with the note referred to in that place, be from henceforth no part of the Preface to the said proposed Book of Common Prayer.

"And it is hereby further determined and declared:

"That the Fourth Article of Religion in the new proposed Book of Common Prayer be altered to render it conformable to the adoption of the Nicene Creed, as follows: 'Of the Creeds. The two creeds, namely, that commonly called the Apostle's Creed and the Nicene Creed, ought to be received and believed because they,' etc., etc."

On the first vote—the question being the restoring of the words "He descended into hell" to the Apostles' Creed—New York, Pennsylvania, and Delaware were divided. New Jersey and South Carolina voted aye. As the divided States did not count, there were two ayes and no negatives, and the words were restored.

The Nicene Creed was restored unanimously. On the question, "Shall the creed commonly called the Athanasian Creed be admitted in the liturgy of the Protestant Episcopal Church in the United States of America?" New Jersey and Delaware were divided, and New York, Pennsylvania, and South Carolina voted in the negative. Maryland, represented by a clerical deputy only, the Rev. Dr. William Smith, was at the outset declared not admitted to the Convention, and was allowed no vote on these important matters.

A brief address to the archbishops was prepared and adopted. The testimonials of Dr. White, bishop elect of Pennsylvania, Dr. Provoost, bishop elect of New York, and Dr. Griffith, bishop elect of Virginia, were signed, and a Committee of Correspondence, with power to convene another General Convention, was appointed.

Although it does not appear on the "Journals," and no direct reference to the circumstance can be found in Bishop White's account of this Convention in his "Memoirs of the Church," the voluminous correspondence of this period, preserved in the archives of the General Convention, acquaints us with the fact that the Wilmington Convention, while availing itself of the presence and the abilities of Dr. William Smith, bishop elect of Maryland, refused to sign the testimonial required, recommending him for consecration. It appears, from letters still on file, that two members only of the Convention voted in favor of Dr. Smith's application for recommendation, and that the opposition was based on moral grounds.

The end desired was near at hand. The bishops elect of Pennsylvania and New York set sail for England early in November, 1786, and arrived at Falmouth on the 21st of that month. We need not trace the story of the successful accomplishment of the long struggle for the episcopate in the English line, as it is detailed at length in the pages of Bishop White's "Memoirs of the Church." It is enough to say that on the fourth day of February, 1787, at Lambeth Chapel, at the hands of the archbishop of Canterbury, Dr. Moore, the archbishop of York, Dr. Markham, the bishop of Bath and Wells, Dr. Moss, and the bishop of Peterborough, Dr. Hinchcliffe, William White and Samuel Provoost were duly and canonically, by the laying on of hands, made bishops of the Church of God.

It was a happy omen for the newly organized American Church that the bishops of Pennsylvania and New York reached their native land amid the Easter festivities of the year 1787. The Church in America was now complete. There only remained the consolidation of the churches of the North with those of the Middle and Southern States in one organization, and the adjustment in the general ecclesiastical constitution of the united churches of those principles and practices which were still unsettled.

Directly on the return of the newly consecrated bishops to their homes, the bishop of Connecticut addressed to each letters of congratulation, adding expressions of his earnest desire to promote "uniformity in worship and discipline among the churches of the different States." Referring to the "present unsettled state of the Church of England in this country, and the necessity of union and concord among all its members in the United States of America, not only to give stability to it, but to fix it on its true and proper foundation," Bishop Seabury proposed that a meeting of the three bishops should be held "before any decided steps be taken," and suggested as a basis of union and comprehension a return to the

English Prayer-book, "accommodating it to the civil Constitution of the United States." "The government of the Church," he adds, "is already settled; a body of canons will, however, be wanted to give energy to the government and ascertain its operation." The terms of union thus suggested were simply an affirmation of the "Fundamental Principle" adopted in New York in October, 1784, respecting the Prayer-book. In the view of Seabury other differences could be settled by conference, and this meeting of the bishops, he was confident, "would promote the great object—the union of all the churches." "May God direct us in all things," was his closing prayer. In making these fraternal overtures Seabury was evidently influenced solely by his earnest desire for union and uniformity. He already occupied a position of absolute independence. Welcomed by the clergy and warmly supported by the laity, his episcopal character had been recognized throughout New England, which had become, practically, his province, and through which, from Stamford and Norwalk in Connecticut to Portsmouth, N. H., he journeyed, confirming, ordaining, and setting in order the churches owing allegiance to his office and to himself. He had exercised his episcopate in New York in spite of the secret opposition of the irate Provoost. Candidates for ordination from New Jersey, Pennsylvania, and the Southern States had sought from him the laying on of hands. There was no dissension among his clergy, no factious opposition among his laity. The Wallingford Convocation of the Connecticut clergy, held in February of this year, resenting the affronts they deemed directed at the bishop at the Philadelphia Convention, had determined to send a representative to Scotland to receive consecration as coadjutor to Seabury; and Leaming and Mansfield were successively chosen to undertake this office, while on their unwillingness, in consequence of age and infirmities, to assume this responsibility, the choice fell on Jarvis, afterward to be the one to fill the place of Seabury. At the same time measures were put in train to secure in Massachusetts the election of Parker as bishop of the Church in that State and in New Hampshire, that thus the college of bishops in the Scottish line of succession might be complete, and any necessity of union with the churches at the southward, for the consecration of bishops in the time to come, removed. The correspondence of this period affords abundant proof that the great body of the churches and Churchmen of New England shared in this feeling of resentment, and were ready for the initiation of measures for perpetuating the separation and antagonism which seemed inevitable. There was every prospect that there would speedily be in this country two rival Episcopal Churches, each possessing the apostolical succession, but at variance with each other in doctrine, in ritual, and in practices. Had Seabury listened

New London May 1st. 1787.

Right Reverend & dear Sir,

It is with great pleasure I take an opportunity of presenting my congratulations on your safe return to Philadelphia, & on the success of your application to the English Archbishops.

You must be equally sensible with me of the present unsettled State of the Church of England in this country, & of the necessity of union & concord, among all its members in the United States of America, not only to give stability to it, but to fix it on the true Episcopal foundation. Possibly nothing will contribute more to this end, than uniformity in worship & discipline, among the Churches of the different States. It will be my happiness to promote so good & necessary a work: And I take the liberty to propose, That, before any decided steps be taken, there may be a meeting of yourself & Bp. Provost, with me, at such time & place as shall be convenient; to try whether some plan can not be adopted, that shall, in a quiet & effectual way, secure the great object which, I trust, we should all heartily rejoice to see accomplished. For my own part, I cannot help thinking that the most likely method will be, to retain the present Book of Common-Prayer, accomodating it to the Civil constitution of the United States. The government of the Church, you know, is already settled: a body of Canons will however be wanted to

guid

to give energy to the government, & quicken its operations.

I have written to Bp. Provoost on this subject, & have invited him to visit us at the stated Convocation of our Clergy which is to be held at Stamford Thursday after Whitsunday. I regret that the distance & time will not probably permit you to do us that favour; more especially as I think it would greatly promote so essential an object as the union of all our Churches must be esteemed. May God direct us in all things!

Believe me to be, Right Reverend, & dear Sir,

your affectionate Brother,

& humble Servant,

Samuel Bp. Connect.

Rt. Revd. Bp. White

to the urgings of his clergy at home, and his correspondents both in this country and abroad, this deplorable result would have occurred. Union would soon have become impossible, and the Church in the United States—a house divided against itself—would have been at the mercy of old foes and new, each and all bent alike on its utter overthrow.

It is in this connection that we cannot fail to recognize and admire the wise conservatism, the marked self-abnegation, the patient forbearance of the first bishop of Connecticut. He was already practically—he might soon have been in fact and name—the "primus" of the Church in New England. Massachusetts, New Hampshire, Rhode Island, and Connecticut were through their episcopal head closely affiliated with the Scottish communion, from which their episcopate was derived, and were already reproducing at the outset of the history of the New England Episcopal Church the distinctive principles of the body whence they sprang. It was Seabury's choice, however, for the "great object" he had at heart, "the union of all the churches," to enter into a union in which he was to be from the start in a hopeless minority. We find him, therefore, restraining the impetuosity of his friends and sympathizers outside of Connecticut. We find him making most friendly and courteous overtures to the bishop of New York, who had attacked him in public and in private, and who cherished an unreasonable personal animosity toward him. He renewed again and again these efforts for union and comprehension, and at length God, who maketh men to be of one mind in a house, rewarded his self-denying, self-forgetting endeavors and made him for the last few years of his earthly life the presiding bishop of a united American Church.

In these efforts of Seabury for union William White was an earnest and able seconder. Recognizing from the start the official character and the Christian courtesy of Seabury, the bishop of Pennsylvania, while careful to secure the features of our ecclesiastical system he had formulated in "The Case of the Episcopal Churches Considered," was ever ready to further the schemes of Seabury for the comprehension of "all the churches" in one organization comprising the churches in every State. Without this seconding Seabury's efforts would have been of no avail. The personal animosity of Provoost, the machinations of the able and unscrupulous William Smith, the lax Churchmanship and doctrinal unsoundness prevailing in various sections of the Church and uniting in efforts to render the episcopal office as powerless as possible—all these obstacles to union were to be overcome, and in the successful struggle it was William White who contributed the most of labor and influence to secure the desired result. It is of interest to note the hand of God hedging up the way to the completion of the episcopal college in the English line until, in His good time, both a disposition for union had become general and measures to effect this end were in train.

The amiable and devoted Griffith, the friend of Washington, and doubtless the most worthy of the Virginia clergy, was the choice of the Convention of that State for bishop, and his papers were favorably passed upon by the adjourned General Convention at Wilmington in 1786. But this excellent man found his intended journey to England hindered and finally prevented by the indifference of the parishes, leading them to withhold their contributions for its accomplishment. Even when the generous aid of William White was offered to remove this obstacle, the coldness of the clergy toward their bishop elect made it evident that they feared both his piety and his zeal for the Church, should he ever enter upon the episcopate to which their suffrages had called him. There followed, as appears from the unpublished correspondence of Dr. Griffith with Bishop White, a series of petty but annoying persecutions which, as detailed in these letters, reveal a lamentable laxity in doctrine, and even in morals, existing in the Virginia Church. It is a pitiful story, and of interest alone in showing a conspiracy of ministers and members of the Episcopal Church designed to destroy the efficiency, if not the very existence, of the episcopate, the powers of which they evidently felt would be at once exercised for their punishment.

These annoying hindrances at length wore out the patience of Griffith, and wrung from him the resignation of the office he had never sought, but which he would have adorned and honored. It was not till after the death of Griffith and the return of the bishops of Pennsylvania and New York from their successful journey to England that the scholarly Madison, the president of William and Mary College, was chosen to the episcopate of Virginia and sent to England to complete the college in the English line.

No obstacle remained to prevent the consecration of a bishop on American soil who should unite the Scottish and English lines of succession. This long-delayed act was finally accomplished when Thomas John Claggett was made a bishop of the Church of God by the laying on of the hands of Provoost, Seabury, White, and Madison.

Know all Men by these Presents that We, Samuel Provoost D.D. Bishop of the Protestant Episcopal Church in the State of New York - Presiding Bishop, Samuel Seabury D.D. Bishop of Connecticut and Rhode Island - William White D.D. Bishop of the Protestant Episcopal Church in the Commonwealth of Pennsylvania - James Madison D.D. Bishop of the Protestant Episcopal Church in the State of Virginia, under the protection of Almighty God, in Trinity Church in the City of New York, on Monday the seventeenth of Sept. in the year of our Lord one thousand seven hundred and ninety two, did then and there rightly and canonically consecrate our Beloved in Christ Thomas John Claggett D.D. late Rector of St. James's Parish in the State of Maryland, of whose sufficiency in good Learning, soundness in the Faith and purity of Manners we were fully ascertained, into the office of Bishop of the Protestant Episcopal Church in the said State to which the said Thomas John Claggett hath been elected by the Convention of the said State. In testimony whereof We have signed our Names and caused our Seals to be affixed, given in the City of New York, this nineteenth day of September in the Year of our Lord one thousand seven hundred and ninety two.

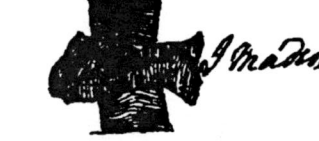

S. Seabury
Wm: White
Samuel Provoost.
J Madison

Endorsement upon
Bishop Claggett's Letter of Consecration.

Certificate of the Consecration of the Rt Reverend Father in God Thomas John Claggett D.D. Bishop of the Protestant Episcopal Church in the State of

Maryland

17th September 1792

Seal of Bishop Provoost, appended to
Bishop Claggett's Letter of Consecration

C. Inglis, 1787; R. Stanser, 1816; J. Inglis, 1825; H. Binney, 1851; F. Courtney, 1888.

Quebec, 1793.
J. Mountain, 1793; C. J. Stewart, 1826;
G. J. Mountain, 1836; J. W. Williams, 1863;
A. H. Dunn, 1892.

Newfoundland, 1839 (independent).
A. G. Spencer, 1839; E. Field, 1844;
J. B. Kelly, coad. 1867, dio. bp. 1876;
L. Jones, 1878.

Fredericton, 1845.
J. Medley, 1845;
H. T. Kingdom, coad. 1881, dio. bp. 1892

Toronto, 1839.
J. Strachan, 1839;
A. N. Bethune, 1867;
A. Sweatman, 1879.

Montreal.
F. Fulford, 1850;
A. Oxenden, 1869;
W. B. Bond, 1879.

Huron.
B. Cronyn, 1857;
I. Hellmuth, 1871;
M. S. Baldwin, 1883.

Ontario.
J. T. Lewis, 1862, abp. 1893.

Algoma.
F. D. Fauquier, 1873;
E. Sullivan, 1882.

Niagara.
T. B. Fuller, 1875;
C. Hamilton, 1885.

PROVINCE OF RUPERT'S LAND.

Rupert's Land, 1849.
D. Anderson, 1849; R. Machray, 1865, primate of all Canada, 1893.

Moosonee, 1872.
J. Horden, 1873;
J. A. Newnham, 1893.

Saskatchewan, 1874.
J. McLean, 1874;
W. C. Pinkham, 1887.

Mackenzie River, 1874 (formerly Athabasca)
W. C. Bompas, 1874;
W. D. Reeves, 1891.

Columbia,[1] 1859.
G. Hills, 1859;
W. W. Perrin, 1893.

Qu'Appelle, 1884 (formerly Assiniboia).
A. J. R. Anson, 1884;
W. J. Burn, 1893.

Athabasca (old, 1874; new, 1884).
R. Young, 1884.

Selkirk, 1891.
W. C. Bompas, cons. 1874, tr. 1891.

New Westminster.[1]
A. W. Sillitoe, 1879;
W. H. Binney, 1895.

Caledonia, 1879.[1]
W. Ridley, 1879.

Since 1878 Newfoundland is properly Newfoundland and Bermuda.
Since 1888 Saskatchewan is properly Saskatchewan and Calgary.

1 Independent of, but represented in Synod of, Rupert's Land.

III.

THE EPISCOPATE OF THE CHURCH IN BRITISH NORTH AMERICA.

THE year of grace 1787 was memorable in ecclesiastical annals as the epoch in which the Church of England gave to the provinces which had maintained their allegiance to the crown the episcopate so long withheld from the American colonists, who for years had persistently craved this boon in vain. The choice had primarily fallen on the excellent Thomas Bradbury Chandler, D.D. Oxon., of Elizabethtown, N. J., whose acknowledged abilities and deep, earnest piety had long pointed him out as the one on whom this honor should be bestowed. But the ravages of incurable disease were even then threatening his life; and although he was spared for several years, and able to render service of inestimable value to the Church in the United States, he was averse to accepting an appointment many of the duties of which it would be impossible to fulfil. It is said that, at the request of the archbishop of Canterbury to suggest one of his brethren to fill the place, he named his friend and former associate in the ministry in America, the late rector of Trinity, New York. On the 12th of August, 1787, Charles Inglis, D.D., sometime missionary at Dover, Del., and later catechist, assistant minister, and rector of Trinity Church, New York, was consecrated, in the chapel of Lambeth Palace, the first colonial bishop of the English Church. His see was the province of Nova Scotia, with New Brunswick, Canada, and Newfoundland included. The newly consecrated bishop proceeded almost directly to his vast jurisdiction.

In a letter addressed to Bishop White, of Philadelphia, soon after the bishop of Nova Scotia had reached America, we have his impressions of his new field:

"HALIFAX, December 10, 1787.

"MY GOOD BROTHER WHITE: . . . You have probably heard of my appointment as bishop of Nova Scotia and my arrival at this place. After many delays of office to which my patent was subject, and much fatigue in forming the arrangements for a new diocese, I was consecrated at Lambeth on Sunday, the 12th of August, embarked for America the 28th of the same month, and arrived at Halifax October 15th. I found the state of this province nearly such as I suppose you found that of your diocese—in great want of the superintending care and inspection of a bishop; and much need I have of the divine aid to enable me to discharge the duties of this station—much prudence, judgment, temper, and zeal guided by discretion are required. Nova Scotia is properly my diocese. I have the same authority given me over the clergy that bishops have in England over their clergy; but the temporal powers vested in English bishops by the constitution are withheld; and this by my own choice, for I drew up the plan that was adopted. By another patent of later date, directed to me as bishop of Nova Scotia, the same authority over the clergy of New Brunswick, Canada, and Newfoundland is given me that was granted before over the clergy of this province. For there are two patents, which I should have mentioned before—one is during my life, by which this province is constituted a bishop's see, and I am appointed the first bishop; the other is during the king's pleasure, and granting me the same authority with the former. This was a prudent measure, and intended to facilitate the appointment of bishops in those other provinces when it would be found expedient. . . . My extreme hurry at present prevents me from mentioning several particulars which I wished to communicate. I shall be always ready by every method in my power to convince you that I am, with great esteem and with sincere wishes for your success,

"Right Reverend Sir,

"Your affectionate brother and humble servant,

"CHARLES, NOVA SCOTIA.

"RIGHT REVEREND BISHOP WHITE."

The correspondence of the first bishop of Nova Scotia with Bishop White is full of interest, and gives in detail most interesting accounts of the bishop's visitations, his interminable journeys, his founding of King's College, Windsor, N. S., his building of churches and schools, his efforts for the spiritual development of his people, and his earnest desire to resent the encroachments of indifference and infidelity. He died full of years and honors, and the hundred years and more that have passed since the first bishop of the Church of England for the colonies was consecrated have witnessed the sending of these missionary apostles throughout the world. We append from data furnished by the Rt. Rev. Dr. Hale, bishop of Cairo, Ill., the succession of bishops in the English line in British North America from Inglis to the present day.

IV.

THE METHODIST SUPERINTENDENCY OR EPISCOPACY.

METHODIST services were first held in America in 1766, by Philip Cushing in New York, and by Robert Strawbridge in Frederick County, Md. Both Cushing and Strawbridge had been Methodist preachers in their native country, Ireland. In 1769 Mr. Wesley sent over Richard Boardman and Joseph Pilmore. In 1771 he appointed Francis Asbury, and two years later Thomas Rankin, to represent him in America. None of these men were ordained, and all of them appear to have confined themselves to such work as Mr. Wesley deemed laymen might undertake, except Robert Strawbridge, who as early as 1769 began to administer the sacraments without any ordination whatever. The minutes of the first American Conference, held in Philadelphia in 1773, show that the following rules were unanimously agreed upon: [1]

[1] "Minutes of the Annual Conferences," vol. i., p. 5 (New York, 1850).

"(1) Every preacher who acts in connection with Mr. Wesley and the brethren in America is strictly to avoid administering the ordinances of baptism and the Lord's Supper. (2) All the people among whom we labor, to be earnestly exhorted to attend their church, and to receive the ordinance there, but in a particular manner to press the people in Maryland and Virginia to the observance of this minute."

Jesse Lee says:

"The necessity of this rule appeared in the conduct of Mr. Strawbridge, a local preacher, who had taken on him to administer the ordinance among the Methodists. . . . We were only a religious society, and not a church."[1]

But Strawbridge would not change his convictions or his course. In 1779 some of the preachers ministering in Virginia and North Carolina "concluded that if God had called them to preach He had called them also to administer the ordinances of baptism and the Lord's Supper. They met together at the Conference held at the Broken Back Church this year, and after consulting together, the Conference chose a committee for the purpose of ordaining ministers. The committee thus chosen first ordained themselves, and then proceeded to set apart other preachers for the same purpose, that they might administer the holy ordinances."[2] Asbury denounced these irregular proceedings, "denying the authority by which the preachers acted, and declaring the ordination to which they had given existence invalid."[3] The Conference in Baltimore, in 1780, "concluded that they did not look upon the Virginia preachers as Methodists in connection with Mr. Wesley; and that Conference neither could nor would consider them as such, unless they came back to their former standing."[4] A compromise was finally adopted by which the recalcitrant preachers agreed temporarily to conform their practice to that of those in Maryland and Pennsylvania, Mr. Asbury promising to write to Mr. Wesley and ask his advice as to the question involved.

At the close of the Revolutionary War Asbury wrote to Mr. Wesley, giving an account of the work under his charge. He spoke especially of the great difficulty of the Methodists' receiving the sacraments, those authorized to administer them being few in number and widely scattered. Still there was reason to believe that as the country returned to its normal state these difficulties would be lessened or wholly obviated. As it was, more than half of the Methodists in America lived in Maryland and Virginia, in both which States there still remained a considerable number of clergy. In Virginia we are told that to meet the existing emergency, and to "prevent so far as possible a renewal of the complaint of the want of sacraments, some at least of the Episcopal clergy traveled over large circuits for the purpose of baptizing the children of Methodists

[1] Lee's "History of the Methodists," p. 47. [2] *Ibid.*, p. 69.
[3] Drew's "Life of Dr. Coke," p. 70 (New York, 1857).
[4] Lee's "History of the Methodists," p. 72.

and administering the eucharist, and continued to do so until the final separation of the Methodists from the Church, without desiring or receiving for their services the smallest compensation."[1]

It is evident that Mr. Wesley formed an exaggerated idea of the destitution of religious privileges in America. In referring to the American Methodists he says: "Since the late Revolution in America these have been in great distress. The clergy, having no sustenance, have been allowed, almost universally, to leave the country and seek their food elsewhere. Hence those who had been members of the Church had none either to administer the Lord's Supper or to baptize their children."[2] He adds the statement that "for some hundred miles together there is none either to baptize or to administer the Lord's Supper."[3]

Wesley had in early life embraced the opinion that "bishops and presbyters were the same order, and consequently have the same right to ordain."[4] For years he had been importuned to put this opinion into practice by ordaining some of the traveling preachers who aspired to a higher station; but he had always refused. A strong pressure was now brought to bear upon him to settle this long-mooted question. At the Conference held at Leeds in July, 1784, a plan was proposed, at first privately, to a few clergymen attending the Conference, that "Mr. Wesley should ordain one or two preachers for the societies in America. But the clergymen approached opposed it. The celebrated Mr. Fletcher was consulted by letter as to this matter. In his reply he counseled that a bishop should be prevailed on, if possible, to ordain these men, and then Mr. Wesley might appoint them to such offices in the societies as he thought proper, and give them letters testimonial of the appointment he had given them."[5]

After much[6] persuasion Wesley finally resolved to "ordain" two of his preachers who had offered to go to America, and determined to send Dr. Coke across the Atlantic as his representative, with such powers as he would give him, to follow his example in "ordaining" a few men chosen out of his preachers there. Wesley's "Journal," under date of Bristol, Sept. 1, 1784, contains the following entry: "Being now clear in my own mind, I took a step I had long weighed in my mind, and appointed Mr. Whatcoat and Mr. Vasey to go and serve the desolate sheep in America."[7] On the same or the following day he "set apart as a superintendent, by the imposition of hands and prayer, . . . Thomas Coke, Doctor of Civil Law,

[1] Hawks's "Contributions to Ecclesiastical History in the United States of America," p. 149 ("Virginia").
[2] John Wesley's "Works," vol. vii., p. 314 (New York, 1840).
[3] Letter to Dr. Coke, Mr. Asbury, and others, in "Facsimiles of Church Documents."
[4] *Ibid.*
[5] Whitehead's "Life of Wesley," vol. ii., p. 255.
[6] *Ibid.*
[7] John Wesley's "Works," vol. iv., p. 139.

New Philad. July 30. 1804

Revd Sir,

I recd your Letter of ye 24th Inst. under Circumstances which prevented my answering by ye Return of ye Post. With it there was delivered a Letter from ye revd John McKlosky; whom I find to be ye Person alluded to in yours. Having written to this Gentleman, my transcribing of ye Information given him will be an Answer to you also.

"I beg it may be understood that I "have never, from ye Suggestion of my own "Mind given Information of ye Matter con-"cerning which you enquire, except to those "whom Dr Coke expected to be informed of it. "Several Years passed after ye Transaction "before I had Reason to suppose it known "to any others. Within these few Years, I "have been spoken to on ye Subject two or "three Times; when I found myself under "a Necessity of stating Facts, in order to "guard against Misrepresentation.

"In ye Spring of ye Year 1791, I recd a "Letter from Dr Coke, on ye Subject ~~on the~~ "~~Subject~~ of uniting ye Methodist Society "with ye Episcopal Church. An Answer was "returned. In consequence of which, Dr "Coke, on his coming to Town, made

"me a Visit; having not then read my Letter
"but having heard that I had written. Our
"Conversation turned chiefly on ye aforesaid
"Subject. The general Outline of Dr Coke's
"Plan were, a Re-Ordination of ye Metho-
"dist Ministers & their continuing under ye
"Superintendence then existing & in the
"Practice of their peculiar Institutions. There
"was also suggested, by him, a Propriety but not
"a Condition made, of admitting to the
"Episcopacy himself & ye Gentleman associ-
"ated with him in ye Superintendence of ye
"Methodist Societies. This Intercourse was
"communicated at ye Time by Dr Coke to Dr
"Magaw. I do not know of any other Person
"then informed of it, unless I may ex-
"cept ye Gentleman above alluded to, by
"whom, if I have been rightly informed
"my Letter to Dr Coke was opened in his
"Absence; such a Freedom being understood,
"as I supposed, to arise out of ye Connection
"between ye two Gentlemen. But for this
"Part of ye Statement I cannot vouch.
"It was understood between Dr Coke & me,
"that ye Proposal should be communicated
"to ye Bishops of ye Episcopal Church, at ye
"next Convention, which was to be in

"Sep 1792 in New-York. This was according
"by Mind after which, I perceived no Use
"of further Communication on ye Subject;
"and I have not since seen Dr Coke nor
"heard from him, nor written to him.

"It appears to me, that ye above compre-
"hends either explicitly or by Implication
"all ye Points to which your Letter leads.
"It would have been more agreeable to me
"if no Occasion of this Testimony had oc-
"curred: & it is now given, merely to prevent
"ye Matters being understood otherwise than it
"really is."

The above is what I have
written to Mr McKlaskey; &
I remain

Your affte Brother:

Wm White

Revd Simon Wilmer.
Chester Town
Maryland.

The following is ye Copy of a Letter addressed to me by ye Revd Dr. Thomas Coke. To ye best of my Recollection, it was never communicated or mentioned by me, except to those to whom it was intended by ye Writer to be made known; untill I heard of it from others, within ye last few Years. My Reserve in this respect was not from any Idea, that there was or could reasonably have been exacted of me Secrecy in such a Transaction; but for Reasons which it is not now necessary to mention. My giving of a Copy of ye Letter is in Consequence of its having been made a Subject of public Controversy; & merely with ye View of preventing Misconstruction & Misrepresentation.

Philad: Oct 30. 1806.

Wm: White.

If ye above Letter of Dr. Coke shd be published it is my Wish, that what I have prefixed may accompany ye Publication.

a presbyter of the Church of England";[1] but of *this* no mention appears in the "Journal." Is it not possible, to quote the words of a careful writer,[2] that "the reason why the one act was mentioned, and not the other, was because he considered the latter one of much less moment than the former—the one an act of *ordination*, the other, one of simple *benediction?* Without entering into the question whether he had the *power* to raise Coke to a higher office than he himself held as a presbyter in the Church, there is nothing in the whole history of the case to imply that he had the slightest *thought* or *wish* to so elevate one who had been, and was to continue to be, subordinate to himself. Coke was sent out to act as joint superintendent, with Asbury, over persons who 'desire to continue under *my* [that is, Wesley's] care, and still adhere to the doctrines and discipline of the Church of England.'[3] And in Wesley's celebrated letter to Asbury, rebuking the latter for assuming the title of bishop, Wesley says: 'There is indeed a wide difference between the relation wherein you stand to the Americans and the relation wherein I stand to all the Methodists. You are the elder brother of the American Methodists; I am, under God, the father of the whole family. Therefore I naturally care for you all, in a manner no other person can do. Therefore I naturally provide for you all; for the supplies which Dr. Coke provides for you, he could not provide were it not for me—were it not that I not only permit him to collect, but support him in so doing.'"[4]

Wesley had long before pointed out that laying on of hands did not necessarily mean ordination: "That the seven deacons were ordained, even to that office, cannot be denied. But when Paul and Barnabas were separated for the work to which they were called this was not ordaining them. St. Paul was ordained long before, and that 'not of men, nor by men.' It was only inducting them to the province for which our Lord had appointed them from the beginning. For this end the prophets and teachers fasted and prayed, and laid their hands upon them—a rite which was used, not in ordination, but in blessing, and on many other occasions."[5]

It is with this view that Dr. Coke, in a letter written shortly before the occurrence in question, and while Mr. Wesley was still undecided, urges Wesley to lay his hands upon him, not so much—if, indeed, at all—for the conveyance of any spiritual power, as because, to use

1 Extract from a Letter of Appointment given Dr. Coke by J. Wesley, in Drew's "Life of Dr. Coke."

2 The bishop of Cairo, Ill., Dr. C. R. Hale, in "The American Church and Methodism," pp. 10, 11.

3 Extract from a Letter of Appointment given Dr. Coke by J. Wesley, in Drew's "Life of Dr. Coke."

4 In Moore's "Life of Wesley," vol. ii., p. 265.

5 John Wesley's "Works," vol. x., p. 237.

Coke's words, "An authority formally received from you will (I am conscious of it) be fully admitted by the people, and my exercising the office of ordination without that formal authority may be disputed, if there be any opposition on any other account." [1]

"Wesley's ordination of Whatcoat and Vasey," to quote again from Bishop Hale,[2] "and his laying on of hands upon Coke, with whatever intent, were acts done in his own chamber in Bristol, and with the utmost secrecy. 'I was then in Bristol,' writes Charles Wesley, 'at his elbow, yet he never gave me the least hint of his intention. How was he surprised into so rash an action?'[3] It seems to have been some time before what was done was generally known in England, and when it was, Wesley's best friends were of one mind in their surprise and disapproval, and in their conviction that he had acted under ill advice. Charles Wesley wrote: 'After we having continued friends for above seventy years, and fellow-laborers for above fifty, can anything but death part us? I can scarcely yet believe that in his eighty-second year my brother, my old intimate friend and companion, should have assumed the episcopal character, ordained elders, consecrated a bishop, and sent him to ordain the lay preachers in America. . . . Lord Mansfield told me last year that *ordination* was *separation!* This my brother does not and will not see, or that he has renounced the principles and practice of his whole life, that he has acted contrary to all his declarations, protestations, and writings, robbed his friends of their boasting, realized the Nag's Head ordination, and left an indelible blot on his name.'[4]"

As has already been said, there seems no reason, from anything Mr. Wesley said or wrote, to conclude that he attempted to make Dr. Coke a bishop, or that he thought of him, after Sept. 2, 1784, as other than a presbyter, subordinate to himself. But when Charles Wesley and others spoke of his act as one of would-be bishop-making, John Wesley preferred to let the charge pass without either admission, denial, or adequate explanation. He was never averse to taking responsibility, and, conscious, as it would seem, that his act was at least liable to be criticized, he would not disarm criticism as to himself by throwing the blame, even where he might justly do so, upon others.

Dr. Whitehead, the physician and one of the literary executors of Wesley, and the one chosen to preach the sermon at his funeral, writes thus: "An old preacher, writing to his friend, delivers his opinion to the following purpose: 'I wish they had been asleep

[1] See the whole of this very curious letter, in Whitehead's "Life of Wesley," vol. ii., p. 255.

[2] "The American Church and Methodism," pp. 12, 13.

[3] Letter of Charles Wesley to Dr. Chandler, in "Facsimiles of Church Documents."

[4] *Ibid.*

when they began this business of ordination. It is neither Episcopal nor Presbyterian, but a mere hodge-podge of inconsistencies. Though it must be allowed that Mr. Wesley acted under the influence of others, yet he had some reasons for the step he took, which at the moment appeared to him to justify it. Perhaps they may not appear in the same light to others, and probably would not to himself had he not been biased by persuasion.'"[1]

Alexander Knox, who was well acquainted with Wesley and held him in high esteem, writes: "Nothing, surely, could have evinced pure weakness of mind more clearly than the strange business of making Coke a bishop. That Dr. C. urged Mr. Wesley to this proceeding, I know with certainty from the doctor himself; and full acquaintance with the well-meaning but very inconsiderate man makes me feel that Mr. Wesley could scarcely have had a more unfortunate adviser. . . . In one of my first interviews with Mr. Wesley after the occurrences in question I thought it right to disclose to him my whole mind upon the subject, and from the manner in which he heard me, and from what he said in reply, I saw clearly that he felt himself in a vortex of difficulties, and that in the steps he had taken, the yielding to what he thought pressing exigencies, he nevertheless had done violence to undissembled and rooted feeling."[2]

In a letter addressed to the English Conference, in 1793, by the trustees of the principal Methodist chapels in London and Bristol, a number of these trustees being persons long intimate with Mr. Wesley, we find this testimony: "Although Mr. Wesley, by dint of importunity, toward the close of his life, was persuaded to ordain a few of his preachers for America and Scotland, he by no means intended to make it general."[3]

To quote again the bishop of Cairo:[4] "In regard to ordinations for America, Mr. Wesley and some of the others concerned approached the matter from different standpoints. He *deprecated* separation from the Church; they *desired* it. He gave such commission as he could to Whatcoat and Vasey, and encouraged or directed Dr. Coke to follow his example, because of the exaggerated idea he had of the fewness of clergy in America, and fearing lest such scarcity should long continue. There were others, however, whose anxiety was to bring about the organization of the Methodists in America into a separate body, before the American Church, which they justly recognized as 'the same Church, though altered in its name,'[5] which had been known before the Revolution as the

[1] Whitehead's "Life of Wesley," vol. ii., p. 258.

[2] In an Appendix to Southey's "Life of Wesley," vol. ii., pp. 358–360 (New York).

[3] See "John Wesley's Place in Church History," p. 162, by R. D. Urlin.

[4] "The American Church and Methodism," pp. 14, 15.

[5] Minutes of 1787, reprinted in "The History of the Discipline," etc., p. 93, by Robert Emory.

'Church of England,' could complete its organization and occupy this land. It was not unknown, to some at least of those, what prompt steps were taken to this end so soon as peace was restored.

"Dr. Coke, in his letter to Bishop Seabury, May 14, 1791, confessed: 'Being educated a member of the Church of England from my earliest infancy, . . . I was almost a bigot in its favor when I first joined that great and good man, Mr. John Wesley, which is fourteen years ago [that is, in 1777]. For four or five years after my union with Mr. Wesley I remained fixed in my attachment to the Church of England, but afterward, for many reasons which it would be tedious and useless to mention, I changed my sentiments and promoted a separation from it, so far as my influence reached.'[1] And in his sermon before the Conference at Baltimore, December, 1784, Dr. Coke, after speaking of the reasons for separating from the Church in America, still known as the Church of England, asks, 'Why, then, did you not separate before?'[2] and gives this answer to the question: 'It has long been the desire of the majority of the preachers and people; but they submitted to the superior judgment of Mr. Wesley.'

"Such being the views of Dr. Coke and 'the majority of the preachers and people,' it is not to be wondered at that, at the Conference over which he presided on his arrival in Baltimore, it was 'unanimously agreed that circumstances made it expedient for the Methodist societies in America to become a separate body from the Church of England, of which until then they had been considered as members.'"[3]

When Dr. Coke came to America, in 1784, his purpose of separating from the Church was not generally known. This appears from a paragraph in his letter to Bishop White, in which he says: "I am not sure whether I have not also offended you, sir, by accepting of one of the offers made me by you and Dr. Magaw, of the use of your churches, about six years ago, on my first visit to Philadelphia, without informing you of our plan of separation from the Church of England. If I did offend, as I doubt I did, . . . I sincerely beg your and Dr. Magaw's pardon. I'll endeavor to amend. But, alas! I am a frail, weak creature." This being the case, there was no opportunity of preventing the schism he was creating before it was an accomplished fact. Still, at the very first opportunity the rector of St. Paul's, Baltimore, the Rev. Dr. West, invited Dr. Coke and Mr. Asbury to spend an evening with him at his residence, and to debate the whole matter at issue. An account of this conference is given in a letter addressed by the Rev. Dr. Andrews to the Rev.

[1] "Facsimiles of Church Documents."

[2] Hampson's "Memoir of Wesley," vol. ii., p. 189.

[3] Rev. Ezekiel Cooper, quoted by John Emory, in "Defense of our Fathers," p. 52 (New York, 1828).

William Smith, D.D.,[1] from which we make a few extracts: "We could not think," said one of the Church clergymen, "so unfavorably of the gentlemen who were at the head of that society as to suppose they would insist on *separating* from us merely for the sake of separating, or cherish in their hearts so unkind a spirit as would not suffer them, even in doing the very same things that we do, to have any satisfaction without doing them in a different manner; that the plan of church government which we had instituted in this State was a very simple and, as we trusted, a very rational plan; that it was to be exercised by a Convention, consisting of an equal number of laity and clergy, and having for their president a bishop, elected by the whole body of the clergy; that such an episcopacy, at the same time that it possessed all the powers requisite for spiritual purposes, would not, on any occasion, or to any person, be either dangerous or burdensome. . . . What occasion, then, could there be for a separation from us on the score of government? And as to articles of faith and worship, they already agreed with us." Dr. West added that "in his opinion the only material point as to which it concerned us at present to inquire was simply this: was the plan upon which the Methodists were now proceeding to act irrevocably fixed?" No decisive or satisfactory answers were given by Dr. Coke or Mr. Asbury to these queries. In this same letter Dr. Andrews states: "A day or two after I took the liberty to wait on Dr. Coke at his lodgings. I expressed the wish that they could be induced to give rise to their orders in a regular manner, and this, I observed, they might do, and yet still continue to manage their own affairs, and remain as distinct a body from us as they might think proper. If they did not esteem it unlawful to *connect the succession*, I contended that it was their duty to connect it. Dr. Coke did not hesitate to acknowledge that it would be more consistent indeed, and more regular, to connect the succession. But it was now too late to think of these things, when their plans were already adopted, and in part even executed; that he himself had received ordination agreeably to the new system, and conferred it on others. . . . Thus," proceeds the Rev. Dr. Andrews, "ended our negotiation, which served no other purpose than to discover to us that the minds of these gentlemen are not wholly free from resentment; and it is a point which among them is indispensably necessary, that Mr. Wesley be the first link of the chain upon which their Church is suspended."

With this sketch of the introduction of the Methodist superintendency or episcopacy in America we give the names of the occupants of this post, as found in the latest records of the Methodist Episcopal Church.

[1] Among the Bishop White papers in the archives of the General Convention.

The present board of bishops numbers eighteen, including two missionary bishops. Four were elected in 1872, three in 1880, five in 1884, and six in 1888. The church has had forty-six bishops since its organization in 1784, as recorded in the following table:

Consecrated.	Names.	Born.	Entered Ministry. Conference.	Yr.	Remarks.
1784	Thomas Coke	Sept. 9, 1747	Brit. Wes.	1778	Died at sea, May 3, 1814, aged 66.
1784	Francis Asbury	Aug. 20, 1745	Brit. Wes.	1767	Died in Virginia, March 31, 1816, aged 70.
1800	Richard Whatcoat	Feb. 23, 1736	Brit. Wes.	1769	Died in Delaware, July 4, 1806, aged 70.
1808	William McKendree	July 6, 1757	M. E. Ch.	1788	Died in Tenn., March 5, 1835, aged 77.
1816	Enoch George	Mar. 10, 1768	M. E. Ch.	1790	Died in Virginia, Aug. 23, 1828, aged 60.
1816	Robert R. Roberts	Aug. 2, 1778	Baltimore	1802	Died in Indiana, March 26, 1843, aged 64.
1824	Joshua Soule	Aug. 1, 1781	New York	1798	Bish. M. E. Ch., South, '46; d. March 6, '67.
1824	Elijah Hedding	June 7, 1780	New York	1801	Died in Poughkeepsie, April 9, 1852, aged 71.
1832	James O. Andrew	Jan. 7, 1794	S. Carolina	1812	Bish. M. E. Ch., South, '46; d. March 2, '71.
1832	John Emory	April 11, 1789	Philadelphia	1810	Died in Maryland, Dec. 16, 1835, aged 46.
1836	Beverly Waugh	Oct. 25, 1789	Baltimore	1809	Died in Maryland, Feb. 9, 1858, aged 68.
1836	Thomas A. Morris	April 28, 1794	Ohio.	1816	Died in Ohio, Sept. 2, 1874, aged 80.
1844	Leonidas L. Hamline	May 10, 1797	Ohio.	1833	Resigned 1852; d. in Ohio, March 23, 1865.
1844	Edmund S. Janes	April 28, 1807	Philadelphia	1830	Died in N. Y. City, Sept. 18, 1876, aged 69.
1852	Levi Scott	Oct. 11, 1802	Philadelphia.	1826	Died in Odessa, Del., July 13, 1882, aged 79.
1852	Matthew Simpson	June 21, 1811	Pittsburg	1833	Died in Philadelphia, June 18, 1884, aged 72.
1852	Osmon C. Baker	July 30, 1812	N. Hampshire	1839	D. in Concord, N. H., Dec. 20, 1871, aged 59.
1852	Edward R. Ames	May 20, 1806	Illinois.	1830	Died in Baltimore, April 25, 1879, aged 72.
1864	Davis W. Clark	Feb. 25, 1812	New York	1843	Died in Cincinnati, May 23, 1871, aged 59.
1864	Edward Thomson	Oct. 12, 1810	Ohio	1832	Died in Wheeling, W. Va., March 22, 1870.
1864	Calvin Kingsley	Sept. 8, 1812	Erie	1841	Died in Beyroot, Syria, April 6, 1870.
1872	Thomas Bowman	July 15, 1817	Baltimore	1839	College president when elected.
1872	William L. Harris	Nov. 4, 1817	Michigan	1837	Died in N. Y. City, Sept. 2, 1887, aged 69.
1872	Randolph S. Foster	Feb. 22, 1820	Ohio	1837	Pres. theological seminary when elected.
1872	Isaac W. Wiley	Mar. 29, 1825	Philadelphia	1849	Died in Foochow, China, Nov. 22, 1884.
1872	Stephen M. Merrill	Sept. 16, 1825	Ohio	1846	Editor when elected.
1872	Edward G. Andrews	Aug. 7, 1825	Oneida.	1848	Pastor when elected.
1872	Gilbert Haven	Sept. 19, 1821	New England.	1851	Died in Malden, Mass., Jan. 3, 1880.
1872	Jesse T. Peck	April 4, 1811	Oneida	1832	Died in Syracuse, N. Y., May 17, 1883.
1880	Henry W. Warren	Jan. 4, 1831	New England.	1855	Pastor when elected.
1880	Cyrus D. Foss	Jan. 17, 1834	New York	1857	College president when elected.
1880	John F. Hurst	Aug. 17, 1834	Newark	1858	Pres. theological seminary when elected.
1880	Erastus O. Haven	Nov. 1, 1820	New York	1848	Died in Salem, Ore., Aug. 2, 1881, aged 60.
1884	William X. Ninde	June 21, 1832	Black River	1856	President Biblical Institute when elected.
1884	John M. Walden	Feb. 11, 1831	Cincinnati	1858	Book-agent when elected.
1884	Willard F. Mallalieu	Dec. 11, 1828	New England.	1858	Presiding elder when elected.
1884	Charles H. Fowler	Aug. 11, 1837	Rock River	1861	Missionary secretary when elected.
1888	John H. Vincent	Feb. 23, 1832	New Jersey	1853	Secretary Sunday-school Union when elected.
1888	James N. Fitzgerald	July 27, 1837	Newark	1862	Recording missionary secretary when elected.
1888	Isaac W. Joyce	Oct. 11, 1836	N'thwest Ind.	1859	Pastor when elected.
1888	John P. Newman	Sept. 1, 1826	Oneida	1848	Pastor when elected.
1888	Daniel A. Goodsell	Nov. 5, 1840	N. Y. East	1859	Secretary Board of Education when elected.
1858	Francis Burns [1]	Dec. 5, 1809	Liberia	1838	Died in Baltimore, April 18, 1863.
1866	John W. Roberts	Sept. 8, 1812	Liberia.	1838	Died in Liberia, Jan. 30, 1875.
1884	William Taylor	May 2, 1821	Baltimore.	1843	Local preacher when elected.
1888	James M. Thoburn	Mar. 7, 1836	Pittsburg	1858	Presiding elder when elected.

[1] Bishops Burns, Roberts, and Taylor, missionary bishops for Africa; Bishop Thoburn, missionary bishop for India and Malaysia.

V.

THE EPISCOPATE OF THE ROMAN CATHOLIC COMMUNION IN THE UNITED STATES.

THE fifteenth day of August, A.D. 1890, was the centenary of a notable event in American ecclesiastical annals. On Sunday, the fifteenth day of August, 1790, the feast of the Assumption of the Blessed Virgin Mary, in the private chapel of Lullworth Castle, Dorsetshire, England, Dr. John Carroll was consecrated the first bishop of Baltimore. It was thus that the Roman Catholic hierarchy of the United States was founded. The consecrator was the Rt. Rev. Dr. Charles Walmesley, titular bishop of Rama and senior vicar apostolic of the English Roman Catholics. By special direction of the papal bull authorizing this consecration, the bishop of Rama was assisted in this solemn function by two attendant priests, no regard being paid to the ancient canon requiring the presence and participation of three bishops in the elevation of a priest to the episcopate. The rare, possibly unique, contemporary pamphlet published by authority, and giving the only account of this event extant, thus describes it:

"By invitation of Thomas Weld, Esq., the consecration of the new bishop was performed during a solemn high mass in the elegant chapel of Lullworth Castle, on Sunday, the fifteenth day of August, 1790, being the feast of the Assumption of the Blessed Virgin Mary; and the munificence of that gentleman omitted no circumstance which could possibly add dignity to so venerable a ceremony. The two prelates were attended by their respective assistant priests and acolytes, according to the rubric of the Roman pontifical; the richness of their vestments, the music of the choir, the multitude of wax lights, and the ornaments of the altar concurred to increase the splendor of the solemnity, which made a lasting impression upon every beholder." [1]

It is of interest in connection with this elevation to the episcopal office of Dr. Carroll to notice that the choice of the first bishop of

[1] "A short account of the establishment of the new see of Baltimore in Maryland, and of consecrating the Rt. Rev. Dr. John Carroll first bishop thereof, on the feast of the Assumption, 1790; with a discourse delivered on that occasion, and the authority for consecrating the bishop and erecting and administering the said see. To which are added extracts from the different bills of right and the Constitution of the United States—that liberty of conscience is the birthright of every man, and an exclusion of any religious test forever." (London, printed by J. P. Coghlan, No. 37 Duke Street, Grosvenor Square, 1790; 8vo, pp. 32.) This tract is in the possession of the bishop of Iowa. It was represented in facsimile by the Historical Club a few years ago. It is to be issued again in facsimile in the "American Catholic Historical Researches," edited by Martin L. Griffin, of Philadelphia. An edition of the original was issued in Dublin in 1790.

Baltimore, with the particular authorization of Pope Pius VI.—"by special grant and for this first time only"; such is the language of the bull—was intrusted to the American priests having cure of souls.

Twenty-six priests assembled in pursuance of this authorization, and after deciding upon Baltimore as the proper place for the establishment of the new see, cast their votes for a bishop. Dr. Carroll (the superior of the Jesuit mission in the United States), the brother of the patriot Charles Carroll, of Carrollton, a signer of the Declaration of Independence, received twenty-four of the whole number of votes cast. The Roman Catholic hierarchy in the United States is thus founded upon a popular election, by papal order and by priests, not bishops. Though "for this first time only," and "by special grant," there was surely here a recognition by the head of the Roman Catholic Church of American institutions and ideas.

Lullworth Castle, where this important function took place, is in Dorsetshire, England. Built on or near the site of an ancient "donjon-keep" referred to in the old chronicles as existing in the earlier half of the twelfth century, the present edifice was not erected till near the close of the sixteenth century. In 1641 it passed into the hands of the Weld family, and at the time of the consecration of Dr. Carroll, Thomas Weld, Esq., was lord of the manor, and a devout and distinguished member of the Roman Catholic Church. Later in life he became a cardinal of the "Holy Roman Church." The chapel, which he had erected but shortly before its use for this great function, is but a short distance from the castle. It is a structure of circular form, increased by four sections of a circle so as to form a cross. It is furnished with a dome and lantern. The altar is composed of choice and costly marbles, and the ornaments of this exquisite little oratory are of unusual magnificence.

The castle of Lullworth has been again and again the abode, for a longer or shorter period, of monarchs; but the fact that it was the scene, on the feast of the Assumption, August 15, 1790, of the consecration of Dr. Carroll and the founding of the hierarchy of the Roman Catholic Church in the United States gives this picturesque structure its chief claim to remembrance.

ARCHDIOCESE OF BALTIMORE.—Comprises all the counties of Maryland lying west of the Chesapeake Bay, as also the District of Columbia.

Most Rev. John Carroll, D.D., cons. Aug. 15, 1790; d. 1815.
Most Rev. Leonard Neale, D.D., cons. Dec. 7, 1800; d. 1817.
Most Rev. Ambrose Marechal, D.D., cons. Dec. 14, 1817; d. 1828.
Most Rev. James Whitfield, D.D., cons. May 25, 1828; d. 1834.
Most Rev. Samuel Eccleston, D.D., cons. Sept. 14, 1834; d. 1851.
Most Rev. Francis Patrick Kenrick, D.D., promoted Aug. 19, 1851; d. 1863.
Most Rev. Martin John Spalding, D.D., cons. Sept. 10, 1848; promoted May 3, 1864; d. 1872.
Most Rev. James Roosevelt Bayley, D.D., cons Oct. 30, 1853; promoted July 30, 1872; d. 1877.
His Eminence James, Cardinal Gibbons, cons. Aug. 16, 1868; trans. to see of Richmond, Va., July 30, 1872; promoted to see of Baltimore, Oct. 3, 1877; created cardinal, June 7, 1886.
Vicar-General, Rt. Rev. Mgr. Edward McColgan.

ARCHDIOCESE OF BOSTON.—See erected 1808; created an archbishopric 1875. Comprises the counties of Essex, Middlesex, Suffolk, Norfolk, and Plymouth, in the State of Massachusetts, the towns of Mattapoisett, Marion, and Wareham excepted.

Rt. Rev. John Cheverus, cons. Nov. 1, 1810; trans to Montauban, thence to Bordeaux; d. cardinal abp. of Bordeaux, July 19, 1836.
Rt. Rev. Benedict J. Fenwick, cons. Nov. 1, 1825; d. Aug. 11, 1846.
Rt. Rev. John B Fitzpatrick, cons. March 24, 1844; d. Feb. 13, 1866.
Most Rev. John Joseph Williams, D.D., cons. March 11, 1866; created first abp. of Boston, Feb. 12, 1875.
Auxiliary bishop, Rt. Rev. John Brady, D.D., titular bp. of Alabanda; cons. Aug. 5, 1891.

ARCHDIOCESE OF CHICAGO.—Established 1844; created an archbishopric 1880. Comprises Illinois north of the south line of Whiteside, Lee, De Kalb, Grundy, and Kankakee counties.

Rt. Rev. William Quarter, D.D., cons. March 10, 1844; d. April 10, 1848.
Rt. Rev. James O. Van DeVelde, D.D., cons. 1848; trans. to Natchez, 1853; d. 1855.
Rt. Rev. Anthony O'Regan, D.D., cons. July 25, 1854; trans. to Dora, 1858; d. 1865.
Rt. Rev. James Duggan, D.D., cons. bp. of Antigone and coad. to the abp. of St. Louis, May 3, 1857; trans. to Chicago, Jan. 21, 1859; removed 1880, on account of infirm health.
Rt. Rev. Thomas Foley, D.D., coad. bp. and administrator of the diocese; cons. bp. of Pergamus, Feb. 27, 1870; d. Feb. 19, 1879.
Most Rev. Patrick A. Feehan, D.D., cons. bp. of Nashville, Nov. 1, 1865; promoted to Chicago, Sept. 10, 1880.

ARCHDIOCESE OF CINCINNATI.—See erected 1821; made an archbishopric 1850. Comprises that part of Ohio lying south of 40° 41′, being the counties south of the northern line of Mercer, Auglaize, Hardin, all west of the eastern line of Marion, Union, and Madison counties, and all west of the Scioto River to the Ohio River.

Rt. Rev. Edward Fenwick, D.D., cons. Jan. 13, 1822; d. Sept. 26, 1832.
Most Rev. John Baptist Purcell, D.D., cons. Oct. 13, 1833; d. July 4, 1883.
Most Rev. William Henry Elder, D.D., cons. bp. of Natchez, May 2, 1857; appointed titular bp. of Avara and coad. to the abp., *cum jure successionis*, Jan. 30, 1880; succeeded to the see of Cincinnati, July 4, 1883; invested with the pallium, Dec. 13, 1883.

ARCHDIOCESE OF DUBUQUE, IA.—The province of Dubuque comprises the States of Iowa, Nebraska, and Wyoming; established 1893. In 1837 the diocese of Dubuque was established; it became a metropolitan see in 1893, and comprises Iowa north of Harrison, Shelby, Audubon, Guthrie, Dallas, Polk, Jasper, Poweshiek, Iowa, Johnson, Cedar, and Scott counties.

Rt. Rev. Matthias Loras, D D., cons. Dec. 10, 1837; d. Feb. 19, 1853.
Rt. Rev. Clement Smyth, D.D., cons. May 3, 1857; d. Sept. 22, 1865.
Most Rev. John Hennessy, D.D., cons. Sept. 30, 1860.

ARCHDIOCESE OF MILWAUKEE.—Established 1844; created an archbishopric 1875. Comprises the south of Wisconsin.

Most Rev. John Martin Henni, D.D., cons. March 19, 1844; created abp., 1875; d. Sept. 7, 1881.
Most Rev. Michael Heiss, D.D., cons. bp. of La Crosse, Sept. 6, 1868; appointed coad. of Milwaukee and titular abp. of Adrianople, March 14, 1880; d. March 26, 1890.
Most Rev. F. X. Katzer, cons. bp. of Green Bay, Sept. 21, 1886; promoted to Milwaukee, Jan. 30, 18.0.
Vicar-General, Rt. Rev. A. Zeininger.

ARCHDIOCESE OF NEW ORLEANS.—Established 1793. Comprises Louisiana between the twenty-ninth and thirty-first degrees of north latitude.

Rt. Rev. Louis Peñalver y Cardenas, D.D., cons. 1793; trans. to Guatemala, 1802.
Francis Porro, D.D., bp. elect.
Rt. Rev. William V. Dubourg, D.D., cons. Sept. 24, 1815; d. abp. of Besançon, December, 1833.
Rt. Rev. Joseph Rosati, D.D., C.M., cons. March 25, 1824, bp. of Tenagre and coad.; trans. to St. Louis, March 27, 1827.
Rt. Rev. Leo De Neckere, D.D., C.M., cons. 1829; d. Sept. 4, 1833.
Most Rev. Anthony Blanc, cons. Nov. 22, 1835; d. June 20, 1860
Most Rev. J. M. Odin, D.D., cons. bp. of Claudiopolis and vicar apostolic of Texas, March 6, 18[illegible], trans. to Galveston, 1847; promoted to New Orleans, 1861; d. at Ambierle, France, May 25, 1870.
Most Rev. Napoleon J. Perché, cons. bp. of Abdera and coad., May 1, 1870; promoted to the see of New Orleans, May 25, 1870; d. December, 1883.
Most Rev. F. X. Leray, D.D., cons. bp. of Natchitoches, April 22, 1877; appointed coad. of New Orleans and bp. of Janopolis, Oct. 23, 1879; promoted to the see of New Orleans, Dec. 27, 1883; d. Sept. 23, 1887, at Châteaugiron, France.
Most Rev. F. Janssens, D.D., cons. bp. of Natchez, May 1, 1881; promoted to the see of New Orleans, Aug. 7, 1888.

ARCHDIOCESE OF NEW YORK.—See erected 1808; created an archbishopric 1850. Comprises the city and county of New York, and the counties of Westchester, Putnam, Dutchess, Ulster, Sullivan, Orange, Rockland, and Richmond; also the Bahama Islands.

Rt. Rev. R. Luke Concanen, O.P., D.D., cons. April 24, 1808; d. 1810.
Rt. Rev. John Connolly, O.P., D.D., cons. Nov. 6, 1814; d. 1825.
Rt. Rev. John Dubois, cons. Oct. 29, 1826; d. 1842.
Most Rev. John Hughes, D.D., cons. titular bp. of Basileopolis and coad. to the bp. of New York, Jan. 7, 1838; succeeded to the see, 1842; created first abp., 1850; d. Jan. 3, 1864.
His Eminence John, Cardinal McCloskey, cons. titular bp. of Axiere and coad. to the bp. of New York, March 10, 1844; trans. to the see of Albany, May 21, 1847; promoted to the see of New York, May 6, 1864; created cardinal priest of the Holy Roman Church, March 15, 1875; d. Oct. 10, 1885.
Most Rev. Michael Augustine Corrigan, D.D., cons. bp. of Newark, N. J., May 4, 1873; promoted to the archiepiscopal see of New York and made coad. to his Eminence Cardinal McCloskey, Oct. 1, 1880; succeeded to the see, Oct. 10, 1885.
Vicar-General, Rt. Rev. Mgr. John M. Farley.

ARCHDIOCESE OF OREGON CITY.—Established 1846. Comprises the State of Oregon.
Most Rev. Francis Norbert Blanchet, abp. of Amida; resigned 1880; d. June 18, 1883.
Most Rev. Charles J. Seghers, cons. bp. of Vancouver's Island, June 29, 1873; coad. to abp. of Oregon City, Dec. 10, 1878; abp., Dec. 20, 1880; resigned 1884, and trans. to Vancouver's Island; d. Nov. 28, 1886.
Most Rev. William H. Gross, D.D., promoted from Savannah, Ga., to the archiepiscopal see of Oregon City, Feb. 1, 1885.

ARCHDIOCESE OF PHILADELPHIA.—See established 1808; erected an archbishopric Feb. 12, 1875. Comprises all the city and county of Philadelphia, and the counties of Berks, Bucks, Carbon, Chester, Delaware, Lehigh, Montgomery, Northampton, and Schuylkill.
Rt. Rev. Michael Egan, D.D., O.S.F., cons. Oct. 28, 1810; d. 1814.
Rt. Rev. Henry Conwell, D.D., cons. 1820; d. 1842.
Rt. Rev. Francis Patrick Kenrick, D.D., cons. June 6, 1830; trans. to Baltimore, 1851; d. July 8, 1863.
Rt. Rev. John Nepomucene Neumann, D.D., C.SS.R., cons. March 28, 1852; d. Jan. 5, 1860.
Most Rev. James Frederic Wood, D.D., cons. coad., *cum jure successionis*, April 26, 1857; bp. of Philadelphia, Jan. 5, 1860; created abp., June 17, 1875; d. June 30, 1883.
Most Rev. Patrick John Ryan, D.D., LL.D., cons. April 14, 1872, bp. of Tricomia and coad., *c. j. s.*, of the abp. of St. Louis; abp. of Salamis, Jan. 6, 1884; abp. of Philadelphia, June 8, 1884.
Vicar-General, Rt. Rev. Mgr. Nicholas Cantwell

ARCHDIOCESE OF ST. LOUIS.—See established 1826; created an archbishopric 1847. Comprises that part of Missouri east of Chariton River and of the west line of the counties of Cole, Maries, Pulaski, Texas, and Howell.
Rt. Rev. Joseph Rosati, D.D., C.M., cons. March 25, 1824, bp. of Tenagre and coad. of New Orleans; trans. to St. Louis, March 27, 1827.
Most Rev. Peter Richard Kenrick, D.D., cons. Nov. 30, 1841, bp. of Drasa and coad.; bp. of St. Louis, 1843; abp., 1847.
Most Rev. John Joseph Kain, D.D., abp. of Oxyrynchia; coad. and administrator of the archdiocese.

ARCHDIOCESE OF ST. PAUL.—See established 1850; made a metropolitan see 1888. Comprises the following counties of the State of Minnesota, viz., Ramsey, Hennepin, Washington, Chicago, Anoka, Dakota, Scott, Wright, Rue, Le Sueur, Carver, Nicollet, Sibley, McLeod, Meeker, Redwood, Renville, Kandiyohi, Lyon, Lincoln, Yellow Medicine, Loc qui-Parle, Chippewa, Swift, Goodhue, Brown, and Big Stone.
Rt. Rev. Joseph Cretin, D.D., cons. Jan. 26, 1851; d. Feb. 22, 1857.
Most Rev. Thomas L. Grace, D.D., cons. July 24, 1859; res. July 31, 1884; titular bp. of Mennith; raised Sept. 24, 1889, to the archiepiscopal dignity and titular of Sinnia.
Most Rev. John Ireland, D.D., cons. Dec. 21, 1875, bp. of Maronea and coad.: succeeded to the see of St. Paul, July 31, 1884; made abp., May 15, 1888.
Vicar-General, Rt. Rev. Mgr. L. E. Caillet.

ARCHDIOCESE OF SAN FRANCISCO.—Established 1853. Comprises the counties of San Francisco, San Mateo, San Joaquin, Stanislaus, Sonoma, Alameda, Contra Costa, Lake, Marin, Mendocino, Napa, Solano, and those portions of Santa Cruz, Santa Clara, and Merced lying north of 37° 5′ northern latitude.
Rt. Rev. Francis Garcia Diego y Moreno, O.S.F., cons. Oct. 4, 1840, bp. of both Californias; d. April 30, 1846.
Most Rev. Joseph Sadoc Alemany, O.S.D., cons. bp. of Monterey, June 30, 1850; promoted to San Francisco, July 29, 1853; res. December, 1884; d. in Valencia, Spain, April 14, 1888.
Most Rev. Patrick W. Riordan, D.D., cons. Sept. 16, 1883, bp. of Cabesa and coad. of Abp. Alemany, *c. j. s.*, and succeeded to the see Dec. 28, 1884.

ARCHDIOCESE OF SANTA FE.—See established 1850; created an archbishopric 1875. Comprises the Territory of New Mexico, Doña Aña and Grant counties excepted.
Most Rev. J. B. Lamy, cons. Nov. 24, 1850; created first abp., 1875; res. July 18, 1885; d. Feb. 13, 1888.
Most Rev. J. B. Salpointe, cons. June 20, 1869; coad. of Santa Fé, April 22, 1884; succeeded to the see, July 18, 1885; res. Feb. 19, 1894; appointed abp. titular of the see of Tomi.
Most Rev. P. L. Chapelle, D.D., appointed bp. of Arabissus and coad. of Santa Fé, *c. j. s.*, Aug. 21, 1891; cons. Nov. 1, 1891; promoted to the titular archiepiscopal see of Sebaste, May 10, 1893; succeeded to the see of Santa Fé, Feb. 19, 1894.

DIOCESE OF ALBANY.—Established 1847; incorporated Oct. 9, 1894, under the laws of the State of New York, with the title "The Roman Catholic Diocese of Albany." Comprises the counties and portions of counties in the State of New York that are bounded on the north by the northern line of the county of Warren, and portions of the counties of Herkimer and Hamilton, north of the northern line of the townships of Ohio and Russia, in the county of Herkimer; on the east by the State of Massachusetts and portions of Vermont; on the south by the southern line of the counties of Columbia, Greene, and Delaware; and on the west by the western line of Otsego and Herkimer and portions of Hamilton.
Most Rev. John McCloskey, D.D., appointed bp. of Axiere and coad. to the bp. of New York, Nov. 21, 1843; cons. March 10, 1844; trans. to Albany, May 21, 1847; promoted to New York, May 6, 1864.
Rt. Rev. John J. Conroy, cons. Oct. 15, 1865; res. Oct. 16, 1877; trans. to the see of Curium, March 22, 1878.

Rt. Rev. Francis McNeirny, D.D., cons. bp. of Rhesina and coad. to the bp. of Albany, April 21, 1872; succeeded to the see, Oct. 16, 1877; d. Jan. 2, 1894.
Rt. Rev. Thomas M. A. Burke, D.D., cons. July 1, 1894.

DIOCESE OF ALTON, ILL.—Formerly diocese of Quincy; erected July 29, 1853; see transferred to Alton, Jan. 9, 1857. Comprises that part of Illinois lying south of the counties of Adams, Brown, Cass, Menard, Sangamon, Macon, Moultrie, Douglas, and Edgar, and north of the southern limits of the counties of Madison, Bond, Fayette, Effingham, Jasper, and Crawford.
Rt. Rev. Henry Damian Juncker, D.D., cons. April 26, 1857; d. Oct. 2, 1868.
Rt. Rev. Peter Joseph Baltes, D.D., cons. Jan. 23, 1870; d. Feb. 15, 1886.
Rt. Rev. James Ryan, D.D., cons. May 1, 1888.

DIOCESE OF BELLEVILLE.—See erected Jan. 7, 1887. Comprises Illinois south of the northern limits of the counties of St. Clair, Clinton, Marion, Clay, Richland, and Lawrence.
Rt. Rev. John Janssen, D.D., cons. April 25, 1888.

DIOCESE OF BOISE CITY.—Established as a vicariate apostolic March 3, 1868; erected a diocese Aug. 25, 1893. Comprises the State of Idaho.
First vicar apostolic, Rt. Rev. Louis Lootens, D.D., cons. bp. of Castabala, Aug. 9, 1868; res. 1876.
Administrators, Most Rev. F. N. Blanchet, D.D., and Most Rev. C. J. Seghers, D.D.
First bishop, Rt. Rev. A. J. Glorieux, D.D., cons. titular bp. of Apollonia, April 19, 1885; trans. to the see of Boisé City, Aug. 26, 1893.

DIOCESE OF BROOKLYN, N. Y.—Established 1853. Comprises Long Island, in the State of New York.
Rt. Rev. John Loughlin, D.D., cons. Oct. 10, 1853; d. Dec. 29, 1891.
Rt. Rev. Charles E. McDonnell, D.D., cons. April 25, 1892.
Vicar-General, Rt. Rev. Mgr. Michael May.

DIOCESE OF BUFFALO.—Established 1847. Comprises the counties of Erie, Niagara, Genesee, Orleans, Chautauqua, Wyoming, Cattaraugus, Steuben, Chemung, Tioga, Allegany, and Schuyler, in the State of New York.
Rt. Rev. John Timon, D.D., C.M., cons. Oct. 17, 1847; d. April 16, 1867.
Rt. Rev. Stephen V. Ryan, D.D., C.M., cons. Nov. 8, 1868.
Vicar-General, Rt. Rev. Mgr. William Gleeson.

DIOCESE OF BURLINGTON.—Established 1853. Comprises the State of Vermont.
Rt. Rev. Louis De Goesbriand, D.D., cons. Oct. 30, 1853.
Rt. Rev. John S. Michaud, D.D., titular bp. of Modra; cons. June 29, 1892, coad. to bp. of Burlington.

DIOCESE OF CHARLESTON.—Established 1820. Comprises the State of South Carolina.
Rt. Rev. John England, D.D., cons. Sept. 21, 1820; d. 1842.
Rt. Rev. William Clancy, D.D., coad.; made vicar apostolic of British Guiana, 1838; d. 1847.
Rt. Rev. Ignatius A. Reynolds, D.D., cons. March 14, 1858; d. Feb. 26, 1882.
Rt. Rev. H. P. Northrop, D.D., cons. titular bp. of Rosalia and vicar apostolic of North Carolina, Jan. 8, 1882; trans. to Charleston, Jan. 27, 1883.
Vicar-General, Rt. Rev. Mgr. D. J. Quigley.

DIOCESE OF CHEYENNE.—Erected Aug. 9, 1887. Comprises the State of Wyoming.
Rt. Rev. Maurice F. Burke, D.D., cons. Oct. 28, 1887.

DIOCESE OF CLEVELAND.—Established October, 1847. Comprises that portion of the State of Ohio lying north of the southern limits of Columbiana, Stark, Wayne, Ashland, Richland, Crawford, Wyandot, Hancock, Allen, and Van Wert counties.
Rt. Rev. Amadeus Rappe, D.D., cons. Oct. 10, 1847; res. Aug. 22, 1870; d. Sept. 8, 1877.
Rt. Rev. Richard Gilmour, D.D., cons. April 14, 1872; d. April 13, 1891.
Rt. Rev. Ignatius F. Horstmann, D.D., cons. Feb. 25, 1892.
Vicar-General, Rt. Rev. Mgr. Felix M. Boff.

DIOCESE OF COLUMBUS.—Established 1868. Comprises that part of the State of Ohio south of 40° 41′, and between the Ohio River on the east and the Scioto River on the west, together with the counties of Franklin, Delaware, and Morrow.
Rt. Rev. S. H. Rosecrans, D.D., cons. titular bp. of Pompeiopolis and auxiliary bp. of Cincinnati, March 25, 1862; trans. to Columbus, March 3, 1868; d. Oct. 21, 1878.
Rt. Rev. John Ambrose Watterson, D.D., cons. Aug. 8, 1880.

DIOCESE OF CONCORDIA.—Established Aug. 2, 1887. Comprises the northwestern part of Kansas, i.e., the counties of Cloud, Republic, Ottawa, Saline, Jewett, Mitchell, Lincoln, Ellsworth, Smith, Osborne, Russell, Phillips, Rooks, Ellis, Norton, Graham, Trego, Decatur, Sheridan, Gore, Rawlins, Thomas, Logan, Cheyenne, Sherman, and Wallace.
Rt. Rev. Richard Scannell, D.D., cons. Nov. 30, 1887; trans. to Omaha, December, 1890.
Administrator, Rt. Rev. John Joseph Hennessy, D.D., bp. of Wichita; appointed April 3, 1891.

DIOCESE OF COVINGTON.—Established 1853. Comprises Kentucky east of the Kentucky River and of the western limit of Carroll, Owen, Franklin, Woodford, Jessamine, Garrard, Rock Castle, Laurel, and Whitley counties.
Rt. Rev. George Aloysius Carrell, D.D., cons. Nov. 1, 1853; d. Sept. 25, 1868.
Rt. Rev. Augustus Maria Toebbe, D.D., cons. Jan. 9, 1870; d. May 2, 1884.
Rt. Rev. Camillus Paul Maes, D.D., cons. Jan. 25, 1885.

DIOCESE OF DALLAS.—Established 1890. Comprises one hundred and eight counties in the northern and northwestern portions of Texas.
Rt. Rev. Thomas Francis Brennan, D.D., cons. April 5, 1891; res. 1892.
Rt. Rev. E. J. Dunne, D.D., cons. Nov. 30, 1892.

DIOCESE OF DAVENPORT.—Erected 1881. Comprises that part of the State of Iowa lying south of the northern limits of the counties of Harrison, Shelby, Audubon, Guthrie, Dallas, Polk, Jasper, Poweshiek, Iowa, Johnson, Cedar, and Scott.
Rt. Rev. John McMullen, D.D., cons. July 25, 1881; d. July 4, 1883.
Rt. Rev. Henry Cosgrove, D.D., cons. Sept. 14, 1884.

DIOCESE OF DENVER.—Vicariate apostolic established 1868; see erected 1887. Comprises the State of Colorado.

Rt. Rev. Joseph Projectus Machebeuf, D.D., cons. bp. of Epiphany, Aug 16, 1868; trans. to Denver, 1887; d. July 10, 1889.

Rt. Rev. Nicholas C. Matz, cons. October, 1887.

DIOCESE OF DETROIT.—Established 1832. Comprises the lower peninsula of the State of Michigan, south of the counties of Ottawa, Kent, Montcalm, Gratiot, and Saginaw, and east of Saginaw and Bay counties.

Rt. Rev. Frederick Resé, D.D., cons. Oct. 6, 1833; d. Dec. 19, 1871.

Rt. Rev. Peter Paul Lefevre, D.D., cons. bp. of Zela and coad. of Detroit, Nov. 21, 1841; d. March 4, 1869.

Rt. Rev. Caspar H. Borgess, D.D., cons. April 24, 1870; res. April 16, 1887; d May 3, 1890.

Rt Rev. John S. Foley, D D, cons. Nov. 4, 1888.

Vicar-General, Rt. Rev. Mgr. Edward Joos.

DIOCESE OF DULUTH.—Established Oct. 3, 1889. Comprises the counties of Aitkin, Becker, Beltrami, Carlton, Cass, Clay, Cook, Crow Wing, Hubbard, Itasca, Kittson, Lake, Marshall, Norman, Pine, Polk, and St Louis, Minn.

Rt. Rev. James M Golrick, D.D., cons. Dec. 27, 1889.

DIOCESE OF ERIE.—Established 1843. Comprises Erie, Crawford, Mercer, Venango, Forest, Clarion, Jefferson, Clearfield, Cameron, Elk, McKean, Potter, and Warren counties, in northwestern Pennsylvania.

Rt. Rev. Michael O'Connor, cons. Aug. 15, 1843. (See Diocese of Pittsburg.)

Rt. Rev. Josue M. Young, cons. April 23, 1854; d. Sept. 18, 1866.

Rt. Rev. Tobias Mullen, cons. Aug. 2, 1868.

DIOCESE OF FORT WAYNE.—See established 1857. Comprises that part of the State of Indiana lying north of the southern boundary of Warren, Fountain, Montgomery, Boone, Hamilton, Madison, Delaware, and Randolph counties.

Rt. Rev. J. H. Luers, D.D., cons. Jan. 10, 1858; d. June 29, 1871.

Rt. Rev. Joseph Dwenger, cons. April 14, 1872; d. Jan. 22, 1893.

Rt. Rev. Joseph Rademacher, cons. June 24, 1883, as bp. of Nashville; trans. to Fort Wayne, July 14, 1893.

DIOCESE OF GALVESTON.—Established 1847. Comprises that part of Texas between the Colorado River on the west and the Sabine River on the east, and between the Gulf of Mexico on the south and the counties of Lampasas, Coryell, McLennan, Limestone, Freestone, Anderson, Cherokee, Nacogdoches, and Shelby on the north, and including these counties.

Rt. Rev. J M. Odin, D.D., cons. bp. of Claudiopolis and vicar apostolic of Texas, March 6, 1842; trans. to Galveston, 1847; promoted to New Orleans, 1861; d. May 25, 1870, in Ambierle, France.

Rt. Rev. C. M. Dubuis, D.D, cons. Nov. 23, 1862; res. 1881.

Rt. Rev. P. Dufal, D.D., cons. bp. of Delcon and vicar apostolic of Eastern Bengal, Nov. 25, 1860; as coad. to Galveston, May 14, 1878; res. 1880.

Rt. Rev. N. A. Gallagher, D.D., cons. April 30, 1882.

DIOCESE OF GRAND RAPIDS.—See established 1882. Comprises the counties of the lower peninsula of Michigan.

Rt. Rev. Henry Joseph Richter, D.D., cons. April 22, 1883.

DIOCESE OF GREEN BAY.—See established 1868. Comprises that part of the State of Wisconsin lying north of Fox and Manitowoc rivers, and east of Wisconsin River.

Rt. Rev. Joseph Melcher, D D., cons. July 12, 1868; d. Dec. 20, 1873.

Rt. Rev. Francis Xavier Krautbauer, D D., cons. June 29, 1875; d. Dec. 17, 1885.

Most Rev. Frederic Xavier Katzer, D.D., trans. to Milwaukee, Jan. 30, 1891.

Rt. Rev. Sebastian G. Messmer, D.D., cons. March 27, 1892.

DIOCESE OF HARRISBURG.—See established 1868. Comprises the counties of Dauphin, Lebanon, Lancaster, York, Adams, Franklin, Fulton, Cumberland, Perry, Juniata, Mifflin, Center, Clinton, Union, Snyder, Northumberland, Montour, and Columbia, in the State of Pennsylvania.

Rt. Rev. J. F. Shanahan, D.D., cons. July 12, 1868; d. Sept. 24, 1886.

Rt. Rev. Thomas McGovern, D.D., cons. March 11, 1888.

DIOCESE OF HARTFORD.—See established 1844. Comprises the State of Connecticut.

Rt. Rev. William Tyler, D.D., cons. March 17, 1844; d. June 18, 1849.

Rt Rev. Bernard O'Reilly, D.D, cons. Nov. 10, 1850; perished at sea, January, 1856.

Rt. Rev. F. P. McFarland, D.D., cons. March 14, 1858; d. Oct. 12, 1874.

Rt. Rev. Thomas Galberry, O.S.A., cons. March 19, 1876; d. Oct. 10, 1878.

Rt. Rev. Lawrence Stephen McMahon, D.D., cons. Aug. 10, 1879; d. Aug. 21, 1893.

Rt. Rev. Michael Tierney, D.D., cons. Feb. 22, 1894.

DIOCESE OF HELENA.—See erected 1884. Comprises the State of Montana.

Rt. Rev. John Baptist Brondel, D.D., cons. Dec. 14, 1879.

DIOCESE OF JAMESTOWN, N. D.—See established 1889. Comprises the State of North Dakota.

Rt. Rev. John Shanley, D.D., cons. Dec. 27, 1889.

DIOCESE OF KANSAS CITY KAN.—See established 1877; seat changed to Kansas City 1891. Comprises that part of Kansas east of Republic, Cloud, Ottawa, Saline, McPherson, Harvey, Sedgwick, and Sumner counties.

Rt. Rev. J. B. Miége, S.J., cons. bp. of Messenia and vicar apostolic, March 25, 1851; res. December, 1874; d. July 21, 1884.

Rt. Rev. Louis M. Fink, O.S.B., D.D., cons. bp. of Eucarpia, June 11, 1871; trans. to Leavenworth, May 22, 1877; seat changed to Kansas City, Kan., May 29, 1891.

DIOCESE OF KANSAS CITY, MO.—See established 1880. Comprises that part of Missouri south of the Missouri River and west of the eastern boundary of the counties of Moniteau, Miller, Camden, Laclede, Wright, Douglas, and Ozark.

Rt. Rev. John Joseph Hogan, D D., cons Sept 13, 1868; trans. to Kansas City, Sept. 10, 1880.

DIOCESE OF LA CROSSE.—See erected 1868. Comprises that part of Wisconsin lying north and west of the Wisconsin River.

Most Rev. Michael Heiss, D.D., cons. Sept. 6, 1868; appointed titular abp. of Hadrianople and coad. to the metropolitan of Milwaukee, March 14, 1880; promoted to Milwaukee, Sept. 7, 1881; d. March 26, 1890.
Rt. Rev. Kilian C. Flasch, D.D., cons. Aug. 24, 1881; d. Aug. 3, 1891.
Rt. Rev. James Schwebach, D.D., cons. Feb. 25, 1892.

DIOCESE OF LINCOLN.—See established 1887. Comprises that part of Nebraska south of the Platte River.

Rt. Rev. Thomas Bonacum, D.D., cons. Nov. 30, 1887.

DIOCESE OF LITTLE ROCK.—See established 1843. Comprises the State of Arkansas.
Rt. Rev. Andrew Byrne, D.D., cons. March 10, 1844; d. June 10, 1862.
Rt. Rev. Edward Fitzgerald, D.D., cons. Feb. 3, 1867

DIOCESE OF LOUISVILLE.—See established 1808. Comprises that part of Kentucky lying west of Carroll, Owen, Franklin, Woodford, Jessamine, Garrard, Rock Castle, Laurel, and Whitley counties.
Rt. Rev. Benedict Joseph Flagel, D.D., cons. bp of Bardstown, Nov. 4, 1810.
Rt. Rev. John B. David, D.D., cons. bp. of Mauricastro and coad. to the bp. of Bardstown, Aug. 15, 1819.
Rt. Rev. Guy Ignatius Chabrat, D.D., cons. bp. of Bolina and coad. to the bp. of Bardstown, July 20, 1834.
Rt. Rev. Martin John Spalding, D.D., cons. Sept. 10, 1848, bp. of Langone and coad. to the bp. of Louisville
Rt. Rev. Peter Joseph Lavialle, D.D., cons. Sept. 24, 1865.
Rt. Rev. William George McCloskey, D.D., cons. May 24, 1868.

DIOCESE OF MANCHESTER.—See established 1884. Comprises the State of New Hampshire.
Rt. Rev. Denis M. Bradley, D.D., cons. June 11, 1884.

DIOCESE OF MARQUETTE.—Dioceses of Sault Ste. Marie and Marquette, established 1857 and 1865. Comprises the northern peninsula of Michigan.
Rt. Rev. Frederic Baraga, D.D., cons. Nov. 1, 1853; d. Jan. 19, 1868.
Rt. Rev. Ignatius Mrak, D.D., cons. Feb. 7, 1869; res. 1878; trans. to Antinoë, 1881.
Rt. Rev. John Vertin, D.D., cons. Sept. 14, 1879.

DIOCESE OF MOBILE.—See established 1824. Comprises the State of Alabama and western Florida.
Rt. Rev. Michael Portier, D.D., cons. Nov. 5, 1826; d. May 14, 1859.
Rt. Rev. John Quinlan, D.D., cons. Dec. 4, 1859; d. March 9, 1883.
Rt. Rev. Dominic Manucy, D.D., res. October, 1884; d. Dec. 4, 1885.
Rt. Rev. Jeremiah O'Sullivan, D.D., cons. Sept. 20, 1885.

DIOCESE OF MONTEREY AND LOS ANGELES.—See established 1850. Comprises southern California.
Rt. Rev. Joseph Sadoc Alemany, D.D., O.P., cons. June 30, 1850; trans. to San Francisco, June 29, 1853.
Rt. Rev. Thaddeus Amat, C.M., D.D., cons. March 12, 1854; d. May 12, 1878.
Rt. Rev. Franciscus Mora, D.D., cons. bp. of Mossynopolis and coad., Aug. 3, 1873; succeeded May 12, 1878.
Rt. Rev. George Montgomery, cons. bp. of Tmui and coad., *cum jure successionis*, April 8, 1894.

DIOCESE OF NASHVILLE.—See established 1837. Comprises the State of Tennessee.
Rt. Rev. Richard Pius Miles, cons. Sept. 16, 1838; d. Feb. 21, 1860.
Rt. Rev. James Whelan, cons. May, 1859; res. 1863; d. 1878.
Rt. Rev. P. A. Feehan, cons. Nov. 1, 1865; created first abp. of Chicago, 1880.
Rt. Rev. Joseph Rademacher, D.D., cons. June 24, 1883; trans. to Fort Wayne, July 14, 1893.
Rt. Rev. Thomas S. Byrne, D.D., cons. 1893.

DIOCESE OF NATCHEZ.—See erected 1837. Comprises the State of Mississippi.
Rt. Rev. John J. Chance, D.D., cons. March 14, 1841; d. July 22, 1852.
Rt. Rev. J. O. Van De Velde, D.D., trans. from Chicago, July 29, 1853; d. Nov. 13, 1855.
Rt. Rev. William Henry Elder, D.D., cons. May 3, 1857; trans. to Cincinnati, 1880.
Rt. Rev. Francis Janssens, D.D., cons. May 1, 1881; promoted to the archiepiscopal see of New Orleans, Aug. 8, 1888.
Rt. Rev. Thomas Heslin, cons. June 18, 1889.

DIOCESE OF NATCHITOCHES.—See established 1853. Comprises northern part of Louisiana.
Rt. Rev. Augustus M. Martin, cons. Nov. 30, 1853; d. Sept. 29, 1875.
Rt. Rev. Francis Xavier Leray, cons. April 22, 1877; named bp. of Janopolis, coad. of New Orleans, and administrator; promoted to see of New Orleans, December, 1883; d. Sept. 23, 1887.
Rt. Rev. Anthony Durier, D.D., cons. March 19, 1885.

DIOCESE OF NESQUALLY.—See established 1850. Comprises the State of Washington.
Rt. Rev. A. M. A. Blanchet, cons. bp. of Walla Walla, Sept. 27, 1846; trans. to Nesqually, May 31, 1850; res. 1879; made bp. of Ibora; d. Feb. 25, 1887.
Rt. Rev. Ægidius Junger, D.D., cons. Oct. 28, 1879.

DIOCESE OF NEWARK.—See erected 1853. Comprises counties of Hudson, Passaic, Bergen, Essex, Union, Morris, and Sussex, in New Jersey.
Most Rev. James Roosevelt Bayley, D.D., cons. Oct. 30, 1853; promoted to archiepiscopal see of Baltimore, July 30, 1872.
Most Rev. Michael Augustine Corrigan, D.D., cons. May 4, 1873; promoted to archiepiscopal see of New York, Oct. 1, 1880.
Rt. Rev. Winand Michael Wigger, D.D., cons. Oct. 18, 1881.

DIOCESE OF OGDENSBURG.—See erected 1872. Comprises portions of northern New York.
Rt. Rev. Edgar P. Wadhams, D.D., cons. May 5, 1872; d. Dec. 5, 1891.
Rt. Rev. Henry Gabriels, D.D., cons. May 5, 1892.

DIOCESE OF OMAHA.—See created 1885. Comprises that part of Nebraska north of south shore of the Platte River.

Rt. Rev. James O'Gorman, D.D., cons. bp. of Raphanea and vicar apostolic of Nebraska, May 8, 1859; d. July 4, 1874.

Rt. Rev. James O'Connor, D.D., cons. titular bp. of Dibona, Aug. 20, 1876; bp. of Omaha, Oct. 2, 1885; d. May 27, 1890.

Rt. Rev. Richard Scannell, D.D., cons. bp. of Concordia, Nov. 30, 1887; trans. to Omaha, Jan. 31, 1891.

DIOCESE OF PEORIA.—See erected 1877. Comprises southern part of Illinois.
Rt. Rev. John Lancaster Spalding, D.D., cons. May 1, 1877.

DIOCESE OF PITTSBURG.—See erected 1843. Comprises fifteen counties in western Pennsylvania.
Rt. Rev. M. O'Connor, D.D., cons. Aug. 15, 1843; trans. to Erie and then again to Pittsburg; res. May, 1860; d. Oct. 18, 1872.

Rt. Rev. M. Domenec, D.D., cons. Dec. 9, 1860; trans. to Alleghany (from Jan. 11, 1876, to Aug. 3, 1877, divided from Pittsburg), Jan. 11, 1876; res. July 29, 1877; d. at Tarragona, Spain, Jan. 5, 1878.
Rt. Rev. J. Tuigg, D.D., cons. March 19, 1876; d. Dec. 7, 1889.
Rt. Rev. Richard Phelan, D.D., cons. Aug. 2, 1885; titular bp. of Cibyra and coad. to Bishop Tuigg; succeeded to see, Dec. 7, 1889.

DIOCESE OF PORTLAND.—See established 1855. Comprises the State of Maine.
Rt. Rev. David W. Bacon, D.D., cons. April 22, 1855; d. Nov. 5, 1874.
Rt. Rev. James Augustine Healey, D.D., cons. June 2, 1875.

DIOCESE OF PROVIDENCE.—Established 1872. Comprises the State of Rhode Island and portions of Massachusetts lying adjacent.
Rt. Rev. Thomas Hendricken, D.D., cons. April 28, 1872; d. June 11, 1886.
Rt. Rev. Matthew Harkens, D.D., cons. April 14, 1887.

DIOCESE OF RICHMOND.—Established 1821. Comprises eastern Virginia and part of the valley between the Alleghany and Blue Ridge mountains.
Rt. Rev. Patrick Kelly, D.D., cons. 1821; trans. to Waterford and Lismore, Ireland, 1822; d. Oct. 8, 1829.
Rt. Rev. Richard V. Whelan, cons. March 21, 1841; trans. to Wheeling, July 23, 1850; d. 1874.
Rt. Rev. John McGill, D.D., cons. Nov. 10, 1850; d. Jan. 14, 1872.
Rt. Rev. James Gibbons, D.D., cons. Aug. 16, 1868; bp. of Adramyttum, etc.; trans. to see of Richmond, July 30, 1872; trans. to see of Baltimore, Oct. 3, 1877.
Rt. Rev. John J. Keane, D.D., cons. Aug. 25, 1878; trans. to Ajasso, August, 1888.
Rt. Rev. A. Van De Vyver, cons. 1889.

DIOCESE OF ROCHESTER.—See established 1868. Comprises eight counties of western New York.
Rt. Rev. Bernard J. McQuaid, D.D., cons. July 12, 1868.
Vicar-General, Rt. Rev. James F. O'Hare, D.D.

DIOCESE OF SACRAMENTO.—Erected 1886. Comprises the former diocese of Grass Valley, with the addition of ten counties in California and one in Nevada.
Rt. Rev. P. Manogue, D.D., cons. coad. to Bishop O'Connell, of Grass Valley, Jan. 16, 1881; succeeded to the see, March, 1884.

DIOCESE OF ST. AUGUSTINE, FLA.—See erected 1870. Comprises east, middle, and south Florida.
Rt. Rev. Augustus Verot, D.D., cons. April 25, 1858, vicar apostolic of Florida; trans. to see of Savannah, July, 1861; appointed bp. of St. Augustine, March, 1870; d. June 10, 1876.
Rt. Rev. John Moore, D.D., cons. May 13, 1877.

DIOCESE OF ST. CLOUD.—See erected 1889. Comprises sixteen counties in the State of Minnesota.
Rt. Rev. Otto Zardetti, D.D., cons. Oct. 20, 1889.
Administrator, Rt. Rev. Mgr. J. P. Bauer.

DIOCESE OF ST. JOSEPH.—See established 1868. Comprises that part of Missouri between the Missouri and Chariton rivers.
Rt. Rev. M. F. Burke, trans. to St. Joseph, June 19, 1893.

DIOCESE OF SALT LAKE.—See erected 1891. Comprises the State of Utah and six counties in Nevada.
Rt. Rev. Lawrence Scanlan, D.D., cons. bp. of Laranden, June 29, 1887; trans. to Salt Lake, Jan. 30, 1891.

DIOCESE OF SAN ANTONIO.—See erected 1874. Comprises the State of Texas between the Colorado and Rio Grande rivers, except that portion south of the Arroyo de los Hermanos on the Rio Grande, and the counties of Live Oak, Bee, Goliad, and Refugio.
Rt. Rev. Anthony Dominic Pellicer, D.D., cons. Dec. 8, 1874; d. April 14, 1880.
Rt. Rev. John C. Neraz, D.D., cons. May 8, 1881.

DIOCESE OF SAVANNAH.—See established 1850. Comprises the State of Georgia.
Rt. Rev. Francis X. Gartland, cons. Nov. 10, 1850; d. Sept. 20, 1854.
Rt. Rev. John Barry, D.D., cons. Aug. 2, 1857; d. Nov. 21, 1859.
Rt. Rev. Augustus Verot, D.D., trans. to St. Augustine, March 11, 1870.
Rt. Rev. Ignatius Persico, D.D., trans. to this see, March 11, 1870; res. 1872.
Rt. Rev. W. H. Gross, C.SS.R., D.D., cons. April 27, 1873; trans. to Oregon, 1885.
Rt. Rev. Thomas A. Becker, D.D., cons. Aug. 16, 1868, bp. of Wilmington; trans. to Savannah, March 26, 1886.

DIOCESE OF SCRANTON.—See established 1868. Comprises eleven counties in central Pennsylvania.
Rt. Rev. William O'Hara, cons. July 12, 1868.

DIOCESE OF SIOUX FALLS, S. D.—Established 1889. Comprises the State of South Dakota.
Rt. Rev. M. Marty, D.D., O.S.B., cons. 1889.

DIOCESE OF SPRINGFIELD.—Established 1870. Comprises five counties in western Massachusetts.
Rt. Rev. P. T. O'Reilly, D.D., cons. Sept. 25, 1870; d. May 28, 1892.
Rt. Rev. Thomas Daniel Beaven, D.D., cons. Oct. 18, 1892.

DIOCESE OF SYRACUSE.—See established 1886. Comprises seven counties in central New York.
Rt. Rev. P. A. Ludden, D.D., cons. May 1, 1887.

DIOCESE OF TRENTON.—See established 1881. Comprises fourteen counties in the State of New Jersey.
Rt. Rev. Michael J. O'Farrell, D.D., cons. Nov. 1, 1881; d. 1894.
Rt. Rev. James Augustine McFaul, cons. Oct. 18, 1894.

DIOCESE OF VINCENNES.—See established 1834. Comprises southern Indiana.
Rt. Rev. Samuel Gabriel Bruté, cons. 1834; d. 1839.
Rt. Rev. Celestine De la Hailandière, cons. 1839; d. 1882.
Rt. Rev. John S. Bazin, cons. 1847; d. 1848.
Rt. Rev. Maurice De St. Palais, D.D., cons. Jan. 14, 1849; d. June 28, 1877.
Rt. Rev. Francis Silas Chatard, D.D., cons. May 12, 1878.
Vicar-General, Rt. Rev. Mgr. August Bessonies.

DIOCESE OF WHEELING.—See established 1850. Comprises the State of West Virginia, save eight counties, and portions of Virginia.
Rt. Rev. Richard Vincent Whelan, D.D., cons. March 21, 1841, bp. of Richmond; trans. to Wheeling, 1850; d. July 7, 1874.
Rt. Rev. John Joseph Kain, D.D., cons. May 23, 1875; trans. June 15, 1893, to the archiepiscopal see of Oxyrynchia, and appointed July 6, 1893, coad., *c. j. s.*, to the abp. of St. Louis.

DIOCESE OF WICHITA.—See established 1887. Comprises southwestern part of Kansas.
Rt. Rev. James O'Reilly, D.D., bp. elect; d. July 26, 1887.
Rt. Rev. John Joseph Hennessy, D.D., cons. Nov. 30, 1888.

DIOCESE OF WILMINGTON.—See established 1868. Comprises the State of Delaware and the eastern shores of Maryland and Virginia.
Rt. Rev. Thomas A. Becker, D.D., cons. Aug. 16, 1868; trans. to Savannah, 1886.
Rt. Rev. Alfred A. Curtis, D.D., cons. Nov. 14, 1886.

DIOCESE OF WINONA.—See established 1889. Comprises twenty counties in Minnesota.
Rt. Rev. Joseph B. Cotter, D.D., cons. Dec. 27, 1889.

VICARIATE APOSTOLIC OF ALASKA.—Erected 1894. Comprises Alaska Territory.
Rt. Rev. Pascal Tosi, S.J., vicar apostolic.

VICARIATE OF ARIZONA.—Established 1869. Comprises Arizona and southern extreme of New Mexico.
Most Rev. J. B. Salpointe, D.D., cons. bp. of Doryla and vicar apostolic of Arizona, June 20, 1869; appointed coad. of Santa Fé, *c. j. s.*, April 22, 1884.
Rt. Rev. P. Bourgade, cons. May 1, 1885.

VICARIATE APOSTOLIC OF BROWNSVILLE.—Erected 1874. Comprises portions of southeastern Texas.
Rt. Rev. Dominic Manucy, cons. titular bp. of Dulma and vicar apostolic of Brownsville, Dec. 8, 1874; d Dec. 4, 1885.
Rt. Rev. Peter Verdaguer, cons. bp. of Aulon, Nov. 9, 1890.

VICARIATE APOSTOLIC OF NORTH CAROLINA.—Established 1868. Comprises the State of North Carolina.
His Eminence the Most Rev. James, Cardinal Gibbons, D.D., cons. 1868, etc.
Rt. Rev. John J. Keane, D.D., cons. bp. of Richmond, etc., 1878.
Rt. Rev. H. P. Northrop, bp. of Charleston, S. C.; cons. bp. of Rosalia, Jan. 8, 1882; trans. to Charleston, Jan. 27, 1883.
Rt. Rev. Leo Haid, D.D., O.S.B., cons. titular bp. of Messene, July 1, 1888.

VICARIATE APOSTOLIC OF THE INDIAN TERRITORY.—Erected 1891. Comprises Oklahoma and the Indian Territory.
Rt. Rev. Theophile Meerschaert, cons. titular abp. of Sidymorum, Sept. 8, 1891.

VI.

THE FOREIGN CHURCHES RECEIVING THE EPISCOPATE FROM THE AMERICAN CHURCH.

THE CHURCH IN HAITI.

COVENANT BETWEEN THE AMERICAN CHURCH AND THE CHURCH IN HAITI, DATED NOVEMBER 3, 1874.

IN the name of the Most Holy and Undivided Trinity, Father, Son, and Holy Ghost. Amen.

The following Covenant, or Articles of Agreement, Concord, and Union, between the House of Bishops of the Protestant Episcopal Church in the United States of America of the first part, and the Convocation of the Protestant Episcopal Church in the Republic of Haiti of the second part, establishes the ensuing stipulations mutually entered into by the two Churches aforesaid:

ARTICLE 1. The House of Bishops aforesaid, in consideration of the fact that all the clergy, eleven in number, belonging to the Church in Haiti owe no allegiance to the government of these United States, but are Haitian citizens, do hereby recognize the aforesaid Church in Haiti as of right, as also in point of fact, a foreign Church, to all intents and purposes, within the meaning of Article 10 of the Constitution of the Protestant Episcopal Church in the said United States of America. But while the aforesaid House of Bishops doth thus recognize the Church in Haiti to be a foreign Church, yet during its early growth and development it shall continue to enjoy the nursing care of the Church in these United States until the Church in Haiti shall attain to competency for its own support, and to a sufficiency in its episcopate for the administration of its own affairs, according to the requirements of the ancient canons and primitive usages of the Church of Christ.

ART. 2. The House of Bishops, acting under the aforesaid Article 10 of the Constitution of the Protestant Episcopal Church in the United States of America, and availing itself of the concession made to them by the Protestant Episcopal Church in the Republic of Haiti in the stipulation contained in Article 5 following of this Covenant, will designate and consecrate to the office of bishop one of the clergymen of the aforesaid Church in Haiti (making selection of the said person according to the best of its godly judgment as to his fitness and qualifications for such a high and holy vocation).

ART. 3. The said House of Bishops furthermore agrees to name from among its own members a commission of four bishops, with whom the aforesaid bishop or bishops to be consecrated for the Church in Haiti shall be associated. And this commission shall form a temporary Board of Administration for the episcopal government of the Church in Haiti. And, as such, a majority of the same shall be competent to take order for the designation and consecration of future bishops in Haiti, as the necessity may arise, on the demand of the Convocation of the Church in that republic. The said temporary Board of Administration shall be furthermore empowered to administer all the discipline pertaining to the episcopal order of the ministry for the Church in Haiti until at least three bishops shall be designated, consecrated, and canonically established in said Church. It being understood that this commission of bishops shall be governed in the exercise of their episcopal administration, judgments, and acts by the provisions contained in the Constitution and canons of the Protestant Episcopal Church in the United States of America, so far as the same can be applied to the divergent circumstances of the Church in Haiti.

ART. 4. The Protestant Episcopal Church in Haiti on its part agrees always to guard in all their essentials a conformity to the doctrine, worship, and discipline of the Protestant Episcopal Church in the United States of America, as the same are set forth in the duly authorized standards of the said Church, and that it will not depart therefrom any further than local circumstances shall make it necessary.

ART. 5. The Protestant Episcopal Church in Haiti further agrees to concede to the House of Bishops of the Protestant Episcopal Church in the United States of America the choice of its first bishop to be consecrated; and thereafter to concede the same prerogative to a majority of the commission of bishops forming the temporary Board of Administration to choose or designate among the Haitian clergy future bishops on the demand of the Convocation in Haiti. And this prerogative shall continue until, in the good providence of God, three bishops shall be canonically resident and exercising jurisdiction in the Church of Haiti. Then this prerogative shall cease on the part of the aforesaid commission, and all its functions revert to those three bishops thus established in Haiti.

In testimony whereof, these Articles have been signed in duplicate, on the part of the House of Bishops by the bishops appointed for that purpose, and on the part of the Convocation of the Church in Haiti by its dean, who has exhibited duly authenticated credentials clothing him with full power to act in this matter in the name and in the behalf of the Convocation aforesaid.

Done in the city of New York, on the third day of November, in the year of our Lord one thousand eight hundred and seventy-four.

(Signed) JAMES THEODORE HOLLY,
Dean, etc.
WILLIAM R. WHITTINGHAM,
Bishop of Maryland.
ALFRED LEE,
Bishop of Delaware.
THOMAS ATKINSON,
Bishop of North Carolina.
HORATIO POTTER,
Bishop of New York.
G. T. BEDELL,
Bishop of the Diocese of Ohio.
A. CLEVELAND COXE,
Bishop of Western New York.

Done in my presence, and duplicates exchanged.

Attest: HENRY C. POTTER,
Secretary of the House of Bishops.

James Theodore Holly.

THE first bishop consecrated by the Church in the United States for the Haitian Church—a man of African descent, but of free-born ancestors—was born in Washington, D. C., 1829.

Reared in the faith and communion of the Holy Roman Church, he obtained his education in the schools of New York and Brooklyn, in which cities his parents successively resided.

Turning his attention to the ministry, he was admitted to the diaconate in St. Paul's Church, Detroit, Mich., June 17, 1855, by Bishop McCoskry. The Rt. Rev. Dr. Williams, of Connecticut, advanced him to the priesthood in St. Luke's Church, New Haven, Jan. 3, 1856.

Visiting Haiti in the interest of the Foreign Committee, with a view of reporting as to its openings for mission work, he returned after two months spent in careful examination of the spiritual needs of the people; and finding the funds of the committee inadequate to undertaking the work, he took charge of St. Luke's, New Haven, where he ministered until 1861. In May of that year he took out a missionary colony of one hundred and eleven persons to Haiti, landing at Port au Prince. Hardships, sickness, death, hindered the success of the plan. In six months forty-three of the settlers died. The missionary's family of eight was reduced to three. Most of the colonists returned to the United States; but the devoted Holly, with about a score of others, remained behind and persevered in the plan they had undertaken.

In 1863 Bishop Alfred Lee confirmed, on a visitation to Port au Prince, twenty-six persons. In 1865 the Foreign Committee assumed the charge of the mission, and the following year Bishop George Burgess made a visitation, ordaining a deacon and a priest and holding several confirmations, dying at sea on his return home.

Toward the close of 1872 and early in 1873 Bishop Cleveland Coxe spent six weeks in Haiti, consecrated the Memorial Church of the Holy Trinity, Port au Prince, dedicated an educational building, confirmed fifty-three, ordained six deacons and five priests, and participated in numerous services.

In 1874 Holly was elected bishop of the Haitian Church, and was consecrated in Grace Church, New York, Nov. 8, 1874, by Bishops Bosworth Smith, Alfred Lee, Horatio Potter, Stevens, Coxe, Kerfoot, and Dr. Reginald Courtenay, bishop of Kingston, W. I.

Bishop Holly attended, by invitation of the archbishop of Canterbury, the Lambeth Conference of 1878, the government of the republic meeting the charges of this visit.

The work of the Haitian Church has gone on, though retarded by many adverse circumstances. It bids fair to prove an important element in the regeneration of the island.

THE CHURCH IN MEXICO.

DECLARATION READ AT THE CONSECRATION OF THE FIRST BISHOP OF THE VALLEY OF MEXICO.

WHEREAS, a Covenant, or Articles of Agreement, Concord, and Union, have been entered into between the bishops of the Protestant Episcopal Church in the United States of America and the Mexican branch of the Catholic Church of our Lord Jesus Christ, militant upon earth; said Covenant having been adopted and confirmed by the said bishops of the Protestant Episcopal Church, assembled in council, in the city of New York, on the twenty-ninth day of October, in the year of our Lord one thousand eight hundred and seventy-five, and having been adopted and confirmed by duly appointed representatives of the said Mexican Church, in the city of Mexico, on the fifth day of January, in the year of our Lord one thousand eight hundred and seventy-six;

In which Covenant the said bishops did recognize the aforesaid Mexican Church as being of right, as also in point of fact, a foreign Church, to all intents and purposes, within the meaning of the tenth article of the Constitution of the Protestant Episcopal Church in the United States of America; and did agree to consecrate to the office of bishop one or more persons, duly elected by the said Mexican Church, after receiving satisfactory evidence of their election by the said Church, and of their fitness and qualifications for such a high and holy vocation;

And WHEREAS it was further stipulated, in the Covenant above mentioned, that the said bishops of the Protestant Episcopal Church in the United States would name from among themselves a commission of seven bishops, with whom the bishop or bishops so to be consecrated for the said Mexican Church should be associated as a temporary Board of Administration for the episcopal government of the said Mexican Church, and that a majority of the said commission should be competent to take order for the consecration of bishops for said Church, as the necessity may arise, on the demand of said Church;

And WHEREAS it was further resolved by the said bishops of the Protestant Episcopal Church, in council assembled, that, when the ratification of the aforesaid Covenant shall have taken place, the commission, so appointed as above stated, is empowered to receive, examine, and report to the presiding bishop of the Protestant Episcopal Church, upon the evidence of election and testimonials of qualification of the person or persons presented by the synodical authority of the said Mexican Church for consecration to the episcopate;

And it was further resolved that the presiding bishop is hereby requested and empowered, when he shall have received any such report from the said commission, to take order for the consecration of such person or persons as may be reported to him by the said commission as duly elected and qualified;

And WHEREAS the said bishops in council, on the twenty-ninth day of October, A.D. 1875, did appoint the Rt. Rev. William R. Whittingham, bishop of Maryland; the Rt. Rev. Alfred Lee, bishop of Delaware; the Rt. Rev. Gregory Thurston Bedell, bishop of Ohio; the Rt. Rev. William Bacon Stevens, bishop of Pennsylvania; the Rt. Rev. Arthur Cleveland Coxe, bishop of Western New York; the Rt. Rev. John Barrett Kerfoot, bishop of Pittsburg; and the Rt. Rev. Abram Newkirk Littlejohn, bishop of Long Island, to be their commission, for the purposes above recited;

Now, therefore, we, the bishops above named, composing the said commission so appointed and empowered, do certify that, after examination of the evidence of election and testimonials of qualification of the Rev. Henry Chauncey Riley, D.D., certified to us as duly elected bishop of the Valley of Mexico, having found the same satisfactory, we reported to the Rt. Rev. Benjamin Bosworth Smith, D.D., presiding bishop, that the said Henry Chauncey Riley was duly elected and qualified.

Henry Chauncey Riley.

HENRY CHAUNCEY RILEY was born in Santiago de Chile, South America, Dec. 15, 1835. He was graduated at Columbia College, New York, 1858, and studied theology under the Rev. Charles Dallas Marston, London. He was ordained deacon and priest by Bishop Horatio Potter, in New York, 1866. After a short service at the Spanish Church of Santiago, New York, he removed to the city of Mexico.

He was consecrated in Trinity Church, Pittsburg, Pa., June 24, 1879, with the title of "Bishop of the Valley of Mexico." The consecrators were Bishops Alfred Lee, Bedell, Stevens, Coxe, Kerfoot, Littlejohn, and Peterkin.

He was invited to resign by the House of Bishops, in October, 1883, and yielded to the request April 24, 1884.

The original organization of the Church is temporarily in abeyance. The government is now in the Cuerpo Ecclesiastico, which consists of the clergy and lay representatives of the congregations; the episcopal authority being, by election of the Cuerpo, in the presiding bishop of the American Church. The bishop of New Mexico and Arizona is the commissary of the presiding bishop, with power to act for him.

RIGHT REVEREND SAMUEL SEABURY, D.D.

Samuel Seabury.

BORN Nov. 30, 1729, at North Groton (now Ledyard), Conn., Samuel Seabury was the son of a Congregationalist minister who had been graduated at Harvard College, and who became a convert to the Church of England.

It was but natural that the son of a missionary of the Venerable Society for the Propagation of the Gospel in Foreign Parts should, on his graduation at Yale College in 1748, turn his attention toward the ministry of the Church. Crossing the ocean for holy orders, he prefaced his application for admission to the diaconate by a course of study in medicine at the University of Edinburgh, where, there is every reason to believe, he became acquainted with the Episcopal Church in Scotland, then, as for many subsequent years, under the ban of the government for its adhesion to the cause of the house of Stuart.

Returning to England, Seabury was ordered deacon by the bishop of Lincoln, Dr. John Thomas, acting for the bishop of London, Dec. 21, 1753, and, two days later, was advanced to the priesthood by the bishop of Carlisle, Dr. Osbaldeston, who was administering holy orders for the same bishop of London, then incapacitated by disease from the exercise of his episcopal functions.

Returning to his native land, Seabury became successively rector of Christ's Church, New Brunswick, N. J. (1754); Grace Church, Jamaica, L. I. (1757); and St. Peter's, Westchester, N. Y. (1766). At the latter place he established a Church school, which met with no little success until political complications compelled the closing of its doors.

On the breaking out of the War of the Revolution, Seabury, who had already attained prominence among the New York clergy, adhered to the crown. For the bold avowal of his loyalty, he became an object of the malevolence of the "Sons of Liberty," and was arrested and taken into Connecticut by an armed mob under circumstances which reflected no credit upon the patriot cause. His home was broken up, his family despoiled and exposed to personal violence, and he was finally driven within the British lines. Never relaxing his devotion to his ministerial work, he became a chaplain to the royal forces, and performed the duties of his calling throughout the war.

On Lady-day, 1783, at Woodbury, Conn., in the house occupied by the incumbent of the cure, the Rev. John R. Marshall, A.M., ten of the Connecticut clergy, who had remained with their people through the war, met in convocation, and after passing a complimentary vote of recognition of the services and devotion of the excellent though infirm Dr. Jeremiah Leaming, elected Samuel Seabury, who had received his doctorate from the University of Oxford during the strife, to the episcopate of Connecticut.

Recognizing the difficulties in the way of the attainment of their desire, these far-seeing men instructed their bishop elect to seek for consecration first in England, and, failing there, to claim it at the hands of "the Catholic remainder of the Church in Scotland."

When the bishop elect of Connecticut reached England on his quest for consecration the relations between the mother-land and the now independent American States were still in a measure strained; and although bearing the highest testimonials and recommendations from leading men of both the patriot and the royalist parties, Dr. Seabury found himself politely but effectually denied the accomplishment of his object. Wearied by delays in the way of his obtaining consecration in England, he turned toward the Church in Scotland. His application to the Scotch bishops was seconded by eminent dignitaries of the English Church, and he was finally consecrated bishop of Connecticut, Nov. 14, 1784, in an "upper room" at Aberdeen. His consecrators were Dr. Robert Kilgour, the primus, bishop of Aberdeen; Dr. Arthur Petrie, bishop of Ross and Moray; and Dr. John Skinner, bishop coadjutor of Aberdeen. A "Concordat" or "Bond of Union" was agreed upon and signed by the Scottish bishops who participated in the consecration, and by the bishop of Connecticut, which was intended to unite the Churches in Scotland and Connecticut in a mutual fellowship in doctrine, discipline, and worship, as well as in brotherly love. This document was the first "state paper" of the American Church.

Welcomed most enthusiastically on his return to his native State, the bishop of Connecticut convened his clergy in convocation at Middletown, Aug. 2, 1785, received their pledges of canonical obedience and fealty, gave them his first episcopal address, and, in connection with this auspicious gathering of the clergy (together with numbers of the laity) for the first time in the United States to welcome their episcopal head, held his first ordination, when four young men were ordered deacons. The Rev. Ashbel Baldwin, who had been active during the War of the Revolution on the patriot side, was the first of the four to receive the laying on of hands.

The bishop of Connecticut, by virtue of his episcopal office, and through his charm of manner and his entire consecration to his

Registred in the Registry of London

John by divine permission Bishop of Lincoln
To all to whom these presents shall come or whom
they may in any wise concern, Know ye—
that at an Ordination holden by us with the aid
and Assistance of Almighty God at the request
and in the stead of the Right Reverend Father
in God Thomas by divine permission Lord
Bishop of London in his Lordship's palace at
Fulham in the County of Middlesex on Friday
the twenty first day of December in the year of our
Lord one thousand seven hundred and fifty three
We did admit and promote our beloved in Christ
Samuel Seabury
to the holy Order of a Deacon according to the
Rights and Ceremonies of the Church of England
in that behalf published and provided he having
been well recommended to his Lordship for his
good Life and virtuous Attainments and
Proficiency in Learning with a sufficient Title
and having been also first examined and approved
by the Examiner of the said Lord Bishop. In
Testimony whereof We have caused the
Episcopal Seal of London to be hereto
affixed Dated the day and year above written and
in the tenth year of our Translation.

W. K. Skelton Reg.r

John [ ] Lincoln

Registred in the Registry of London

Richard by divine permission Bishop of Carlisle To all to whom these presents shall come or whom they may in any wise concern. Know Ye that at an Ordination holden by us with the aid and assistance of Almighty God at the request and in the stead of the Right Reverend Father in God Thomas by divine permission Lord Bishop of London in his Lordship's Palace at Fulham in the County of Middlesex on Sunday the twenty third day of December in the year of our Lord one thousand seven hundred and fifty three We did admit and promote our beloved in Christ Samuel Seabury to the holy Order of a Priest according to the Rights and Ceremonies of the Church of England in that behalf published and provided, he having been well recommended to his Lordship for his good Life and virtuous Attainments and proficiency in Learning with a sufficient Title, and having been also first examined and approved by the Examiner of the said Lord Bishop. In Testimony whereof we have caused the Episcopal Seal of London to be hereto affixed Dated the day and year above written and in the seventh year of our Consecration.

W. Shelton Registr

Rich^d. Carlisle

Samuel, by divine permission, Bishop of the Episcopal Church in Connecticut; To all whom it may concern, Know Ye, That on the sixteenth day of September One thousand, seven hundred and eighty five, We the Bishop afore mentioned solemnly administering Holy Orders under the protection of Almighty God in Trinity Church in the City of New Haven in the State of Connecticut did admit and promote our beloved in Christ Thomas Fitch Oliver A.M. (concerning whose Morals, Learning, Age and Title we were well satisfied) unto the Holy Order of Priests and him the said Thomas Fitch Oliver did then and there rightly and canonically Ordain Priest: He having first in our presence made and subscribed a declaration of his Assent and Conformity to the Articles and Liturgy of the Church of England, except in matters affected by the Civil Constitution of the American States. In Testimony whereof We have caused our Episcopal Seal to be hereunto affixed the day and year above written, and in the first year of our Consecration.

Samuel Bp: Epis: Chh Connect.

work, became almost at once the bishop of New England and portions of New York, while exercising his apostolic powers for the advantage of the Church to the southward as well. His episcopal progresses extended to the north as far as Portsmouth, N. H., and to the south to Long Island; while candidates for orders from the Middle and Southern States sought orders at his hands. Great numbers received confirmation from this apostolic man; while as the rector of St. James's Church, New London, he instituted the weekly eucharist, and by his discourses, as delivered on his visitations and subsequently published to the world, made the Church's teaching and usage the rule of the diocese, and thus laid the foundation for the prevalence of that type of belief and practice which is known as "Connecticut churchmanship."

Bishop Seabury died suddenly on Feb. 25, 1796. For some years before his decease he had been bishop of Rhode Island as well as Connecticut. When the Connecticut Church united with the Churches of the Middle and Southern States at the second General Convention of 1789, he became the first presiding bishop of the American Church.

As a leader of American religious thought, Samuel Seabury stands preëminent among the divines of his communion. His writings served to shape the theological belief of John Henry Hobart, and were not without their potent influence on the Oxford Movement itself. He was an intellectual giant among his fellows, and after a century has passed since he entered into rest, "his works follow him;" and his name shall endure forever.

WORKS.—1. Occasional sermons printed during and subsequent to the war; 2. "Charges to the Clergy of Connecticut"; 3. "On the Recommendation of Candidates for Holy Orders, and on the Rite of Confirmation" (1785); 4. "On the Conduct of the Clergy, the Religious Errors of the Times, and on the Holy Eucharist" (1786); 5. "The Communion Office; or, Order for the Administration of the Holy Eucharist, etc. With Private Devotions" (1786. Two editions of an Annotated Reprint of this office have been issued by the Rev. Prof. Samuel Hart, D.D., of Trinity College, Hartford. It was earlier reprinted in vol. iii. of Perry's "Half-century of Legislation: A Reprint of the General Convention Journals, 1785–1835. With Illustrative Notes and Documents," 8vo, 1871); 6. "An Address to the Ministers and Congregations of the Presbyterian and Independent Persuasions of the United States" (1790); 7. Two volumes of "Discourses Dedicated to the Episcopal Clergy of Connecticut and Rhode Island" (1793, second edition 1795); 8. "An Earnest Persuasion to the Frequent Receiving of the Holy Eucharist" (1794, republished again and again); 9. "The Psalter" (issued for use at St. James's, New London); 10. "Sermons," a single volume, issued in 1798; 11. "Discourses" (2 vols., Hudson, N. Y., 1815). In the Hon. George Shea's "Life of Alexander Hamilton" there is an interesting discussion of the authorship of the "Westchester Farmer's Pamphlets," which the writer attributes to Seabury.

RIGHT REVEREND WILLIAM WHITE, D.D.

William White.

THE son of prominent and most worthy parents, William White was born in Philadelphia, April 4, 1748, and was baptized at Christ Church, in that city, May 25, 1748. He was graduated in 1765 at the College and Academy of Philadelphia, then lately founded—in large measure through the exertions of Benjamin Franklin,—and of which the celebrated William Smith, D.D. Oxon., was the provost.

Determining to devote his life to the sacred ministry, he visited English relatives, remaining abroad until of canonical age for admission to orders. He was ordered deacon in the Chapel Royal of St. James's Palace, Westminster, London, Dec. 23, 1770, by the bishop of Norwich, Dr. Young, at that time acting for the bishop of London. He was ordained to the priesthood in the chapel of Fulham Palace, June 25, 1772, by the bishop of London, Dr. Richard Terrick.

On his return to Philadelphia he entered directly upon his life-work as one of the assistant ministers of the united parishes of Christ Church and St. Peter's, to the rectorship of which he was advanced on the resignation (during the War of the Revolution) of the Rev. Jacob Duché, remembered as having offered the first prayer in the Continental Congress, in Carpenter's Hall, in 1774.

Sympathizing from the first with the patriotic side, at the breaking out of the war, White became one of the chaplains to Congress at a period when the prospects of the American cause were far from promising; and after the national independence was secured, and while Philadelphia remained the capital, he served in this capacity from 1787 to 1801.

The University of Pennsylvania, which had succeeded the College and Academy of Philadelphia, on its reorganization toward the close of the war gave to its distinguished alumnus its first honorary degree, that of D.D.

During the progress of the strife which resulted in the separation of the American colonies, White had been a careful student of the condition and needs of the Church in this country, which, by the severance of political connection with the English state and Church, had become independent as well as, and at the same time with, the nation. Prior to the announcement of peace, in a remarkable pamphlet entitled "The Case of the Episcopal Churches Considered" (1782–83), the young rector of the united churches of Philadelphia had with consummate skill outlined and elaborated a plan of organization for the independent and autonomous Church in the United States, which in its originality, its adaptation to the exigencies of the times, and its far-seeing provision for a growth and development which at that time few Churchmen, however loyal and sanguine, believed to be possible, fully entitles its author to recognition as the foremost ecclesiastical statesman of his times. In this masterly state paper, among other suggestions which have in nearly every instance commended themselves to our acceptance, the idea of comprehending the laity in the councils of the Church was for the first time propounded. There is little doubt that through the wise forecasting of White in this respect the organization of the American Church was made both possible and practicable at a time when in the judgment of many its continued existence seemed problematical. The men who in the halls of Congress or on the fields of battle had won for us our independence, and afterward had framed our federal constitution, were those who in the State or General Conventions gave their willing efforts for the organization of "the free Church in the free State," as proposed by White. The incorporation of laymen in the Church Conventions or Councils, begun under the presidency of White in the historic Christ Church, Philadelphia, was repeated in each successive ecclesiastical gathering, till, through the successful working of this new principle in ecclesiastical legislative bodies, there was gained for the Church in the United States a close conformity in her organization with that of the Republic of which her members and ministers formed so important a part.

It was only to be expected that one so evidently a leader should be foremost in all the efforts for the rehabilitation of the Church in the United States, as independent of the mother-Church of England. In the early Conventions of the Churches in the Middle and Southern States the youthful rector of the united Philadelphia churches, by his presence, his counsels, his persuasive personal magnetism, and his knowledge of men, took a prominent part. He was without opposition chosen by the Pennsylvania State Convention for the episcopate in the English line, which, now that Seabury in Scotland had secured the coveted prize of the apostolical succession, was found to be ready for the asking at the hands of the mother-Church. It was in the chapel of the archbishop of Canterbury, at Lambeth Palace, on Feb. 4, 1787, that William White, D.D., bishop elect of Pennsylvania, and Samuel Provoost, D.D., bishop elect of New York, received consecration to the episcopate at the hands of the archbishop of Canterbury, Dr. John Moore; the archbishop of York, Dr. William Markham; the bishop of Bath and Wells, Dr.

Palace at Lambeth in the County of Surry admit our beloved in Christ William White Clerk D.D. a Subject or Citizen of the State of Pennsylvania in North America, and Rector of Christ Church and St Peters in the City of Philadelphia in the said State, of whose sufficiency in good Learning, Soundness in the Faith, and Purity of Manners We were fully ascertained into the Office of a Bishop of the Protestant Episcopal Church in the State of Pennsylvania aforesaid to which the said William White hath been elected by the Convention for the said State as appears unto Us by due Testimony thereof by him produced, and him the said William White did then and there rightly and canonically consecrate a Bishop according to the Manner and Form prescribed and used by the Church of England, his taking the Oaths of Allegiance Supremacy and Canonical Obedience only excepted, he being exempted from the Obligation of taking the said Oaths by virtue of the above recited Act. Provided that neither He the said Bishop nor any Person or Persons deriving their Consecration from or under him, nor any Person or Persons admitted to the Order of Deacon or Priest by him or his Successor or Successors, shall be enabled to exercise his or their respective Office or Offices within his Majesty's Dominions. In Testimony whereof We have caused our Archiepiscopal Seal to be affixed to these Presents. Given at Lambeth House the Day and Year above written and in the Fourth Year of our Translation.

J. Cantuar.

To all Persons to whom these Presents shall come, or whom the same shall or may in anywise or at anytime concern: We John, by Divine Providence Lord Archbishop of Canterbury, Primate of all England and Metropolitan, send Greeting.

Whereas by an Act of Parliament passed at Westminster in the Twenty sixth year of the Reign of our Sovereign Lord George the Third King of Great Britain France and Ireland, intitled "An Act to empower the Archbishop of Canterbury or the Archbishop of York, for the Time being, to consecrate to the Office of a Bishop, Persons being Subjects or Citizens of Countries out of his Majesty's Dominions": It is enacted That it shall and may be lawful to and for the Archbishop of Canterbury or the Archbishop of York, for the Time being, together with such other Bishops as they shall call to their Assistance to consecrate Persons, being Subjects or Citizens of Countries out of his Majesty's Dominions, Bishops, for the Purposes aforesaid, without the King's License for their Election, or the Royal Mandate under the Great Seal, for their Confirmation and Consecration, and without requiring them to take the Oaths of Allegiance and Supremacy, and the Oath of due Obedience to the Archbishop for the Time being. Provided always, That no Persons shall be consecrated Bishops in the Manner herein provided until the Archbishop of Canterbury or the Archbishop of York, for the Time being shall have first applied for and obtained his Majesty's License, by Warrant under his Royal Signet and Sign Manual, authorising and empowering him to perform such Consecration and expressing the Name or Names of the Persons so to be consecrated, nor until the said Archbishop has been fully ascertained of their sufficiency in good Learning, of the Soundness of their Faith, and of the Purity of their Manners. Provided also, and be it hereby declared, That no Person or Persons consecrated to the Office of a Bishop in the Manner aforesaid, nor any Person or Persons deriving their Consecration from or under any Bishop so consecrated, nor any Person or Persons admitted to the Order of Deacon or Priest by any Bishop or Bishops so consecrated, or by the Successor or Successors of any Bishop or Bishops so consecrated, shall be thereby enabled to exercise his or their respective Office or Offices within his Majesty's Dominions. Provided always and be it further enacted, That a Certificate of such Consecration shall be given under the Hand and Seal of the Archbishop who consecrates, containing the Name of the Person so consecrated, with the Addition, as well of the Country whereof he is a Subject or Citizen, as of the Church in which he is appointed Bishop, and the further Description of his not having taken the said Oaths, being exempted from the Obligation of so doing by virtue of this Act. Now know all Men by these Presents that We the said John Lord Archbishop of Canterbury having obtained his Majesty's License by Warrant under his Royal Signet and Sign Manual, did, in pursuance of the said Act of Parliament, on Sunday the Fourth day of February in the Year of our Lord One thousand seven hundred and Eighty seven, in the Chapel of our

[illegible] William White [illegible]

We William Lord Archbishop of York. Charles Lord Bishop of Bath & Wells and John Lord Bishop of Peterborough were present and assisting at the Consecration within mentioned.

W. Ebor
C. Bath & Wells
J. Peterborough

The Signatures of the Archbishops of Canterbury and York, and of the Bishops of Bath & Wells and Peterborough were made in my Presence Feby 4th 1787

Wm Dickes Secretary to the Archbishop of Canterbury.

Certificate of the Consecration of the Rt Revd Father in God William White D.D. Bishop of the State of Pensylvania in North America

Feby 4th 1787

Charles Moss; and the bishop of Peterborough, Dr. John Hinchcliffe. The addition of two bishops of the English line of succession to Seabury, deriving his episcopate from the Scotch prelates, completed a college of bishops for America, and gave an impetus to the adoption of measures for the union in one confederation of the Churches North and South, which was at length happily accomplished at the second General Convention, held in Philadelphia, 1789. From this date the history of the Church in the United States as an autonomous and independent branch of the Church Catholic begins.

Bishop White held his first ordination at Christ Church, May 28, 1787, on which occasion Joseph Clarkson, whose grandson, R. H. Clarkson, became, many years afterward, the first bishop of Nebraska, was ordered deacon. In the same historic church the bishop of Pennsylvania, during the more than half a century of his episcopate, presided at the consecration of six bishops.

Bishop White was the personal friend and, during his official residence in Philadelphia, the pastor of Washington. His episcopate was as full of honors as of years; and at the time of his death (July 17, 1836) he was undoubtedly the most revered and widely known of the bishops of the Anglican communion throughout the world. Buried in the churchyard of his beloved Christ Church, his remains were removed, on Dec. 23, 1870, to their fitting resting-place in the chancel of the church to which he had ministered for so many years, and where they now await the resurrection day.

WORKS.—Besides numerous occasional sermons, addresses, charges, and theological treatises, as well as countless contributions to the religious press, Bishop White will be chiefly remembered in literature by his "Memoirs of the Protestant Episcopal Church," of which three editions have appeared: the first in 1820, the second, under the editorship of the Rev. Francis Lister Hawks, D.D., LL.D., in 1836, and the third, under the editorship of the Rev. Dr. B. F. De Costa, in 1880. We have already referred to the able state paper, "The Case of the Episcopal Churches Considered" (1782–83). His theological writings, besides the above, were chiefly his "Comparative View of Calvinism and Arminianism" (2 vols., 8vo, 1817); "Commentary on the Ordinal and on the Duties of the Public Ministry" (8vo, 1833). His "Addresses," at the General Theological Seminary in the years 1822, 1824, 1827, 1828, 1829, were really theological treatises. The "Pastoral Letters" of the House of Bishops, 1808–35 inclusive, were the composition of the presiding bishop. Although on the committee of Convention appointed to prepare and publish what is known in American liturgical literature as the "Proposed Book of Common Prayer" (12mo, Philadelphia, 1786), this work is incorrectly spoken of as "Bishop White's Prayer-book." The bulk of the changes in this volume were made by the other members of the committee, notably by Provost Smith; and the substitution of the revision of 1789, which was practically a return to the English original, and which became the "standard" of the American Church for the first century of its independent existence, was heartily acquiesced in by Bishop White.

RIGHT REVEREND SAMUEL PROVOOST, D.D.

Samuel Provoost.

THE "patriot" rector of Trinity Church, and the first bishop of New York, was born March 11, 1742, in New York City.

After graduating at King's College (now Columbia), Provoost, in 1761, matriculated at the University of Cambridge, England, and became a fellow-commoner at St. Peter's House (now St. Peter's College). He was ordered deacon in the Chapel Royal of St. James's Palace, Westminster, London, Feb. 3, 1766, by the bishop of London, Dr. Richard Terrick, and was advanced to the priesthood March 25th of the same year, by the bishop of Chester, Dr. Edmund Keene, acting for the bishop of London. On his return to his native land he became one of the clergy of Trinity Church, New York, to the rectorship of which he was elected, on the final evacuation of the city by the British, by the patriotic vestry, who thus recognized his unflagging support of the American cause. In 1785 he was appointed one of the chaplains of Congress, and in 1789 was made the chaplain of the Senate. After the public exercises of the inauguration of Washington, the President, having taken the oath of office, proceeded on foot to St. Paul's Chapel (Trinity then being in ruins), where Provoost read prayers, using, without doubt, the form as prescribed in the "Proposed Book," then in use in New York.

The doctorate in divinity was conferred on Provoost by the University of Pennsylvania, 1786. He was consecrated bishop of New York at Lambeth Palace chapel, Feb. 4, 1787, by the two archbishops and the bishops of Bath and Wells and Peterborough, at the same time with White.

Bishop Provoost resigned his see in 1801; but the House of Bishops declined to accept his resignation, and authorized the consecration of a bishop coadjutor for New York. He afterward only appeared in public at the consecration, on May 29, 1811, of Hobart and Griswold. He died Sept. 6, 1815.

WORKS.—Although a scholar of varied and even profound attainments, Bishop Provoost published nothing. While at Cambridge he prepared an index to the "Historia Planetarum" of Baubin. In his theological opinions he appears to have leaned toward the views of the celebrated Samuel Clark, D.D., although he refused the overtures made to him by the authorities of King's Chapel, Boston, on their lapse into Unitarianism, for the ordination of their lay reader, Mr. James Freeman. Provoost's partizan antagonism to Seabury forms an interesting and unique chapter in the annals of the consolidation of the Churches North and South.

RIGHT REVEREND JAMES MADISON, D.D.

James Madison.

THE life of the first bishop of Virginia was the uneventful career of a college professor and president. Born in Rockingham, Va., Aug. 27, 1749, he was graduated at William and Mary College 1772. He took up the study of law and was admitted to the bar, but almost directly turned his attention to divinity, while serving his alma mater as professor of mathematics.

In 1775 he crossed the ocean for ordination, and was ordered deacon in the chapel of Fulham Palace, Sept. 29, 1775, by the bishop of London, Dr. Terrick, and was advanced to the priesthood by the same prelate, in the same place, Oct. 1, 1775.

On his return he was made president of William and Mary College, which position he held with distinguished ability until his death.

On the resignation of the amiable and godly David Griffith, the friend and rector of Washington, of his election to the Virginia episcopate, Madison was chosen to fill the place. He was consecrated bishop of Virginia in the chapel of Lambeth Palace, Sept. 19, 1790. The consecrators were the archbishop of Canterbury, Dr. John Moore, the bishop of London, Dr. Beilby Porteus, and the bishop of Rochester, Dr. John Thomas.

His episcopate witnessed the gradual decay and almost the extinction of the Church in the state. Conscientiously regarding himself as under primal obligations to the college, his episcopal work was fragmentary and at length practically laid aside. Meade, who received orders at his hands, defends him from the charge of succumbing to the tide of French infidelity which, during his presidency, swept over the college and throughout the land. The bishop's desire to bring about the incorporation of the Methodists in the Church, in which purpose he lacked, unfortunately, the sympathy and support of his brethren in the episcopate, indicates an appreciation of personal religion, of which the adherents of that body were at the time, in many places, almost the sole exponents.

He died March 5, 1812, and was buried at Williamsburg, Va.

WORKS.—1. "Discourse on the Death of General Washington" (1800); 2. "A Thanksgiving Sermon" (1781); 3. "A Letter to Jedediah Morse" (1795); 4. "An Address to the Episcopal Church in Virginia" (1799). These, with a few other less important pamphlets, comprise his printed works.

RIGHT REVEREND THOMAS JOHN CLAGGETT, S.T.D.

Thomas John Claggett.

In the consecration of Claggett as bishop of Maryland the two lines of the apostolical succession existing in the United States, that of the Scottish and that of the English Church, were united; and by this union of divergent lines every American bishop can trace his spiritual lineage to Seabury as representing the line from Aberdeen, and to White, Provoost, and Madison as representing that from Canterbury. The measures leading to this happy union of the Churches North and South, as detailed on the pages of the General Convention "Journals," or as found in fuller detail in the correspondence of the clergy of the day, form a chapter of our annals of deep interest. This union, for which Seabury and White labored, and against the accomplishment of which Provoost contended, was clearly the work of "Him who maketh men to be of one mind in an house."

Thomas John Claggett was born in Prince George's County, Md., Oct. 2, 1742. He was graduated at the College of New Jersey, Princeton, 1762, and received his training for holy orders from his maternal uncle, the Rev. Dr. John Eversfield.

Sept. 20, 1767, he was ordered deacon in the chapel of Fulham Palace, by the bishop of London, Dr. Terrick. At the same place and by the same prelate he was priested, Oct. 11, 1767.

Appointed to the charge of All Saints', Calvert County, Md., he remained there till, on the breaking out of the Revolutionary War, he retired to his estate in Prince George's County, where he remained for two years. In 1779 he began ministering in St. Paul's Church in his native county, and in the following year became rector of the parish.

In 1787 his alma mater conferred on him the doctorate of sacred theology, and in 1792 he received the degree of doctor in divinity from Washington College.

Claggett's consecration took place in Trinity Church, New York, Sept. 17, 1792. The consecrators were Bishops Provoost (presiding), Seabury, White, and Madison. This was the first consecration to the episcopal office in the United States.

Claggett was appointed chaplain to the United States Senate, 1800. In 1808 he became rector of Trinity Church, Upper Marlborough. He died at Croom, Md., Aug. 2, 1816.

WORKS.—Bishop Claggett published only a few occasional sermons, etc.

RIGHT REVEREND ROBERT SMITH, D.D.

Robert Smith.

THE Church in the State of South Carolina entered into federal relations first with the Churches of the Middle and Southern States, and finally with the united Churches of the North and South, with the implied, and at length expressed, condition that no bishop was to be consecrated as its head. The abilities and devotion of Robert Smith led his fellow-Churchmen of the clergy and laity in South Carolina to put aside this determination and to ask for the consecration as their spiritual head of the most gifted and learned divine in the State.

Born in the county of Norfolk, England, Aug. 25, 1732, Smith was matriculated at the University of Cambridge as a member of Gonville and Caius College, taking his degree in 1753, and becoming a fellow of his college.

He was ordered deacon March 7, 1756, by the bishop of Ely, Dr. Matthias Mauson, and was advanced to the priesthood by the same prelate, Dec. 21st of the same year.

Coming to South Carolina as assistant at St. Philip's Church, Charleston, 1757, he was made rector in 1759.

Espousing most heartily the popular cause at the beginning of the War of the Revolution, the rector of St. Philip's became a marked man among the Southern patriots, and rendered efficient aid to the cause of liberty. In 1780, on the occupation of Charleston by the British forces, Smith was banished from the city. Removing to Maryland, he took temporary charge of St. Paul's parish, Queen Anne County. Returning to Charleston at the close of the war, in 1783, he opened a classical academy, which was subsequently chartered (in 1786) as the South Carolina College. Of this institution he continued in charge as president until 1798.

In 1789 he received the doctorate in divinity from the University of Pennsylvania.

Dr. Smith's consecration to the episcopate took place Sept. 14, 1795, at Christ Church, Philadelphia. His consecrators were Bishops White, Provoost, Madison, and Claggett. Bishop Smith, after an honored and most useful episcopate, died Oct. 28, 1801, universally revered and lamented. The bishop was, in consequence of his Revolutionary services, one of the first and foremost members of the South Carolina State Society of the Cincinnati.

WORKS.—Bishop Smith, it is believed, published nothing save, possibly, some papers of an ephemeral nature.

RIGHT REVEREND EDWARD BASS, D.D.

Edward Bass.

Born at Dorchester, Mass., Nov. 23, 1726, Bass was graduated from Harvard College, 1744.

Ordered deacon May 17, 1752, at the chapel of Fulham Palace, by Bishop Sherlock, he was priested by the same prelate in the same place, May 24, 1752. He became missionary of the Venerable Society for the Propagation of the Gospel in Foreign Parts at Newburyport, Mass., and incumbent of St. Paul's Church.

At the opening of the War of the Revolution Bass observed the days of fasting and thanksgiving appointed by the Continental Congress, and because of his patriotism was dismissed from the service of the Venerable Society. Though deprived of the chief means for his support, he still remained at his post. His parishioners sympathized with him. He omitted the "state prayers," observed the frequent appointments for services in the interest of the patriots, and kept his church open throughout the war.

The presentation to the General Convention of the Churches in the Middle and Southern States of the name of the rector of St. Paul's as the bishop elect of Massachusetts and New Hampshire, accompanied with a request of the clergy of those two States, headed by Samuel Parker, that the Convention should ask the three bishops then in the United States—Seabury, White, and Provoost—to unite in his consecration, paved the way for the completion of the episcopal college in the line of Canterbury by the consecration at Lambeth of Madison, and effected the recognition of the validity of the Scottish consecrations.

On the accomplishment of the union of the New England Churches under Seabury with those of the Middle and Southern States under White and Provoost, the project of Bass's consecration, which had been the means of effecting this result, was not pushed, and it was not until May 7, 1797, that Bass, who had received his doctorate from the University of Pennsylvania in 1789, was consecrated the first bishop of Massachusetts at Christ Church, Philadelphia, by Bishops White, Provoost, and Claggett.

He died at Newburyport, Sept. 10, 1803. In addition to his charge of Massachusetts he had been elected to the episcopate of New Hampshire, Rhode Island, and Vermont.

Works.—1. "A Masonic Address" (1779); 2. "A Sermon before the Merrimac Humane Society" (1800); 3. A pamphlet on his connection with the Venerable Society.

RIGHT REVEREND ABRAHAM JARVIS, D.D.

Abraham Jarvis.

BORN at Norwalk, Conn., May 5, 1739, and graduated from Yale in 1761, Jarvis was ordered deacon in the chapel at Whitehall, London, Feb. 5, 1764, by the bishop of Exeter, Dr. Keppell, acting for the bishop of London, and was advanced to the priesthood in the Chapel Royal of St. James's Palace, Westminster, by the bishop of Carlisle, Dr. Lyttelton, Feb. 9, 1765.

He became the incumbent of Christ Church, Middletown, Conn. Remaining at his post during the war, he took part in the notable convocation of clergy at Woodbury on the feast of the Annunciation, 1783, and was the secretary of the faithful priests who chose Seabury for their bishop. The papers and testimonials of this election were drawn up in his handwriting, and during Seabury's weary months of dancing attendance on the varying moods of the English bishops, it was to Jarvis that his indignant letters were addressed, detailing the obstacles in his way; and it was from the sympathizing secretary of the convocation that encouragement and support came. It was natural that, on the final success of the effort to secure a bishop for the free and independent States, which had at last been effected through the offices of a Church untrammeled by connection with the state, the bishop of Connecticut, on his return, should receive from his clergy, through Jarvis, the pledges and testimonials of their fealty and love.

Later, when the prospects of union with the Churches of the Middle and Southern States seemed hopeless, Jarvis, on whom the bishop of Connecticut had conferred the doctorate in divinity, was designated by Seabury to go to Scotland for consecration as bishop coadjutor of Connecticut, with the view of eventually procuring an episcopal college for the transmission of the succession in the Scottish line. Happily an unexpected turn in affairs made this unnecessary.

On the death of Seabury the vacancy was filled by the choice of Jarvis. He was consecrated in Trinity Church, New Haven, Sept. 18, 1797, by Bishops White, Provoost, and Bass. He received the doctorate in divinity from Yale in 1786.

He died May 13, 1813, and was buried under the altar of Trinity Church, New Haven.

WORKS.—1. "A Sermon on the Death of Bishop Seabury"; 2. "A Sermon on the Witness of the Spirit."

RIGHT REVEREND BENJAMIN MOORE, S.T.D.

Benjamin Moore.

BENJAMIN MOORE was born in Newtown, L. I., Oct. 5, 1748. He was graduated at King's College, New York, 1768. His ordination to the diaconate took place in the chapel of Fulham Palace, June 24, 1774; and he was advanced to the priesthood the following day in the same place and by the same prelate, Dr. Richard Terrick, bishop of London.

On his return to New York he was appointed an assistant minister of Trinity Church; and such was the moderation of his course, and such the confidence inspired by the purity of his life and the singular devoutness of his mien and ministry, that he retained his position throughout the trying scenes of the war for independence, giving no offense to Whigs or Tories alike, and contenting himself with ministering in spiritual things to all alike until the return of peace. In 1789 his alma mater (now called Columbia College) conferred on him the doctorate in divinity, and on Dec. 22, 1800, he was chosen rector of Trinity Church.

Dr. Moore was consecrated bishop coadjutor of New York in St. Michael's Church, Trenton, N. J., Sept. 11, 1801, during the session of the General Convention at that place. His consecrators were Bishops White, Claggett, and Jarvis. He was elected to the presidency of Columbia College the year of his consecration, and held this honorable post for ten years in connection with his episcopal and rectoral duties. He died Feb. 27, 1816, at Greenwich, N. Y.

WORKS.—Three occasional discourses and a single pamphlet comprise all the writings of Bishop Moore published during his life. Two volumes of his sermons, edited by his distinguished son, Professor Clement C. Moore, LL.D., of the General Theological Seminary, appeared after his decease.

RIGHT REVEREND SAMUEL PARKER, D.D.

Samuel Parker.

BORN in Portsmouth, N. H., Aug. 17, 1744, and graduating at Harvard, 1764, Samuel Parker was invited to become assistant minister of Trinity Church, Boston, before his ordination.

He was admitted to deacon's orders at Fulham Palace chapel, Feb. 24th, and was priested on Feb. 27, 1774, by Bishop Terrick.

Left in charge of Trinity on the retirement of the rector to Halifax, Parker, with the consent of his vestry, on the receipt of the news of the Declaration of Independence, adapted the services of the church to the new order of things by the omission of the "state prayers," and thus gave early proof of stable purpose. In June, 1779, he accepted the rectorship of Trinity, conditioned on the recognition by the parish of his predecessor's rights, should he return to his former charge and accept the new condition of affairs.

Parker was among the clergy assembled at Middletown to welcome Seabury, and there began at this meeting a friendship which had a marked influence on the fortunes of the rising Church. He took, at Seabury's request, a leading part in adapting the Prayer-book to the change in civil affairs, being associated in this important work with Jarvis and Moore. The results of this, the first American revision, were subsequently adopted by the Massachusetts Convention at Parker's suggestion, and prevailed throughout New England.

Urged by Seabury to seek in Scotland the consecration to the episcopate of Massachusetts, Parker entered into a correspondence with White in the interest of the union of the American Churches. It was chiefly to Parker that the union of 1789 was due, and it was in recognition of his preëminent services, on the nomination of White, that the University of Pennsylvania conferred on him the doctorate in divinity in 1789.

He had refused the episcopate at the time that Bass was first named for this office, and later, when, through Parker's influence, Bass was again chosen. On his death, Parker's opposition was not suffered to prevail longer, and he received consecration in Trinity, New York, Sept. 14, 1804, during the session of the General Convention. His consecrators were Bishops White, Claggett, Jarvis, and Moore. He died, three months from the day of his consecration, Dec. 6, 1804.

WORKS.—1. An annual "Election Sermon" (1793); 2. "A Charitable Discourse Delivered in Behalf of the Female Asylum of Boston" (1803).

RIGHT REVEREND JOHN HENRY HOBART, D.D.

John Henry Hobart.

NEXT to the name of Samuel Seabury as preëminent among the leaders of thought in the American Church, and as wielding a constantly increasing influence, must be placed that of John Henry Hobart, the third bishop consecrated for the New York diocese.

Born in Philadelphia, Sept. 14, 1775, baptized and confirmed by White in Christ Church, prepared for his college course at the Episcopal Academy of his native city, and graduating, after two years spent at the College of Philadelphia, at Princeton, 1793, Hobart at first turned his attention to mercantile affairs. Finding a business life uncongenial, he accepted (1796) a tutorial position at Princeton, which he held for two years.

Having determined to enter the ministry, he returned to Philadelphia and prepared for ordination under the direction of White, who admitted him to deacon's orders, June 3, 1798, in Christ Church. After serving various parishes in Pennsylvania, New Jersey, and New York, he was, September, 1800, elected an assistant minister of Trinity Church, New York, entering at once upon the duties of this important post. He had earlier (June 3, 1799) been elected secretary of the House of Bishops. In 1801 he was chosen secretary of the New York State Convention, as well as a deputy to the General Convention which convened at Trenton, N. J., in the autumn of that year.

He was priested by Bishop Provoost, April 5, 1801. He was chosen secretary of the House of Deputies of the General Convention of 1804. In 1806 he received the doctorate in divinity from Union College, Schenectady, N. Y.

Hobart was consecrated bishop coadjutor of New York in Trinity Church, May 29, 1811, by Bishops White, Provoost, and Jarvis. At the same time Dr. Alexander Viets Griswold was consecrated for the newly created "Eastern Diocese," which composed all of the New England States save Connecticut.

Agreeably to the English precedent established at the consecration, in Lambeth Palace chapel, of White and Provoost, Hobart, although the younger man and elected to his office of coadjutor subsequently to the date of Griswold's election, first received the laying on of hands as the senior doctor in divinity.

The omission of a portion of the sentence of consecration by the bishop presiding at the time of this double ordination to the episcopate was made the occasion of a bitter controversy in New York, and an attempt to impugn the regularity of Hobart's consecration, though it is believed there was no faulting of the consecration of Griswold.

On the decease of Moore (1816), Hobart became the diocesan of New York, and also rector of Trinity Church. His episcopal duties were not confined to his own see. He rendered abundant and efficient service in New Jersey prior to the election of Croes, and was provisional bishop of Connecticut, 1816–19.

Hobart was one of the founders of the General Theological Seminary, of which he was for years the professor of pastoral theology. He originated, or furthered, the Bible and Prayer-book Society, the Tract and Homily Society, and similar organizations for the defense of Church principles and the instruction of Churchmen.

Besides the promotion of these objects through the agency of societies which are still fulfilling their mission, Hobart found time for editing approved works in support of the Church's teachings, discipline, and worship. To these compilations the bishop added original works of a high order, and thus made for himself an enviable reputation as an accurate theologian, an exact polemic, and a scholar of rare and varied attainments. Personally, and by his numerous and opportune contributions to theological literature, he impressed his views upon the Churchmen of his day and generation; and he shares with Seabury the distinction of founding and making popular in this country the school of thought known as "High-church" Anglicanism.

Hobart visited England in 1823, where he was received with every possible distinction due to his merit and his exalted position. It is noticeable that although afforded an opportunity of preaching while in Rome, Italy, the "proviso" to the Act of Parliament, authorizing the consecration of Wente and Provoost, prevented the bishop of New York from exercising his office "within his Majesty's dominions." It was not until the repeal of this "proviso," in 1840–41, that an American bishop was at liberty to preach or officiate in his episcopal character in any church of the mother-land.

Hobart's death occurred at Auburn, N. Y., Sept. 10, 1830, and is supposed to have resulted from his conscientious unwillingness to resort to stimulants when suffering from disease. He was buried under the chancel of Trinity Church.

WORKS.—It would require several pages to give in detail the list of sermons, addresses, charges, pastoral letters, essays, etc., which owe their authorship to Hobart. The following are among the volumes he wrote or edited, in many cases revising and adapting the work of some English writer to an extent quite equal to the rewriting of the book: 1. "Companion for the Altar" (12mo, 1804. Issued in countless editions, appended to copies of the Book of Common Prayer, and still regarded as of value and authority); 2. "Companion for the Festivals and Fasts" (12mo, 1805. An adaptation of Robert Nelson's excellent work to meet the requirements of American Church readers); 3. "Companion to the Book of Common Prayer" (12mo, 1805. A compilation from the standard liturgical works of the day, and, in common with the preceding compilations, having a wide circulation for years); 4. "The Clergyman's Companion" (12mo, 1806. A *vade-mecum* for the use of the clergy on occasions and at services for which no special provision is found in the Book of Common Prayer); 5. "Collection of Essays on Episcopacy" (8vo, 1806. An invaluable treasury of the arguments for Church defense); 6. "Apology for Apostolic Order" (8vo, 1807. A masterly statement of the Church's position as opposed to Presbyterianism and other forms of dissent); 7. "The Christian's Manual of Faith and Devotion" (12mo, 1814. Prepared from various sources for household and individual use); 8. "The Candidate for Confirmation Instructed" (12mo, 1816); 9. "A Treatise on the Place of Departed Spirits and Christ's Descent into Hell," appended to a "Funeral Address" at the interment of Bishop Benjamin Moore (8vo, 1816. Numerous editions of this treatise appeared in successive years); 10. "D'Oyly and Mant's Bible with Notes" (8vo, 1823); 11. "Sermons on the Principal Events and Truths of Redemption" (2 vols., 8vo, 1824). Bishop Hobart's "Life" appeared shortly after his decease, and was reprinted in England.

RIGHT REVEREND ALEXANDER VIETS GRISWOLD, S.T.D.

Alexander Viets Griswold.

BORN in Simsbury, Conn., April 22, 1766, educated privately by his uncle, the Rev. Roger Viets, Griswold received deacon's orders from Bishop Seabury, at St. Andrew's Church, Simsbury, June 3, 1795. He was priested by the same prelate Oct. 1st, 1795, in Christ Church, Hartford.

The first decade of his ministry was spent in his native State in charge of country parishes at East Plymouth, Northfield, and Harwinton. He became rector of St. Michael's, Bristol, R. I., 1804. He accepted a call to St. Michael's, Litchfield, Conn., 1810, but while the preparations for his removal were still incomplete he was elected, May 31, 1810, to the bishopric of the Eastern Diocese, a jurisdiction comprising all of New England save Connecticut.

Griswold was consecrated in Trinity Church, New York, May 29, 1811, by Bishops White, Provoost, and Jarvis, at the same time with Hobart.

In 1830 the bishop of the Eastern Diocese, who had thus far continued in charge of St. Michael's, removed to Salem, Mass., where he became rector of St. Peter's Church. From 1835 he devoted himself exclusively to the care of his abnormally extensive see.

He received the doctorate in theology from Brown University in 1811; from Princeton in 1811; and from Harvard in 1812. He succeeded White as presiding bishop. He was fellow of Brown, 1812–15; trustee, 1815–28; chancellor, 1815–28.

The last episcopal act of Griswold was the consecration of the Rev. Dr. Manton Eastburn, of New York, as his coadjutor and successor in the see of Massachusetts, Dec. 29, 1842. On Feb. 15, 1843, the venerable bishop, full of years and honors, dropped dead at the threshold of Bishop Eastburn's house in Boston.

Griswold was a man of great personal holiness. He was modest and retiring in his bearing, yet gifted with a sound judgment and inspired with a spirit of self-consecration which made his life one of continual labor and sacrifice. His theological views were those of the "Evangelical" school; and his published "Life" by the late Rev. John S. Stone, D.D., is an interesting contribution to the history of the Church in New England, as well as to that of the "Evangelical" party in the United States.

WORKS.—1. "Discourses on the Most Important Doctrines and Duties of the Christian Religion" (8vo, 1830); 2. "The Reformation and Apostolic Office" (1843); 3. "Remarks on Social Prayer Meetings" (1858); 4. Occasional sermons, addresses, etc.

RIGHT REVEREND THEODORE DEHON, S.T.D.

Theodore Dehon.

THEODORE DEHON was born in Boston, Mass., Dec. 8, 1776. He was graduated at Harvard College, 1795. Having, on Oct. 9, 1797, received an election to the rectorship of Trinity Church, Newport, R. I., he presented himself for ordination to Bishop Bass, and was ordered deacon at St. Paul's, Newburyport, Dec. 24, 1797, and was priested by the same prelate and in the same church, Oct. 9, 1800.

Dehon remained at Trinity Church, Newport, until 1810, when he removed to South Carolina, having accepted the charge of St. Michael's Church, Charleston. Prior to his removal to the South he had received (1809) the doctorate from Princeton. He was a deputy from the Eastern Diocese to the General Convention of 1808.

He was consecrated to the episcopate of South Carolina in succession to the distinguished Robert Smith, in Christ Church, Philadelphia, Oct. 15, 1812, by Bishops White, Jarvis, and Hobart. His short and brilliant episcopate was terminated by his death, Aug. 6, 1817. He left behind him a reputation for eloquence and personal attractiveness which is still cherished in the diocese where he ministered in holy things, and throughout the Church in the United States as well.

WORKS.—Bishop Dehon's "Sermons on Public Means of Grace" were published in two volumes, 8vo, shortly after his death. An English edition of these remarkable discourses brought in to the committee of publication a large sum. Besides this volume, only a few episcopal addresses and occasional sermons ever appeared in print.

RIGHT REVEREND RICHARD CHANNING MOORE, D.D

Richard Channing Moore.

THE Church in Virginia, unjustly despoiled of its glebes, with a clergy list annually recording losses by removals, deaths, and absorptions in secular pursuits, had reached its lowest point when, in the choice of Moore to succeed the scholarly but inactive Madison, a new life was infused into the dying body; and that life is vigorous still.

Moore was born in New York, Aug. 21, 1762. Originally a student of medicine, after a few years' practice he entered upon a course of theological study under the direction of Bishop Provoost.

He was ordered deacon in St. George's Chapel, New York, July 15, 1787, by the bishop of New York; and was priested by the same prelate in St. Paul's Chapel, Sept. 19, 1787.

Beginning his ministry as rector of Christ Church, Rye, N. Y., where he remained for about two years, he removed to Staten Island, where he was the beloved and successful incumbent of St. Andrew's Church for twenty-one years. He received his doctorate in divinity, 1805, from Dartmouth College.

In 1809 he removed to New York, where he became the rector of St. Stephen's Church. Before leaving his Staten Island parish he had represented the State of New York in the General Convention which met in Baltimore, 1808; and at this Convention, which gave us our first collection of hymns, he did excellent service as chairman of the committee of the House of Deputies on hymnody.

Chosen to the episcopate by the few Virginia clergy and laity who still had hope of the Church's revival, Moore's consecration took place in St. James's Church, Philadelphia, May 18, 1814. His consecrators were Bishops White, Hobart, Griswold, and Dehon.

On his taking up his abode in Richmond, the Monumental Church was placed under his pastoral charge and became the center of his activities. It was not long before the Virginia Church was made again the Church of the oldest and most influential families of the State.

The second bishop of Virginia, after an episcopate covering nearly three decades, died at Lynchburg, Nov. 11, 1841. He will ever be held in grateful remembrance for the results of his abundant labors, seen in the revival of the Virginia Church.

WORKS.—1. "A Sermon Preached before the General Convention in St. James's Church, Philadelphia" (1820); 2. The annual addresses, pastorals, and charges.

RIGHT REVEREND JAMES KEMP, D.D.

James Kemp.

THE only suffragan bishop of the Church in the United States was born in Keith Hall parish, Aberdeenshire, Scotland, May 20, 1764.

Graduating at Marischal College, Aberdeen, in 1786, Kemp emigrated to Maryland the following year. After pursuing his theological studies under the direction of the Rev. Dr. John Bowie, rector of Great Choptank parish, Md., he received deacon's orders in Christ Church, Philadelphia, Dec. 26, 1789, and was priested the following day in the same place, the ordainer in each case being Bishop White. Kemp succeeded his theological instructor, Dr. Bowie, in the rectorship of Great Choptank parish in August, 1790; and after an incumbency of more than twenty years removed to Baltimore, where he became associate rector of St. Paul's Church. Columbia College conferred on him the doctorate in divinity, 1802.

There being need of additional episcopal services in Maryland, Kemp was consecrated as suffragan to Bishop Claggett, in Christ Church, New Brunswick, N. J., Sept. 1, 1814, by Bishops White, Hobart, and Channing Moore.

As suffragan to the bishop of Maryland, Kemp was placed in charge of the "Eastern Shore," which is now the see of Easton. In 1815 Kemp was elected provost of the University of Maryland, which honorable position he held during the remainder of his days.

On the death of the bishop of the see, in 1816, Kemp succeeded to the bishopric of Maryland.

The circumstances of his death were trying. Returning from the consecration of Dr. Henry U. Onderdonk as assistant to Bishop White, he was so severely injured by the upsetting of his stage-coach near New Castle, Del., that he passed away after three days of intense suffering, regretted not alone in Maryland, but throughout the American Church.

WORKS.—1. "Sermon on the Death of Washington" (1800); 2. "Sermon before the Convention of the Church in Maryland" (1803); 3. "Sermon before the Free Masons" (1806); 4. "Sermon before the General Convention, together with a Tract on Conversion" (1807); 5. "Letters in Vindication of Episcopacy" (1808); 6. "Sermon on Death-bed Repentance" (1816); 7. "Sermon on the Death of Bishop Claggett" (1816); 8. "An Address before the Students of the General Theological Seminary" (1825).

RIGHT REVEREND JOHN CROES, D.D.

John Croes.

THE first bishop of New Jersey was born in Elizabethtown, in that State, June 1, 1762.

Toward the close of the War of the Revolution he served as a non-commissioned officer on the patriotic side. It was after he had for some time successfully pursued the vocation of a classical instructor, and had opened a private academy which subsequently developed into a prominent institution of learning, that he determined to apply for holy orders. His theological studies were pursued during the intervals of teaching, and were directed by Bishop White, who ordered him deacon in St. Peter's, Philadelphia, Feb. 28, 1790, and advanced him to the priesthood March 4, 1792, in the same church. His first cure was at Swedesborough, N. J., where he served as the incumbent of Trinity Church for twelve years. In 1793, and again in 1814, he was a deputy from New Jersey to the General Conventions held in those years. At the session of this body in 1814 he was elected president of the House of Deputies.

In 1801 Croes removed from Swedesborough to New Brunswick, N. J., where he united the rectorship of Christ's Church with the care of St. Peter's, Spotswood. With his fondness for teaching, he also maintained an academy of classical learning. In 1811 he received the doctorate in divinity from Columbia College.

In June, 1815, he was elected to the episcopate of Connecticut, but declined this unlooked-for distinction. In August of the same year he was chosen to the episcopate of his native State. His consecration took place in St. Peter's Church, Philadelphia, Nov. 19, 1815, Bishops White, Hobart, and Kemp being the consecrators. The death of this excellent man and devoted bishop occurred July 26, 1832.

WORKS.—1. "A Sermon on the Duty of Contributing Liberally to the Promotion of Religious and Benevolent Institutions"; 2. "A Sermon before the General Convention of 1823"; 3. "Addresses to his Conventions."

RIGHT REVEREND NATHANIEL BOWEN, D.D

Nathaniel Bowen.

THE son of a clergyman who was a convert from the Congregationalists, Nathaniel Bowen was born in Boston, June 29, 1779.

His father removed with his family to Charleston, S. C., 1787. On the death of the elder Bowen, shortly after his arrival, the Rev. Robert Smith, subsequently the first bishop of South Carolina, took charge of the orphan boy and provided for his education. The lad was an apt scholar, and on his graduation at Charleston College, 1794, received an appointment as tutor at his alma mater, where he continued for several years.

Returning to his native city, Bowen prepared himself for holy orders, under the charge of Dr. (afterward Bishop) Parker, and was admitted to the diaconate in Trinity Church, Boston, June 3, 1800, by Bishop Bass. He was advanced to the priesthood in October, 1802, at St. Paul's Church, Newburyport, by the same prelate. The day of his ordination is not known with certainty. After a brief pastorate at St. John's Church, Providence, R. I., Bowen returned, March, 1802, to Charleston, where he became the assistant minister of St. Michael's Church, succeeding to the rectorship, 1804. Five years later he removed to New York and became rector of Grace Church in that city. He received his doctorate in divinity, 1814, from the University of Pennsylvania and from the College of South Carolina.

Bowen received consecration in Christ Church, Philadelphia, Oct. 8, 1818, Bishops White, Hobart, Kemp, and Croes being his consecrators. After an episcopate of upward of twenty years, Bishop Bowen died at Charleston, S. C., Aug. 25, 1839. His remains were interred in the chancel of St. Michael's Church. To unusual pulpit powers he added great executive ability and a commanding influence over men. He was an accomplished scholar, a wise theologian, and a holy man.

WORKS.— 1. "Sermon before the Bible and Common Prayer-book Society" (1812); 2. "Six Sermons on Christian Consolation" (1831); 3. "Pastoral Advice: An Essay" (1831); 4. "The Duty of being Confirmed" (1831); 5. "On Responding Aloud" (1833); 6. "Fast-day Circular" (1833); 7. "Sermon on the Death of Bishop White" (1836); 8. "An Address before the Students of the General Theological Seminary" (1836); also other occasional sermons.

RIGHT REVEREND PHILANDER CHASE, D.D., LL.D.

Philander Chase.

THE first American bishop consecrated for the territory lying west of the Alleghanies was born in Cornish, N. H., Dec. 14, 1775.

He was graduated at Dartmouth College, 1796. Admitted to the diaconate by Bishop Provoost in St. Paul's Chapel, New York, June 10, 1798, and priested by the same prelate, in the same place, Nov. 10, 1799, Chase began his ministry by missionary work in the northern and western portions of New York. During these itinerant labors he organized parishes at Utica, Canandaigua, and Auburn, each of which became a center of strength and usefulness. In 1800 he assumed the charge of the Poughkeepsie and Fishkill churches. In 1805 he went to New Orleans, where he organized and entered upon the rectorship of Christ Church. Returning to the North, 1811, he became rector of Christ Church, Hartford, Conn.; but finding the work of a city parish unsuited to his tastes, he entered upon mission work in the territory to the west of the Alleghanies, whither the stream of emigration was steadily tending.

Holding his first service in Ohio at a town called Salem, March 16, 1817, Chase organized parishes at numerous points, and in June of the same year took charge of the church at Worthington, with outlying work at Delaware and Columbus, and adding to his missionary and pastoral duties the oversight of an academy at Worthington.

It had long been the purpose of the Churchmen in the United States to secure the Western territory for Christ and His Church. An "act of the General Convention" adopted in 1798 had proposed measures for the extension of the kingdom of Christ in the regions beyond the Alleghanies. The appeals of the frontier clergy, who (as in the case of the celebrated Rev. Joseph Doddridge, M.D.) were laboring almost single-handed at various points in the lands but lately opened up to immigration, were not wholly refused a hearing. Bishop White, though but once in his episcopate reaching the western boundaries of his own see at Pittsburg, still recognized the Church's duty of providing for the actual and intending settlers of the West. The abundant labors and the marked success of Chase's missionary journeys indicated his special fitness for an appointment to a Western episcopate, and he was therefore consecrated bishop of Ohio, Feb. 11, 1819, in St. James's Church, Philadelphia, by Bishops White, Hobart, Kemp, and Croes.

The new bishop at once entered upon the duties of his charge. Chosen to the presidency of Cincinnati College, 1821, he retained the headship of this institution for two years, while taking measures for the establishment of a theological seminary in his see for the training of his candidates for orders in theology as well as in arts. In the prosecution of this purpose, which resulted in the foundation and partial endowment of a theological seminary and Kenyon College, at Gambier, O., the bishop visited England, where his earnestness, his devotion, and the evident advantage of founding a Church college and divinity school in the Western world, gained for him, and for the cause he advocated, noble, influential, and liberal friends, and made the Western mission work of the American Church for the first time known in England.

Difficulties having arisen in the development of his work, Bishop Chase, in September, 1831, resigned the presidency of the theological seminary and Kenyon College, as well as his episcopate.

Removing to Michigan in 1832, where he remained and faithfully labored for several years, he was chosen by the clergy of Illinois, in 1835, as their bishop; and on accepting this new administration he proceeded to organize a diocese and found a college, for which, on visiting England in its interest, he secured a handsome sum. This institution he named Jubilee College. It was situated in Peoria County, Ill., at a spot to which he gave the name of Robin's Nest. Liberal gifts were obtained for this new venture, and the last days of the good bishop were brightened by the sympathy and support of Churchmen at home and abroad.

On the death of Bishop Griswold, 1843, the bishop of Illinois became presiding bishop. His death occurred Sept. 20, 1852.

Chase received the doctorate in divinity from Columbia College, 1819, and the doctorate of laws from Cincinnati College, 1823.

He was a man of intense feelings, marvelous powers of endurance, unusual pertinacity, and great impatience of opposition. As a pioneer bishop he rendered services throughout the middle West which can never be forgotten. His unfailing wit and humor made him welcome in the settlers' cabins, on the stage-coach, on the canal and steamboat,—wherever travelers congregated. He was raised up of God for his work, and the results of his self-denying efforts will be seen forever. The story of his controversies have little interest to-day. It is enough to recall the fact that this great-hearted man was naturally misunderstood by the men about him, who were incapable of judging of his measures or of recognizing his vast superiority. They have long since passed into a merited obscurity, while the bishop they annoyed with their petty provocations is remembered with ever increasing veneration. It is given to few to whom is intrusted the Episcopal office to found two dioceses and establish two institutions of the higher learning, one of which at least will ever perpetuate his name and fame.

Full of energy, perseverance, and zeal, he will ever be remembered as a master builder of the Church of God.

WORKS.—1. "A Plea for the West" (1826); 2. "The Star in the West" (1828); 3. "Defense of Kenyon College" (1831); 4. "A Plea for Jubilee" (1835); 5. "Reminiscences: An Autobiography" (2 vols., 8vo, 1847); 6. The "Pastoral Letters" of the House of Bishops from 1844 to 1850, inclusive. His "Life" has been published. See also "Malignity Exposed: A Vindication of Bishop Chase," by Rev. Samuel Chase (1847), and "Sermon in Memory of Bishop Chase," by Rev. D. Chase (Jubilee College, 1852).

RIGHT REVEREND THOMAS CHURCH BROWNELL, D.D.

Thomas Church Brownell.

THE successor of Seabury and Jarvis in the episcopate of Connecticut was born at Westport, Mass., Oct. 19, 1779.

He was graduated at Union, 1804, becoming tutor (1805–06), professor of logic and belles-lettres (1806–11), lecturer on chemistry (1811–14), and professor of rhetoric and chemistry (1814–17) in his alma mater. He was admitted to the diaconate in Trinity Church, New York, April 11, 1816, and was advanced to the priesthood, Aug. 4, 1816, by Bishop Hobart, in the same church.

The vacancy in the episcopate in Connecticut had continued for six years. The Rev. Dr. Croes, of New Jersey, had declined an election to the see in 1815. It was natural that the clergy and laity, to whom Bishop Hobart had provisionally ministered with great acceptance for several years, should turn their thoughts to the rising scholar and divine who had entered upon so distinguished a career at Schenectady. Receiving the doctorate in divinity in 1819 from Columbia and Union, he was consecrated in Trinity Church, New Haven, Oct. 27, 1819, by Bishops White, Hobart, and Griswold.

On entering upon his see, Brownell founded at Hartford, the city of his residence, Washington College, of which he became the president. In after-years the name of this institution of Christian learning was changed to Trinity, and a bronze statue of its founder, with hand extended as in benediction, stands on the campus of this noble foundation.

The duties of the episcopate, to which were added the cares of the direction of a college, were not enough to exhaust his energy and devotion. Undertaking, at the request of the Domestic Missionary Board, an extensive visitation through the Southern States, not then organized into dioceses, he rendered a service the results of which will ever be seen and felt.

In 1852, on the decease of Chase, Brownell became presiding bishop. He died, after a most honored and useful episcopate, at Hartford, Jan. 13, 1865. It would be quite impossible to overestimate the influences for good to the Church, the college, and the community resulting from his laborious and self-forgetful life.

WORKS.—1. "Commentary on the Book of Common Prayer" (8vo, numerous editions); 2. "Consolation for the Afflicted"; 3. "The Christian's Walk and Consolation"; 4. "An Exhortation to Repentance"; 5. "Family Prayers"; 6. "Religion of the Heart" (5 vols.); 7. "Religious Inquirer Answered"; 8. "The Youthful Christian's Guide"; 9. "New-Englandism not the Religion of the Bible"; 10. Occasional sermons, etc. See "Commemorative Discourse," by E. E. Beardsley (1865).

RIGHT REVEREND JOHN STARK RAVENSCROFT, D.D.

John Stark Ravenscroft.

THE first bishop of North Carolina entered upon the work of the ministry at the age of forty-five years.

Born near Blanford in Prince George's County, Va., 1772, his early life was spent in Scotland, and it was not until he had reached the age of twenty-seven that he determined upon a profession, and entered William and Mary College, with the view of preparing for the law. A return to Scotland, rendered necessary for the final settlement of his paternal estate, prevented the accomplishment of this purpose. Returning to Virginia, Ravenscroft lived as a country gentleman on his lands in Lunenburg County for eighteen years, during which period, it is said, "he never bent his knees in prayer, nor did he once open a Bible."

About the year 1810 the wild enthusiasm of a religious body known as "Republican Methodists" made an impression on his mind; but after a brief connection with these fanatics he withdrew from their membership and received the grace of confirmation at the hands of Bishop Channing Moore.

The knowledge of his purpose to enter upon the ministry secured for this gifted man an invitation to a Virginia rectorship some months before his ordination. April 25, 1817, Bishop Moore admitted him to the diaconate in the Monumental Church, Richmond, and, May 6th of the same year, advanced him to the priesthood in St. George's Church, Fredericksburg. He had not exercised his ministerial functions for five years when his shining abilities, which had secured him numerous invitations to important posts, gained for him the election to the episcopate of North Carolina. He was consecrated in St. Paul's Church, Philadelphia, May 22, 1823, by Bishops White, Griswold, Kemp, Croes, Bowen, and Brownell. His doctorates in divinity were conferred upon him, in the year of his consecration, by Columbia, William and Mary, and the University of North Carolina at Chapel Hill.

The administration of Ravenscroft was energetic, wise, and successful, and the Church under his charge grew in power. His death occurred March 5, 1830. The Church throughout the land mourned his loss.

WORKS.—Besides the usual occasional sermons, addresses, charges, and pastoral letters, two volumes of sermons were published after his death, and are still held in high esteem. See Wainwright's "Memoir"; also his "Correspondence with Professor Mitchell" (1825).

RIGHT REVEREND HENRY USTICK ONDERDONK, D.D.

Henry Ustick Onderdonk.

THE choice of an assistant to the venerable White involved a bitter partizan controversy, which left its baleful effects on the Church for many years. The successful candidate was one of the most noted Churchmen of his day, and his brilliant episcopate, though clouded toward its close, still realized the inspired prediction that "at evening-time it shall be light."

Onderdonk was born in New York, March 16, 1789, and was graduated at Columbia College, 1805. Having devoted his life to medicine, he studied in London and Edinburgh, receiving his degree of M.D. from the university of the latter city. On his return to New York he became actively engaged in his profession.

After a few years, Onderdonk studied theology under the direction of Hobart, who ordered him deacon in St. Paul's Chapel, Dec. 8, 1815, and priested him in Trinity Church, April 11, 1816. After a four years' pastorate at Canandaigua he became rector of St. Ann's, Brooklyn, where he remained until his consecration to the episcopate.

Chosen assistant bishop of Pennsylvania, he was consecrated, Oct. 25, 1827, in Christ Church, Philadelphia, by Bishops White, Hobart, Kemp, Croes, and Bowen. He received his doctorate in divinity the same year from Columbia and from Geneva (now Hobart) College. In 1836 he became, on the death of White, the bishop of Pennsylvania.

He resigned his bishopric, 1844. The resignation was accepted, and because of charges of having contracted habits of intemperance (which he did not deny) he was suspended from the exercise of his office and ministry. Humbly receiving this act of discipline, Onderdonk lived for the remainder of his days a life of sanctity; and in 1856, was, with singular unanimity, restored to the exercise of his office. He died in Philadelphia, Dec. 6, 1858, with the regained confidence and regard of all men.

WORKS.—1. "An Appeal to the Religious Public of Canandaigua" (1818); 2. "Episcopacy Tested by Scripture" (1830); 3. "Episcopacy Examined and Reëxamined" (1835); 4. "Essay on Regeneration" (1835); 5. "Family Devotions from the Liturgy" (1835); 6. "Thoughts on the Objections to Christianity" (1835); 7. "Sermons and Charges" (2 vols., 8vo, 1851).

Onderdonk was an exact theologian, a controversialist of the highest order, an able logician, and a poet of decided merit. In the Collection of Psalms and Hymns appended to the Prayer-book of the time, Nos. 14, 105, 106, 109, 131, 195, 203, 208 and 211 of the hymns, and Nos. 16, 23, and 59 of the psalms are his.

See Horace Binney's "Case" (1853); Bishop Meade's "Counterstatement" (1854), etc.

RIGHT REVEREND WILLIAM MEADE, D.D.

William Meade.

It was at a day when nearly all men despaired of the Virginia Church that, in the consecration of his life to the ministry, Meade entered upon a career to which, under God, the revival of the Church in his native State is largely due.

Born near Millwood, Clark County, Va., Nov. 11, 1789, and graduated at Princeton, 1808, he was ordered deacon by Bishop Madison, in Bruton parish church, Williamsburg, Feb. 24, 1811, and was advanced to the priesthood by Bishop Claggett, Jan. 29, 1814, in St. Paul's Church, Alexandria, Va.

Beginning his ministry as curate to the Rev. Alexander Balmaine, the rector of Millwood, with the exception of two years (1811–13, when he took charge of Christ Church, Alexandria) his ministrations were given to Millwood, of which he subsequently became rector. In 1827 the College of William and Mary conferred upon him the doctorate in divinity.

Meade had become a leader of the "Evangelical" party, and had been the candidate of that school for the assistant bishopric of Pennsylvania. Losing that appointment by a single vote, he was chosen to the assistant bishopric of Virginia. He was consecrated in St. James's Church, Philadelphia, Aug. 19, 1829, by Bishops White, Hobart, Griswold, Channing Moore, Croes, Brownell, and H. U. Onderdonk.

On the death of Moore he became, without opposition, bishop of Virginia, although he had been originally elected without the right of succession. The bishops, at the time of his consecration, protested against this disability, and it was never urged.

Meade, with no little reluctance, entered into the confederation of the Churches of the South during the Civil War, and became, by virtue of seniority of consecration, the presiding bishop of the Church in the Confederate States. He died March 14, 1862, at Richmond, Va. His remains, first interred in Hollywood, now rest in the cemetery of the Theological Seminary of Virginia. He was "a good man, and full of the Holy Ghost."

Works.—1. "Family Prayers" (1834); 2. "Lectures on the Pastoral Office" (1849); 3. "Old Churches, Ministers, and Families of Virginia" (2 vols., 8vo, 1856); 4. "The Bible and the Classics" (1861). Bishop Meade reprinted Bacon's "Sermons to Servants," originally issued in colonial days. His sermons, addresses, pastorals, etc., had a wide circulation. To his fostering care the Virginia Theological Seminary is deeply indebted. See "Memoir" by Bishop Johns.

RIGHT REVEREND WILLIAM MURRAY STONE, D.D.

William Murray Stone.

THE episcopate of the third bishop of Maryland was comparatively brief and uneventful. It was a period of transition in the diocesan history. The clergy of ante-Revolutionary ordination, those who, on the one side or the other, had participated in the stirring scenes of the Revolution, and even the few who at the introduction of the episcopate into this country had entered upon the ministry at the first ordinations of the earliest bishops, were now at rest or incapacitated. The party spirit which had begun to manifest itself throughout all sections of the church was now at its height in Maryland. It was not long before the first schismatic organization was effected, and the founder of the short-lived "Evangelical Episcopal Church" in Maryland was the theological instructor of the bishop who succeeded the able and inflexible Kemp. Ranged under opposing banners, and using the shibboleth of party, the clergy, not alone of Maryland, but elsewhere, wasted in intestine strifes the strength and effort which, if directed to secure the Church's advance, would have "made glad the city of our God."

Born in Somerset County, Md., June 1, 1779, Stone was graduated at Washington College, Kent County, Md., and, directly on receiving his degree, began the study of theology under the tutorship of the eloquent and accomplished George Dashiel, of Baltimore.

He was admitted to deacon's orders by Bishop Claggett, in St. Paul's Church, Prince George's County, Md., May 17, 1802, and received the priesthood at the hands of the same prelate, in the same place, Dec. 27, 1802.

For more than a quarter of a century Stone served as rector of Stepney parish, Somerset County, removing in 1829 to St. Paul's Church, Chestertown, in the county of Kent.

In 1830 he received the doctorate in divinity from Columbia College, New York, and on Oct. 21st of the same year was consecrated bishop of Maryland in St. Paul's Church, Baltimore, by Bishops White, Channing Moore, H. U. Onderdonk, and Meade.

Bishop Stone died Feb. 26, 1838, after a life consecrated to Christ and His Church.

WORKS.—1. "A Charge to the Clergy and Laity of Maryland" (1831); 2. "A Pastoral Letter" (1835); 3. "Sermon before the General Convention" (1835).

RIGHT REVEREND BENJAMIN TREDWELL ONDERDONK, D.D.

Benjamin Tredwell Onderdonk.

A BULKY octavo records the "Trial of Bishop B. T. Onderdonk." With the scores of other pamphlets called out by this proceeding, there will be preserved for all time to come the story of one of the most painful chapters of the annals of the American Church. Reviewed after the lapse of fifty years, a sober judgment will possibly question the wisdom of the court's decision, and believe that party differences (though quite unintentionally) hindered the more charitable construction of acts and purposes deemed at the time conclusive of guilt. Certainly, if a holy and humble walk during the long years of his suspension, and consistent and unwavering protestations of innocence of conscious sin, are to enter into our consideration, Onderdonk may be regarded as sinned against, even if sinning.

Born in New York, July 15, 1791, and graduated from Columbia, 1809, Onderdonk was admitted to the diaconate by Hobart, in St. Paul's Chapel, New York, Aug. 2, 1812, and was priested by the same prelate, in Trinity Church, Newark, N. J., July 26, 1815.

In 1816 he was elected secretary of the Diocesan Convention, which position, with an assistancy at Trinity, New York, he held until he was raised to the episcopate. The professorship of ecclesiastical history in the General Theological Seminary, with the chair of the nature, ministry, and polity of the Church, he nominally retained until his death. In 1826 Columbia College gave him a D.D.

Onderdonk was consecrated bishop of New York in St. John's Chapel, New York, Nov. 26, 1830, by Bishops White, Brownell, and H. U. Onderdonk. His episcopate was vigorous and aggressive. Untiring in labors, pronounced in his judgments, impatient of opposition, he was naturally a leader; and his "High-Church" position secured for him enemies as well as friends.

Bishop Onderdonk was suspended Jan. 3, 1845. The request of the Diocesan Convention to the General Convention of 1859 to terminate the suspension, which had been adopted by a clerical vote of 147 to 19, and by a lay vote of 75 to 46, was not granted. Dr. S. H. Tyng, a leader of the opposition, earnestly advocated the remission of the sentence, and the bishop's restoration was repeatedly urged by the diocese. Before the next General Convention, Onderdonk died, April 30, 1861, still protesting his innocence.

WORKS.—Episcopal addresses, charges, and pastorals.

RIGHT REVEREND LEVI SILLIMAN IVES, D.D., LL.D.

Levi Silliman Ives.

Born in Meriden, Conn., Sept. 16, 1797, the subject of this sketch entered Hamilton College, N. Y., 1816, with the Presbyterian ministry in view. Failing health compelled the abandonment of his purpose. He left college without graduating, and on removing to New York began his preparation for holy orders under the direction of Bishop Hobart.

Ordered deacon by this prelate, Aug. 4, 1822, in Trinity, New York, and advanced to the priesthood in Trinity (Southwark), Philadelphia, Dec. 14, 1823, by Bishop White, Ives served at St. James's, Batavia, N. Y.; Trinity (Southwark), Philadelphia; as assistant minister at Trinity, New York; and as rector of St. Luke's, New York, and St. James's, Lancaster, Pa. In 1824 Columbia conferred upon him the doctorate in divinity. He received the doctorate of laws from the University of North Carolina at Chapel Hill, 1834. He was consecrated to the see of North Carolina, in Trinity Church (Southwark), Philadelphia, Sept. 22, 1831, by Bishops White, H. U. and B. T. Onderdonk.

After serious difficulties with his clergy and laity, resulting in an utter loss of confidence on the part of the diocese in his judgment and integrity, Bishop Ives, quite suddenly, made his submission to the Roman obedience, and was solemnly deposed from his episcopal office and administration, October, 1853.

The perversion of Bishop Ives was not attended with serious injury to the American Church, and in his new relations he failed to attain the prominence that was anticipated. He was appointed professor of rhetoric in St. Joseph's Seminary, Fordham, N. Y., lecturer on English literature and rhetoric in the Convent of the Sacred Heart, and president of the Order of St. Vincent de Paul. He died Oct. 13, 1867.

Works.—1. "A Catechism"; 2. "Manual of Devotion"; 3. "Sermons on the Apostles' Doctrine and Fellowship"; 4. "Trials of a Mind in its Progress to Catholicism" (published in Boston, 1853, and reprinted in London the following year); 5. Occasional sermons, addresses, charges, and pastorals.

RIGHT REVEREND JOHN HENRY HOPKINS, D.D., LL.D.

John Henry Hopkins.

SOON after the close of the War of the Revolution the erratic Samuel Peters, LL.D., a refugee clergyman of Connecticut then residing in London, was chosen to the episcopate of Vermont, and measures were set on foot to secure his consecration either in England or from the bishops of the United States. The plan failed, and the Churchmen of Vermont at a later day placed themselves under the charge of the excellent Bass, of Massachusetts, who never visited them, and who was, possibly, unaware of his election to the see. Vermont afterward became a part of the Eastern Diocese, and enjoyed the apostolic ministrations of Griswold till, in the development of the Church in this State, and in the recovery of much of its old endowments arising from grants of land made prior to the war to the Venerable Society for the Propagation of the Gospel in Foreign Parts, it was deemed expedient to form an independent see and to elect a bishop of its own.

John Henry Hopkins, first bishop of Vermont, was born in Dublin, Ireland, Jan. 30, 1792. During the future bishop's boyhood his father removed with his family to the United States, making his home in Philadelphia.

After varied experiences, in all of which appears the guiding hand of Providence, the young Hopkins was admitted to the bar, and speedily attained a successful and lucrative practice at Pittsburg, Pa. During a vacancy in the rectorship of Trinity Church, of which he was a devoted member, his services as a lay reader and in the conduct of the church music, as well as in the Sunday-school and other parish activities, were so acceptable to the congregation that the vestry elected him, even before he had become a candidate for orders, to the rectorship of the church. After consultation with Bishop White, the young lawyer determined to accept the vestry's invitation. He was admitted to the diaconate in Trinity Church (Southwark), Philadelphia, Dec. 14, 1823, by Bishop White, who advanced him to the priesthood in St. John's, Norristown, Pa., May 12, 1824. In 1826, and again in 1829, Hopkins was a deputy to the General Convention from the diocese of Pennsylvania, taking from the first a leading part in its debates and measures.

In 1831 he was called to Boston, where he became the assistant minister of Trinity Church, and was designated the professor of systematic divinity in the proposed theological school of the diocese. It was in the midst of preparations for the establishment of this school that Hopkins was chosen bishop of Vermont. His consecration took place in St. Paul's Chapel, New York, Oct. 31, 1832. His consecrators were Bishops White, Griswold, and Bowen.

On his entrance upon his episcopate he became rector of St. Paul's, Burlington, and at once began the educational, literary, and missionary work that with unfailing vigor he never lost sight of till death. He was preëminently a leader of men, and his active part in the controversies of the day is shown by his writings, which had great weight at the time of their appearances, and still attest his wide reading and analytical powers.

Bishop Hopkins was a prominent figure at the first Lambeth Conference, in 1868. The manly and independent course taken by the distinguished American prelate with reference to the "Colenso scandal" gained for Bishop Hopkins the respect of those who opposed him, and gave great satisfaction to the Church he represented. The American Church, independent of state complications, had recognized the validity of the deposition of the heretical bishop by the metropolitan of South Africa, the sainted Robert Gray. This position the English prelates found themselves unable to take, and in this Conference the bishop of Vermont was a leader of those who contended for the supremacy of the Church in matters ecclesiastical over any opposition arising from the state. It was to Hopkins, as appeared when the proceedings of the first Lambeth Conference first saw the light ten years later, that this stand in defense of the sound Churchmanship and fearless bravery of Robert Gray (*pro ecclesia Dei*) was due.

There appears in the works of this great bishop a marked development of Churchly feeling and an increased conservatism in Churchly news, when we compare the printed pamphlets and works of his earlier years with those of later days. The trenchant pen that was used in support of the tenets of the "Evangelical" school in the bishop's youth, was found in his maturity equally powerful on behalf of a more pronounced teaching and a more unequivocal advocacy of Church teaching. The literary history of the bishop is quite as interesting and instructive as the story of his life. He was a seeker after truth, and he was never ashamed to own the convictions he had reached, even if they were at variance with those he had earlier avowed. He took a leading part in efforts to prevent the rending of the Church at the breaking out of the Civil War, as well as in bringing together the bishops of the North and South when the strife was over. He was made a doctor in divinity by the University of Vermont, and received the doctorate of laws from Jubilee

College, Illinois. On the decease of Bishop Brownell he succeeded to the primacy in the House of Bishops and in the American Church.

A man of varied accomplishments, of extensive reading, of broad culture, of Catholic tastes, logical, judicial, and argumentative, the administration of the first bishop of Vermont left the impress of his powers, his genius, and his marvelous capacity for labor on the Church in the diocese, and on the Church at large as well. The story of his life, " by one of his sons," published in 1873, reads like a romance, and is a most interesting and valuable contribution to the history of the times.

Bishop Hopkins died at Burlington, Vt., Jan. 9, 1868, beloved and regretted by all men.

WORKS.—1. "Christianity Vindicated" (1833); 2. "The Primitive Creed Examined and Explained" (1834); 3. "The Primitive Church" (1835); 4. "Essay on Gothic Architecture" (4to, 1836); 5. "The Church of Rome Contrasted," etc. (1837); 6. "The Novelties which Disturb our Peace" (1844); 7. "Sixteen Lectures on the Reformation" (1845); 8. "History of the Confessional" (1850); 9. "The 'End of Controversy' Controverted" (1854, 2 vols.); 10. "The American Citizen" (1857); 11. "A Scriptural, Ecclesiastical, and Historical View of Slavery" (1864); 12. "The Law of Ritualism" (1866); 13. "The History of the Church in Verse" (1867). After his death there was published his "Candid Examination of the Question whether the Pope of Rome is the Great Antichrist of Scripture" (1868).

He issued numerous occasional sermons, addresses, letters, and tracts, in addition to his printed volumes.

RIGHT REVEREND BENJAMIN BOSWORTH SMITH, D.D., LL.D.

Benjamin Bosworth Smith.

BORN in Bristol, R. I., June 13, 1794, and graduating at Brown University, Providence, 1816, Smith was admitted to deacon's orders by Bishop Griswold at St. Michael's Church in his native town, April 23, 1817, and was advanced to the priesthood in St. Michael's, Marblehead, Mass., June 24th of the following year.

His first pastoral work was rendered at Marblehead, where he remained for two years, and at St. George's, Accomack County, Va., where he remained in charge for about the same length of time. He then combined the cure of Zion Church, Charlestown, with that of Trinity, Shepherdstown, Va. Returning to New England, he was rector of St. Stephen's Church, Middlebury, Vt., from 1823 to 1828. From 1828 to 1832 he had charge of Grace Church mission, Philadelphia. Removing to Kentucky, he was, 1832, in charge of Christ Church, Lexington, and was consecrated bishop of the diocese in St. Paul's Chapel, New York, Oct. 31, 1832, by Bishops White, Brownell, and H. U. Onderdonk. In 1837 he gave up his rectorate of Christ Church, Lexington, and devoted himself wholly to the work of the episcopate. In 1868, on the death of Bishop Hopkins, he became presiding bishop. During his term of office as presiding bishop fifty-two bishops were consecrated, of which number fifty were living at the time of his decease. He received the degree of D.D. from Geneva College 1832, and was made an LL.D. by Griswold College, Davenport, Ia., 1870, and by his alma mater, Brown University, 1872. He was for a time State superintendent of education in Kentucky.

Smith died in New York, May 31, 1884, after a long, useful, and honored episcopate.

WORKS.—1. "Five Charges to the Clergy of Kentucky"; 2. "The Position of the Protestant Episcopal Church in the United States" (a sermon before the General Convention, 1850); 3. "Saturday Evening; or, Thoughts on the Progress of the Plan of Salvation" (1876); 4. "Apostolic Succession: Facts which Prove that a Ministry Appointed by Christ Himself Involves this Position" (1877). Bishop Smith was editor of the "Episcopal Register" of Vermont, 1823–28; of the "Episcopal Recorder," Philadelphia, 1828–32.

RIGHT REVEREND CHARLES PETTIT McILVAINE, D.D., D.C.L., LL.D.

Charles Pettit McIlvaine.

THE successor of the pioneer Chase was born in Burlington, N. J., Jan. 18, 1799, and was graduated at Princeton, 1816.

He studied at the Princeton Theological Seminary, and was ordered deacon in St. Peter's, Philadelphia, June 28, 1820. He was advanced to the priesthood by Bishop Kemp in St. Paul's, Baltimore, March 20, 1821, and entered upon his ministry at Christ Church, Georgetown, D. C. He became professor of ethics and chaplain in the U. S. Military Academy, West Point, 1825, where he remained two years. In 1830 he became rector of St. Ann's Church, Brooklyn, and, 1831, professor of the evidences of revealed religion and sacred antiquities in the University of the City of New York.

On the resignation of Chase, McIlvaine was chosen bishop of Ohio, and was consecrated in St. Paul's Chapel, New York, Oct. 31, 1832, by Bishops White, Griswold, and Meade. He received his doctorate in divinity from Princeton and Brown, 1832, and an LL.D. from Brown, 1867. Oxford conferred upon him a D.C.L., 1853, and Cambridge an LL.D., 1858. He held the presidency of Kenyon College, 1832–40, and was the head of the theological seminary of the diocese. He was a member of the U. S. Sanitary Commission during the Civil War, and visited England on a mission for the government.

McIlvaine was a pronounced "Evangelical," and was for years a leader of that party. His most earnest efforts, however, were directed, at the time of the deposition of Cheney, toward discountenancing the steps which led to the formation of the "Cummins Schism," 1873–74.

McIlvaine died at Florence, Italy, March 13, 1873. His body rested in state in Westminster Abbey on its way to America for burial. Eloquent and accomplished, a ready writer, a skilled polemic, with great personal magnetism and influence, he will ever be held in memory as a godly and devoted bishop.

WORKS.—1. "The Evidences of Christianity in their External Division" (1832; republished in numerous editions); 2. "Oxford Divinity Compared with that of the Roman and Anglican Churches" (1841); 3. "The Sinner's Justification before God" (1851); 4. "The Holy Catholic Church" (1844); 5. "No Priest, no Altar, no Sacrifice but Christ" (1846); 6. "Valedictory Offering" (five sermons, 1853); 7. "A Word in Season to Candidates for Confirmation"; 8. "The Doctrine of the Protestant Episcopal Church as to Confirmation"; 9. "The Chief Danger of the Church" (many editions of the last three tracts); 10. "The Truth and the Life" (twenty-two discourses, 1855); 11. "Select Family and Parish Sermons" (2 vols., 8vo, 1839; a compilation of popular English "Evangelical" discourses); 12. Numerous addresses, etc.

RIGHT REVEREND GEORGE WASHINGTON DOANE, D.D., LL.D.

George Washington Doane.

THE second bishop of New Jersey was born at Trenton, N. J., May 27, 1799.

He was graduated at Union, 1818; was admitted to the diaconate by Hobart, in Christ Church, New York, April 19, 1821, and priested by the same prelate in Trinity, New York, Aug. 6, 1823. After two years' service at Trinity he became professor of rhetoric and belles-lettres in Washington (now Trinity) College. He became assistant minister at Trinity, Boston, 1828, of which he soon became the rector.

He was consecrated bishop of New Jersey, Oct. 31, 1832, by Bishops White, B. T. Onderdonk, and Ives. He then became rector of St. Mary's Church, Burlington, holding that cure until his death. Columbia and Trinity conferred upon him the degree of D.D., 1831, and in 1841 St. John's College, Maryland, gave him the LL.D. He died at Burlington, April 27, 1859, and was buried in St. Mary's churchyard.

Doane was the founder of St. Mary's Hall, 1837, and Burlington College, 1846. He may be regarded as the father of Church schools in America. He was a lifelong friend of the cause of missions, and a leading spirit in the development of our first missionary enthusiasm. To him is due the recognition of the principle that the Church itself is the true missionary organization, and that every member is, by virtue of holy baptism, a pledged supporter of missions.

In developing plans for his schools Doane found himself financially embarrassed. This was made the occasion for a petty trial fomented by disaffected laymen. Doane, announcing his intention to "make the trial of a bishop hard," triumphed over his opponents.

He had a commanding presence; possessed great intellectual powers, together with a capacity for almost infinite work; attracted all classes; was a polished writer, a graceful poet, an impassioned speaker.

WORKS.—"The Life and Writings of Bishop Doane" (4 vols., New York, 1860), edited by his son, contains many of his numerous prose and poetical works. To record his publications seriatim would require nearly a hundred titles. His charges, pastorals, etc., still command attention. A volume of his sermons was published in England, where he preached at the consecration of St. Saviour's, Leeds, the first time an American bishop had been heard from an English pulpit.

RIGHT REVEREND JAMES HERVEY OTEY, S.T.D.

James Hervey Otey.

THE first bishop of Tennessee was a Virginian, having been born in Liberty, Bedford County, Jan. 27, 1800.

He was graduated at the University of North Carolina, at Chapel Hill, 1820, and became a tutor in this institution the academic year following. He was admitted to the diaconate in St. John's Church, Williamsboro', N. C., Oct. 16, 1825, by Bishop Ravenscroft, who advanced him to the priesthood in St. Matthew's Church, Hillsboro', June 17, 1827.

Removing to Tennessee, and making his home at Franklin in that State, he opened a classical school for his support, while ministering at Franklin, Columbus, and Nashville.

Columbia College conferred on the young divine his doctorate in divinity, 1833; and the following year, Jan. 14th, he was consecrated bishop of Tennessee in Christ Church, Philadelphia, by Bishops White, the two Onderdonks, and Doane.

Besides the duties devolving upon him in his own see, Otey acted for several years as provisional bishop of Mississippi and Florida, and as missionary bishop of Arkansas, the Indian Territory, and Louisiana. He founded a diocesan school of the higher education for girls at Columbia, Tenn., which, with the usual vicissitudes attending such ventures of faith, has proved of great advantage to the Church in the South. The bishop was one of the original projectors of the University of the South at Sewanee, Tenn.

Otey died, April 23, 1863, during the troubles and desolations of the Civil War. On his monument he had directed these words to be inscribed:

FIRST BISHOP OF THE HOLY CATHOLIC CHURCH
IN TENNESSEE.

"The blood of Jesus Christ cleanseth us from all sin."

WORKS.—Otey was a man of strong intellectual powers, a forcible and argumentative preacher, a theologian, a scholar, and a man of affairs. Under circumstances requiring less of wearying episcopal labor and travel he would have been an acceptable contributor to the theological literature of the day, as well as to that of culture and social science. He has left in print, besides his charges, episcopal addresses, pastorals, etc., but a single work: "Doctrine, Discipline, and Worship of the American Branch of the Catholic Church, Explained and Unfolded in Three Sermons" (1852).

RIGHT REVEREND JACKSON KEMPER, D.D.

Jackson Kemper.

THE first missionary bishop of the American Church was born in Pleasant Valley, N. Y., Dec. 24, 1789.

Graduated at Columbia, 1809, Kemper studied theology under Hobart; was made deacon and priested in Christ Church, Philadelphia, by White, March 10, 1811, and Jan. 23, 1814, respectively. For twenty years he was assistant minister of the united parishes of Christ Church, St. Peter's, and St. James's, Philadelphia, adding to this work the duties of diocesan secretary, 1811–18, and giving special attention to outlying mission stations. In 1819–20 he was engaged in securing funds for the General Theological Seminary. Columbia gave him the divinity doctorate, 1829.

He became rector of St. Paul's Church, Norwalk, Conn., 1831. He was consecrated, Sept. 25, 1835, missionary bishop for Missouri and Indiana, in St. Peter's Church, Philadelphia, by Bishops White, Moore, Chase, the two Onderdonks, Smith, and Doane,—the last consecration in which the venerable White took part.

The annals of Kemper's missionary apostolate are of the deepest interest. In addition to his own extensive see, his care of the churches was extended over the territory now embraced by Iowa, Wisconsin, Minnesota, Nebraska, and Kansas, into which immigrants were pouring. His visitations were undertaken under circumstances of the greatest difficulty. Traversing vast reaches of country just opened for settlement; with only the most primitive facilities for journeying; making his temporary home in the rough cabin or the miserable tavern—Kemper gave full proof of his apostolic ministry, and in his care for the churches never cared for himself. He made extensive visitations in Arkansas, Mississippi, Louisiana, Alabama, Georgia, and Florida, 1837–38. The experiences of this tour were apostolic.

The see of Maryland was offered Kemper, 1838, and declined. He was chosen diocesan of Wisconsin, 1847, but this was also declined. Twelve years later he was again offered Wisconsin, and in view of increasing years and infirmities he accepted the see.

He died at Delafield, Wis., May 24, 1870.

WORKS.—His life is yet to be written. It will be the history of the founding of the Church in the middle West. His reports in "The Spirit of Missions" and "The Proceedings of the Board of Missions" are of the deepest interest. He left a few pamphlets, etc.

RIGHT REVEREND SAMUEL ALLEN McCOSKRY, S.T.D., LL.D.

Samuel Allen McCoskry.

BISHOP CHASE, on his resignation of Ohio (1831), had removed to Michigan, and made purchases of lands for Church purposes, when he was called (1835) to Illinois. The impetus given to the development of the Church in Michigan during this period resulted in the organization of a diocese.

McCoskry was born in Carlisle, Pa., Nov. 9, 1804. He entered the U. S. Military Academy, 1820, where he remained for two years. He then entered Dickinson College, Carlisle, and was graduated 1825. Studying law, he was a successful practitioner for six years, holding for a time the deputy attorney generalship for Cumberland County. He began his preparation for orders, 1831; was ordered deacon, in Christ Church, Reading, March 28th, and priested in the same church, Dec. 13, 1833, by H. U. Onderdonk. After a brief term of service at Reading he became rector of St. Paul's Church, Philadelphia.

He was consecrated, July 7, 1836, bishop of Michigan, in St. Paul's Church, Philadelphia, by Bishops H. U. Onderdonk, Doane, and Kemper. On entering upon his see, McCoskry accepted the rectorship of St. Paul's, Detroit, which he retained for twenty-seven years. Columbia College and the University of Pennsylvania conferred upon him the doctorate in divinity, 1837. On his visit to England at the jubilee of the Venerable Society for the Propagation of the Gospel in Foreign Parts, he received from Oxford the degree of D.C.L.

His administration was marked by great growth and development. After nearly forty-two years of service he tendered his resignation, March, 1878, "owing to failing health and infirmities of age, which hinder the efficient administration of the affairs of the diocese." He was then in his seventy-fifth year. Charges having been made against his character, he withdrew his resignation, demanding an investigation. With the vacillation of age, and weakened mentally and physically, he renewed his resignation, but before the House of Bishops could investigate, sailed for Europe.

At a meeting of the House in New York, Sept. 3, 1878, he was deposed. It is but just to say that at this meeting a quorum was obtained with great difficulty, and that many are not satisfied with the decision there reached. He died in New York, August, 1886.

WORKS.—McCoskry left nothing but his official addresses, etc.

RIGHT REVEREND LEONIDAS POLK, D.D.

Leonidas Polk.

BORN at Raleigh, N. C., April 10, 1806, Leonidas Polk was graduated at the U. S. Military Academy, West Point, 1827. It was during his connection with the academy that he received holy baptism at the hands of the Rev. Charles Pettit McIlvaine, and shortly after his graduation he was confirmed in Christ Church, Raleigh, by Ravenscroft.

Resigning his commission in the army with a view to entering the ministry, he was admitted to the diaconate in the Monumental Church, Richmond, Va., by Bishop Channing Moore, April 11, 1830, and was advanced to the priesthood by the same prelate in Christ Church, Norfolk, Va., May 22, 1833.

His service as assistant to the bishop at the Monumental Church was terminated by loss of health, which made a visit to Europe necessary, and on his return he removed to Tennessee, where he became rector of St. Peter's, Columbia. In 1835 he was a deputy to the General Convention. In 1838 Columbia College conferred upon him the doctorate in divinity.

Chosen by the General Convention to the missionary episcopate, he was consecrated bishop of Arkansas and the Indian Territory south of 36° 30′ of latitude, with provisional charge of Alabama, Mississippi, and the republic of Texas, in Christ Church, Cincinnati, Dec. 9, 1838. His consecrators were Bishops Meade, Smith, McIlvaine, and Otey. In 1841 he was elected first bishop of Louisiana, and resigned his missionary episcopate.

Polk was a judicious administrator, a scholarly theologian, an eloquent preacher, and an influential member of the Upper House. His views were those of the "Evangelical" school; and his broad culture and sympathetic interest in the young led him to take an active part in the first foundation of the University of the South, at Sewanee, Tenn.

Intense in his Southern sympathies, and still retaining his interest in military matters, on the breaking out of the Civil War he threw himself heartily into the secession movement, and was commissioned a major-general of the Confederate forces. While on duty in the vicinity of Marietta, Ga., he was mortally wounded, and died in the faith and peace of God, June 14, 1864.

WORKS.—Other than his official addresses, etc., Polk left nothing in print.

RIGHT REVEREND WILLIAM HEATHCOTE DE LANCEY, S.T.D., LL.D., D.C.L.

William Heathcote de Lancey.

THE descendant of one of the most prominent and devout Churchmen of the colonial Church, the first bishop of Western New York was born on the family estates in Mamaroneck, N. Y., Oct. 8, 1797, and was graduated at Yale College, 1817.

He studied under Hobart, and was ordained by him to the diaconate in St. John's Chapel, New York, Dec. 28, 1819, and to the priesthood in Trinity Church, March 6, 1822. He then became an assistant minister of the united parishes in Philadelphia, under the charge of White, and was afterward appointed for duty at St. Peter's Church. He was secretary of the Pennsylvania Convention, 1823–30, and of the House of Bishops, 1823–29. In 1828 he was chosen provost of the University of Pennsylvania, which position he retained for five years. In 1833 he resumed his duties as assistant minister at St. Peter's; and on the death of White he was chosen to the rectorship of the parish, which now for the first time became independent of Christ Church.

On the division of the diocese of New York by the creation of the western portion of the State as an independent see, De Lancey was chosen the first Bishop of Western New York. The consecration took place in St. Peter's Church, Auburn, May 9, 1839. The consecrators were Bishops Griswold, the two Onderdonks, and Doane.

De Lancey established his home at Geneva, making Trinity Church in that town his pro-cathedral, and giving special attention to the development of Geneva, afterward known as Hobart, College.

Yale conferred upon him the doctorate in divinity, 1828; Union gave him the degree of LL.D., 1847; and Oxford made him a D.C.L., 1852.

After a judicious and successful administration, with the evidence of growth on every side, and possessing the love, the confidence, and the profound respect of his diocese and the Church at home and abroad, De Lancey "fell asleep" at his home in Geneva, April 5, 1865.

WORKS.—1. Several tracts (one on the "Duties of Churchwardens and Vestrymen"); 2. "An Historical Sermon on the Centennial of St. Peter's, Philadelphia"; 3. The "Annual Addresses" to his diocese (one of which gives in detail the account of his visit to England at the time of the jubilee of the Venerable Society); 4. Charges and pastorals.

RIGHT REVEREND CHRISTOPHER EDWARDS GADSDEN, D.D.

Christopher Edwards Gadsden.

THE successor of Robert Smith, Theodore Dehon, and Nathaniel Bowen in the episcopate of South Carolina was born in Charleston, Nov. 25, 1785, and was graduated at Yale in the class of 1804.

Ordered deacon in St. Paul's Chapel, New York, July 25, 1807, by Bishop Benjamin Moore, and priested in Bruton Church, Williamsburgh, Va., by Bishop Madison, April 14, 1810, Gadsden served for two years at St. John's, Berkeley, S. C., and then removing to his native city, he was first assistant minister, and, 1814, rector of St. Philip's Church. In this cure of souls he remained until his consecration to the episcopal office. In 1815 he received the degree of D.D. from South Carolina College.

Gadsden's consecration took place in Trinity Church, Boston, June 21, 1840. The consecrators were Bishops Griswold, Doane, and McCoskry. After an administration marked by growth and spiritual development, and made noteworthy by his untiring labors and marked successes, he entered into rest at Charleston, June 24, 1852, and his remains were interred in the chancel of St. Philip's Church. "He, being dead," by the holiness of his life and conversation "yet speaketh."

WORKS.—1. "Sermon on the Death of Bishop Dehon, and an Essay on his Life" (1833); 2. "The Prayer-book as it Is"; 3. Three charges to the clergy.

RIGHT REVEREND WILLIAM ROLLINSON WHITTINGHAM, S.T.D., LL.D.

Photographed by W. C. Babcock, from painting by Mrs. Rollinson Colburn.

William Rollinson Whittingham.

Born in the city of New York, Dec. 2, 1805, educated privately, and chiefly by his mother, a woman of the highest culture, Whittingham was graduated with distinguished honors at the General Theological Seminary; was made deacon by Hobart in Trinity Church, March 11, 1827; was advanced to the priesthood by Croes, in St. Mark's Church, Orange, N. J., Dec. 17, 1829; and was instituted to the rectorship of that church by the same prelate on the following day.

He became rector of St. Luke's, New York, 1831, and in 1836 was made professor of ecclesiastical history in the General Theological Seminary, which position he retained until his consecration. In 1837 Columbia conferred upon him the doctorate in divinity. In 1859 St. John's, Annapolis, gave him the doctorate of laws.

His consecration to the episcopate of Maryland took place in St. Paul's Church, Baltimore, Sept. 17, 1840. His consecrators were Bishops Griswold, Channing Moore, B. T. Onderdonk, and Doane.

Whittingham was a scholar of rare attainments, a sound theologian, an impassioned speaker, a clear debater, and a most devoted bishop. Outspoken, fearless in his defense of the right, scrupulously conscientious, and self-denying, he will ever be remembered among the foremost bishops of the American Church. His vast collection of books, the largest private library in the country at the time of his death, it is believed, he bequeathed to the diocese, and with his usual modesty gave to it the name of the friend through whose liberality the building which contained it was erected. He died at Orange, N. J., Oct. 17, 1879.

Works.—While in New York Whittingham was the editor of several Church serials, and of a " Parish Library of Standard Works," in 13 volumes, annotated and prefaced with great care. He published a reprint of " Palmer's Church History " (12mo, 1862), which has been several times reissued. With the Rev. J. F. Schroeder, D.D., and other associates, he edited a series of " Essays and Dissertations on Biblical Literature " (8vo, 1829). In connection with the Rev. Prof. S. H. Turner, D.D., he edited Jahn's " Introduction to the Old Testament." His charges and addresses, together with his occasional sermons, pastorals, essays, etc., were numerous and of great value.

RIGHT REVEREND STEPHEN ELLIOTT, D.D.

Stephen Elliott.

BORN at Beaufort, S. C., Aug. 31, 1806, Elliott received his collegiate training for two years at Harvard, and for the remainder of his course at South Carolina College, where he was graduated, 1825.

Admitted to the bar, he continued in the practice of law for five years, and then abandoned the legal profession for the study of theology.

He was admitted to deacon's orders by Bishop Bowen, in St. Paul's Church, Charleston, Nov. 8, 1835, and was advanced to the priesthood by the same prelate, June 22, 1838.

After a brief service during his diaconate at Christ Church, Wilton, S. C., he was elected professor of sacred literature and the evidences of Christianity in South Carolina College. He retained this post until called to the episcopate. He received the doctorate in divinity in 1840 from Columbia College, New York, and Trinity, Hartford.

Elliott was consecrated to the episcopate of Georgia in Christ Church, Savannah, Feb. 28, 1841. His consecrators were Bishops Meade, Ives, and Gadsden.

On establishing his home in his new see, he became rector of St. John's Church, Savannah. He was appointed, 1845, provisional bishop of Florida. At the same time he established at Montpelier a diocesan school for girls. After seven years of effort this venture of faith proved unsuccessful and involved the loss of the bishop's entire fortune. Returning to Savannah, he became rector of Christ Church, which position he retained till death.

Bishop Elliott entered heartily into the secession movement, and throughout the Civil War was a prominent and influential leader in the efforts for the establishment of the Church in the Confederate States. He died in Savannah, Dec. 21, 1866, beloved and revered of all men.

WORKS.—Besides his official publications, addresses, pastorals, charges, etc., a volume of "Sermons" was published in New York after the bishop's decease, with a prefatory sketch of his life.

RIGHT REVEREND ALFRED LEE, S.T.D., LL.D.

Alfred Lee.

ALFRED LEE was born in Cambridge, Mass., Sept. 9, 1807.

He was graduated at Harvard, 1827. On taking his degree he studied law, and was admitted to the bar. Turning his attention toward the sacred ministry, he entered the General Theological Seminary, where he was graduated, 1837. He was admitted to the diaconate in Trinity Church, Norwich, Conn., May 21, 1837, by Bishop Brownell, who advanced him to the priesthood in Christ Church, Hartford, June 12, 1838. A few months of his early ministry were spent at St. James's, Poquetanuck, Conn. In September, 1838, he became rector of Calvary Church, Rockdale, Pa., where he remained until he was raised to the episcopate. In 1841 Trinity and Hobart gave him the divinity doctorate. He received the same degree from Harvard in 1860, and in 1877 Delaware College, Newark, Del., gave him the doctorate of laws.

He was consecrated bishop of Delaware in St. Paul's Chapel, New York, Oct. 12, 1841, by Bishops Griswold, Moore, Chase, Brownell, H. U. Onderdonk, Meade, and McIlvaine. He became rector of St. Andrew's Church, Wilmington. On the death of Smith (1884) he became presiding bishop. He died at Wilmington, April 12, 1887, and his remains rest in the "Old Swedes'" churchyard.

Lee was a scholar of wide erudition, well read in the theology of the Calvinistic and Puritan schools; a graceful writer, an earnest and effective preacher, and a mild, though firm and fearless, administrator. His views were "Evangelical." He was deeply interested in the Church's missions abroad, in the work of Christian education, and in all the leading charities and organizations of the "Evangelical" party. He was specially prominent in the conduct and development of the Mexican mission, and visited Mexico in its behalf, participating in the work of the Mexican Commission, which resulted in the consecration of Dr. H. C. Riley as bishop of the Valley of Mexico. Of great personal holiness, courteous, cultured, and refined, he lived the life of a true-hearted bishop.

WORKS.—1. "Life of St. Peter"; 2. "Life of St. John"; 3. "Voice in the Wilderness"; 4. Five episcopal charges; 5. "A Life Hid in Christ with God," memoir of Susan Allibone, chiefly from her diary and letters (8vo, 1855); 6. Ordination sermon on 1 Timothy iv. 16; 7. Six sermons, viz.: "The Unsearchable Riches of Christ"; "The Uncertainty of the Morrow"; "The Society of Divine Origin"; "The Lamb the Light of the Church"; "The Voice of the Spirit to His Church"; Sermon before the General Convention of 1868; 8. "Coöperative Revision of the New Testament" (1881); 9. "Eventful Nights in Bible History" (1886); 10. Occasional addresses, etc.

RIGHT REVEREND JOHN JOHNS, D.D., LL.D.

John Johns.

JOHN JOHNS, fourth bishop of Virginia, was born in New Castle, Del., July 10, 1796.

He was graduated at Princeton, 1815, admitted to the diaconate by White, in St. James's Church, Philadelphia, May 6, 1819, and advanced to the priesthood by Kemp, in All Saints' Church, Fredericktown, Md., July 26, 1820. Johns remained at Fredericktown for eight years. Removing at the end of this period to Baltimore, he became rector of Christ Church in that city, retaining this cure of souls until his consecration. In 1834 he received the doctorate in divinity from Princeton and from the University of New York; and in 1855 William and Mary College conferred on him the doctorate of laws.

Johns was consecrated assistant bishop of Virginia, in the Monumental Church, Richmond, Oct. 13, 1842. His consecrators were Bishops Griswold, Meade, Ives, and Whittingham. In 1844 Bishop Johns accepted the presidency of William and Mary College, which he retained for five years. He was also at the head of the Theological Seminary of Virginia for a number of years. On the death of Meade (1862) he became bishop of Virginia. He died April 5, 1876.

Johns was eloquent, earnest, and devout. In fullest sympathy, doctrinally and personally, with the leaders of the "Evangelical" school of thought, his personal magnetism impressed the views he held upon several successive generations of the young Southern clergy, and his influence is still felt. He was a man of God, true-hearted, lovable, and holy in life; beloved and venerated in death.

WORKS.—Besides "A Memoir of Bishop Meade" (12mo, Baltimore, 1867), which is minute, interesting, and a most valuable contribution to Virginia Church history, Bishop Johns published but little. His episcopal addresses, pastorals, charges, and a few tracts, are all that are to be found in print.

RIGHT REVEREND MANTON EASTBURN, S.T.D., LL.D.

Manton Eastburn.

THE coadjutor and successor in Massachusetts of the venerable Griswold was born in Leeds, England, Feb. 9, 1801.

Brought by his father to the United States in childhood, he entered Columbia College in his thirteenth year, and was graduated 1817. Pursuing his studies for orders at the General Theological Seminary, he completed his course, 1821; was admitted to deacon's orders by Hobart, in St. John's Chapel, New York, May 16, 1822; and the same bishop advanced him to the priesthood, Nov. 13, 1825.

For the first five years of his ministry Eastburn was assistant minister of Christ Church, New York; in 1827 he became rector of the Church of the Ascension in the same city; in 1835 he received the doctorate in divinity from Columbia; and in 1870, Griswold College, Davenport, Ia., conferred upon him the doctorate of laws. In 1838 he declined an election to the episcopate of Maryland.

He was consecrated bishop coadjutor to Griswold in Trinity Church, Boston, Dec. 29, 1842, by the presiding bishop, assisted by Bishops Brownell, B. T. Onderdonk, and De Lancey. On the death of the bishop of the Eastern Diocese, Eastburn became the bishop of Massachusetts. He died in Boston, Sept. 12, 1872, and was buried at Dedham, Mass.

The third bishop of Massachusetts was an excellent classical scholar, a theologian, a man of culture. Strongly partizan in his prejudices and prepossessions, an "Evangelical of the Evangelicals," fearless in defense of his views, and intolerant of contradiction or opposition, his episcopate was not free from strife. He was a critical admirer of "our inestimable liturgy," ever contending, with Herbert, as to "the prayers of our mother, the Church of England," that "there are no prayers like hers." His strong insistence upon "Evangelical" principles brought him into collision with the "High Churchmen," but men of all shades of opinion learned to appreciate and admire the honesty and truthfulness of one who consistently held through life to the principles that had made his pastorate memorable, and that gave to his episcopate a distinctive character that is still remembered with respect.

WORKS.—1. "Four Lectures on Hebrew, Latin, and English Poetry" (1825); 2. "Lectures on the Philippians" (8vo, 1833); 3. "Oration at the Semicentennial of Columbia College" (1837). He was a contributor to the volume of "Essays and Dissertations on Biblical Literature" (1829). He printed numerous charges, etc., and edited Thornton's "Family Prayers."

RIGHT REVEREND JOHN PRENTISS KEWLEY HENSHAW, D.D.

John Prentiss Kewley Henshaw.

THE Church in Rhode Island had formed part of the see of Seabury, and the signature of the first American bishop—"S. Bp. Conn. et Rho. Ins."—is found attached to many official documents and letters. Bass of Massachusetts, and Jarvis of Connecticut, succeeded to the episcopal oversight of Rhode Island. On the dissolution of the Eastern Diocese the see made choice of its first bishop who was unassociated with another charge.

Henshaw was born in Middletown, Conn., June 13, 1792. He was graduated at Middlebury College, Vt., 1808, pursuing post-graduate studies at Harvard. He was admitted to deacon's orders in St. Michael's, Bristol, R. I., by Griswold, and was advanced to the priesthood in St. Ann's, Brooklyn, N. Y., June 13, 1816. His diaconate was spent at St. Ann's. He entered, when priested, upon the rectorship of St. Peter's Church, Baltimore, where he remained until called to Rhode Island.

He was consecrated in St. John's Church, Providence, R. I., Aug. 11, 1843, by Bishops Brownell, B. T. Onderdonk, Hopkins, Doane, Whittingham, and Johns. His alma mater conferred upon him the doctorate in divinity in the year of his consecration. On his coming to Rhode Island, he accepted the rectorship of Grace Church, Providence, which he held till death.

Henshaw was an eloquent preacher and a popular and successful parish priest. His views were those of the "Evangelical" party, and he maintained these principles with an energy and power that won for him a place among the leaders of this school. In later years he grew more conservative in his theological opinions, while his administration was ever just, equitable, and tolerant of conflicting opinions. He had an attractive presence, was courtly, and an accomplished conversationalist. He was a faithful priest and bishop. It was while rendering loving service in the diocese of Maryland, where, after years of absence, he was still most affectionately remembered, that he "fell asleep," near Frederick City, July 20, 1852. He was buried in the cemetery of Grace Church, Providence, R. I.

WORKS.—1. "Theology for the People" (8vo, 1840); 2. "Hymns for Parochial Use at St. Peter's"; 3. "Lectures on the Advent of Christ": 4. "Tract on Confirmation"; 5. "Sermon on the Jubilee of the Society for the Propagation of the Gospel" (1851); 6. Addresses, charges, pastorals, etc.

RIGHT REVEREND CARLTON CHASE, D.D.

Carlton Chase.

SEABURY visited New Hampshire in the course of his progresses through New England, and Bass accepted the charge of the Church in that State in connection with his own see. The signature "Edward, Bp. Mass. and New Hamp.," is still extant, and the connection of the few clergy in New Hampshire with the union of the churches made the connection of the Massachusetts and New Hampshire churches intimate and lasting. At the time of the resolving of the Eastern Diocese into its constituent parts, New Hampshire was ready to choose for its own bishop a native of the State.

Chase was born in Hopkinton, N. H., Feb. 20, 1794. He was graduated at Dartmouth College, 1817; admitted to deacon's orders at St. Michael's Church, Bristol, R. I., Dec. 9, 1818, by Griswold, who advanced him to the priesthood in Trinity Church, Newport, R. I., Sept. 27, 1820. His sole charge prior to his consecration was the rectorship of Immanuel Church, Bellows Falls, Vt. In 1839 the University of Vermont conferred upon him the doctorate in divinity. He was consecrated bishop of New Hampshire, in Christ Church, Philadelphia, Oct. 20, 1844, by Bishops Philander Chase, Brownell, B. T. Onderdonk, Ives, and Bosworth Smith. Removing to Claremont, N. H., he became rector of Trinity Church, which charge he retained for a number of years.

He was invited by the standing committee of the diocese of New York, after the suspension of Onderdonk and before the election of Wainwright, to perform episcopal duties in New York. Under this appointment he made three visitations, 1850, 1851, 1852, giving great satisfaction to a diocese restive under the disabilities consequent upon an ecclesiastical sentence which had failed to commend itself to the popular mind. Chase died at his home in Claremont, Jan. 18, 1870.

The first bishop of New Hampshire was a man of strong intellectual ability, a sound theologian, a faithful and tireless administrator of his see, judicial in his judgments, considerate and affectionate, and possessing the confidence and veneration of all. He was "a good man, and full of the Holy Ghost."

WORKS.—Chase published nothing save his addresses, charges, and a few occasional sermons, together with a valuable contribution on the "History of the Church in Vermont," included in Thompson's "Gazetteer."

RIGHT REVEREND NICHOLAS HAMNER COBBS, D.D.

Nicholas Hamner Cobbs.

Born in Bedford County, Va., Feb. 5, 1796, and educated privately, the early life of Cobbs was spent in teaching, in which vocation he attained a marked success.

On turning his attention toward the sacred ministry he was admitted to the diaconate in Trinity Church, Staunton, Va., May 23, 1824, by Channing Moore, who advanced him to the priesthood, May 22, 1825, in the Monumental Church, Richmond. After fifteen years of pastoral work in the county of his birth, in 1839 he became rector of St. Paul's Church, Petersburg, and in 1843 rector of St. Paul's, Cincinnati, O. The following year he was elected to the episcopate of Alabama.

Cobbs was a deputy from Virginia to the General Conventions, 1829–41 inclusive. In 1842 Geneva College conferred upon him the degree of doctor in divinity. He was consecrated bishop of Alabama in Christ Church, Philadelphia, Oct. 20, 1844, by Bishops Philander Chase, Meade, McIlvaine, Doane, and Otey. He died at Montgomery, Ala., Jan. 11, 1861.

The first bishop of Alabama was an able and argumentative preacher, a thorough logician, and a student of varied attainments and wide culture. He was faithful in his administration, and his memory is cherished by a grateful people.

Works.—1. Sermon on "The Doubting Christian Encouraged" (several times reprinted); 2. Occasional discourses and episcopal addresses.

RIGHT REVEREND CICERO STEPHENS HAWKS.

Cicero Stephens Hawks.

THE successor of the apostolic Kemper in the half of his original missionary jurisdiction, and the first bishop of Missouri elected by the clergy and laity of the diocese, was born at Newbern, N. C., May 26, 1812.

He was graduated at the university of his native State, at Chapel Hill, 1830. He received deacon's orders in St. Thomas's Church, New York, Dec. 8, 1834, from Bishop B. T. Onderdonk, who advanced him to the priesthood in Trinity Church, Ulster, N. Y., July 24, 1836. His diaconate was spent at Trinity Church, Ulster. On becoming a priest he accepted the rectorship of Trinity Church, Saugerties, N. Y. In 1837 he became rector of Trinity Church, Buffalo, N. Y. In 1843 he removed to Missouri, and was rector of Christ Church, St. Louis, until his election to the episcopate.

He was consecrated bishop of Missouri in Christ Church, Philadelphia, Oct. 20, 1844, by Bishops Philander Chase, Kemper, McCoskry, Polk, and De Lancey. He died in St. Louis, April 19, 1868.

The administration of the first bishop of Missouri was uneventful, save in the rapid growth and development of the Church throughout the State. The bishop was an eloquent preacher, a man of culture and refinement, and a wise, conservative, and tolerant diocesan. He died universally beloved and regretted.

WORKS.—Hawks published nothing save his official addresses, charges, and pastorals, which are found in the Convention "Journals" of Missouri.

RIGHT REVEREND WILLIAM JONES BOONE, M.D.

William Jones Boone.

THE first foreign missionary bishop sent forth to his apostolic labors by the Church in the United States was born at Walterborough, S. C., July 1, 1811.

He was graduated at the College of South Carolina, 1829. He was admitted to the bar after a full course of study, 1833; but turning his thoughts toward the work of the ministry, he abandoned the profession of the law, and after taking the course at the Theological Seminary of Virginia, he gave himself to the foreign missionary work of the Church. With a view of adding to his qualifications for successful labor in China he pursued a course of medical study at the College of South Carolina, and received the degree of M.D.

Boone was made deacon in St. Peter's Church, Charleston, Sept. 18, 1836, by Bishop Bowen, who advanced him to the priesthood in St. Michael's Church, March 3, 1837. His appointment as a missionary to China immediately followed his admission to priest's orders, and he sailed for his distant field, July 8, 1837. In 1844 he was chosen to the missionary episcopate of China by the Church in General Convention, and was consecrated in St. Peter's Church, Philadelphia, Oct. 26, 1844, by Bishops Philander Chase, Doane, Otey, and Henshaw. He sailed on his return to China, Dec. 14, 1844, and ministered for twenty years with great assiduity and success in the field to which he had devoted his life, dying at Shanghai, July 17, 1864.

Bishop Boone was preëminently a man of God. Cultured in manner, winning in his intercourse with others, with unusual linguistic powers, and widely read on all subjects connected with his calling, he labored with all the faithfulness and zeal of an apostle, and laid down his life willingly for the cause of Christ.

WORKS.—Besides the missionary reports published in "The Spirit of Missions," Boone printed only his contributions to the discussions attending the translation of the Bible into Chinese.

RIGHT REVEREND GEORGE WASHINGTON FREEMAN, D.D.

George Washington Freeman.

LITTLE is known of the early life and studies of Bishop Freeman. Born in Sandwich, Mass., June 13, 1789, of an old Puritan family, he had reached the age of thirty-eight years when he was admitted to the diaconate in Christ Church, Raleigh, N. C., Oct. 8, 1826, by Bishop Ravenscroft, who advanced him to the priesthood in Christ Church, Newbern, N. C., May 20, 1827.

The first years of his ministry were spent in mission work in North Carolina. In 1829 he accepted the rectorship of Christ Church, Raleigh, which he retained until 1840, when he removed to Columbia, Tenn. Here he spent about a year of service, and then, after a short time given to Swedesborough, N. J., he became rector of Immanuel Church, New Castle, Del. Chosen by the Church in General Convention to the missionary episcopate of "Arkansas and the Indian Territory south of 36½°, with supervision of the Church in Texas," Freeman, who had received his degree in divinity from the University of North Carolina in 1839, was consecrated in St. Peter's, Philadelphia, Oct. 26, 1844. The consecrators were Bishops Philander Chase, Kemper, Doane, Otey, Henshaw, Polk, Alfred Lee, Whittingham, Elliott, and Johns. He died, after a laborious but useful episcopate, at Little Rock, Ark., April 29, 1858.

WORKS.—Bishop Freeman left nothing of importance in print save his annual reports to the Board of Missions, found in "The Spirit of Missions."

RIGHT REVEREND HORATIO SOUTHGATE, D.D.

Horatio Southgate.

THE first missionary bishop of the American Church to the Orient was born in Portland, Me., July 5, 1812.

Graduating at Bowdoin College, 1832, he entered the Andover Theological Seminary, intending to become a Congregationalist minister. The study of church history led him to ask for confirmation at the hands of Griswold. He was ordered deacon in Trinity, Boston, July 12, 1835. Appointed by the Domestic and Foreign Missionary Society to investigate the openings for mission work in Turkey and Persia, he sailed for his field of labor, April 24, 1836, and continued his investigations for two years. He was advanced to the priesthood in St. Paul's Chapel, New York, Oct. 3, 1839, by B. T. Onderdonk, and in the following spring sailed for Constantinople as missionary to the dominions of the sultan of Turkey.

He received consecration to the missionary episcopate in Turkey in St. Peter's, Philadelphia, Oct. 26, 1844. The consecrators were Bishops Philander Chase, Whittingham, Elliott, Johns, and Henshaw. He returned to Constantinople in 1845, continuing in his work until 1849, when he tendered his resignation, which was accepted, 1850.

He organized St. Luke's Church, Portland, 1851; became rector of the Church of the Advent, Boston, 1852, remaining there for over five years; 1859–1872 was rector of Zion Church, New York. He received the doctorate in divinity from Columbia, 1845, and from Trinity, 1846. He died, April 12, 1894, at Astoria, N. Y.

The principles of missionary operations under which he attempted the introduction of a purer practice among the Oriental Churches were those which were determined by the American Church. The principles of non-interference with the Christian Churches existing in those countries, save in educational work, the circulation of the Word, etc., are now accepted by nearly all missionaries. The failure of the Church to support him in his judicious and conservative work is to be regretted. He was a half-century ahead of his times.

WORKS.—1. "A Tour through Armenia, Kurdistan, and Mesopotamia" (2 vols., 12mo); 2. "A Visit to the Syrian Church of Mesopotamia" (12mo, 1844); 3. "A Treatise on the Antiquity, Doctrine, Ministry, and Worship of the Anglican Church" (12mo, 1849; published in modern Greek at Constantinople); 4. "Practical Directions for the Observance of Lent" (1850); 5. "The War in the East" (1855); 6. "Parochial Sermons" (1860); 7. "The Cross above the Crescent" (1877); 8. "Christus Redemptor: Life, Character, and Teachings of Our Lord"; 9. "Gone Before"; 10. "Manual of Consolation"; 11. "Many Thoughts about Our Lord" (1880); 12. Occasional papers.

RIGHT REVEREND ALONZO POTTER, D.D., LL.D.

Alonzo Potter.

THE third to fill the chair of the venerable William White, first bishop of the American Church in the line of succession from Canterbury, was born in Beekman (La Grange), Dutchess County, N. Y., July 6, 1800.

Graduating at Union College, 1818, he was the following year appointed to a tutorship in his alma mater, and, 1821, became professor of mathematics and natural philosophy.

Potter was admitted to the diaconate by Bishop Hobart, May 1, 1822, and was advanced to the priesthood by Bishop Brownell, Sept. 16, 1824. In 1826 he became rector of St. Paul's, Boston, where he remained for five years. In 1831 he was appointed professor of moral philosophy in Union College, which post he held with distinguished success until his election to the see of Pennsylvania. In 1834 Kenyon College conferred on him the degree of doctor in divinity, which was also given him by Harvard, 1843. He received the doctorate of laws from Union, 1846.

Potter was consecrated in Christ Church, Philadelphia, Sept. 23, 1845, by Bishops Philander Chase, Brownell, Hopkins, Doane, McCoskry, Whittingham, Alfred Lee, and Freeman. After a brilliant episcopate, fruitful in every good word and work; with an unprecedented development of Church activities; with an increase of communicants, congregations, clergy, never attained before; with the addition to the diocesan institutions of schools, hospitals, retreats, colleges, to an extent difficult to realize, the beloved and revered bishop of Pennsylvania died on shipboard in the harbor of San Francisco, July 4, 1865. The Church and country mourned the loss of this great-hearted bishop of souls.

WORKS.—1. "Political Economy"; 2. "Handbook for Readers"; 3. "Principles of Science Applied to the Arts"; 4. "The School and the Schoolmaster" (written in connection with George B. Emerson); 5. "The Three Witnesses" (a posthumous volume of the Lowell Lectures); 6. Sermons, addresses, charges, pastoral letters, etc. Bishop Potter edited "The Memorial Papers" and a course of lectures on "The Evidences of Christianity." See Bishop M. A. DeW. Howe's "Memoirs."

RIGHT REVEREND GEORGE BURGESS, D.D.

George Burgess.

THE first bishop of Maine was born at Providence, R. I., Oct. 31, 1809.

He was graduated at Brown University, 1826, and was, 1826–29, a tutor in his alma mater. He studied at the universities of Bonn, Göttingen, and Berlin, 1831–34, and on his return was ordered deacon in Grace Church, Providence, June 10, 1834, by Bishop Griswold. On Nov. 2, 1834, Bishop Brownell advanced him to the priesthood in Christ Church, Hartford, Conn., of which parish he had been chosen rector. He received the doctorate in divinity from Trinity College, 1845, and from Union and Brown, 1846.

He was consecrated in Christ Church, Hartford, Conn., Oct. 31, 1847, by Bishops Philander Chase, Brownell, Eastburn, Henshaw, and Carlton Chase. After an episcopate of singular devotion, self-sacrifice, and success, he died at sea near Hayti, where he had just completed an episcopal visitation, April 23, 1866, and was buried at Gardiner, Me., which had been his home, and of which he had been the rector since his entrance upon his see.

The first bishop of Maine was beloved of all. Retiring in manner and unconscious of the subtle personal magnetism which drew all hearts to himself, it only required the occasion to bring out the stores of learning, covering almost the entire range of knowledge, which made him the most agreeable of conversationalists and the most ready of debaters. He seemed never to forget any information he had once acquired, and his stores of recondite learning were ever at the use of his friends. Strong in his integrity, impartial in his judgments, conservative in his administration, he lived a life of saintliness, and his end was peace.

WORKS.—1. Academic poem, "The Strife of Brothers" (1844); 2. "The Book of Psalms Translated into English Verse" (1844); 3. "The Last Enemy Conquering and Conquered" (1850); 4. "Pages from the Ecclesiastical History of New England between 1740 and 1840" (1854); 5. "Sermons on the Christian Life" (1854); 6. "Catechism on the Church Catechism"; 7. "List of Persons Admitted to the Order of Deacons in the Protestant Episcopal Church, 1785–1857." Bishop Burgess's five Charges were compositions of unusual merit. He published several tracts: "The Stranger in the Church," "Swedenborgianism," etc., which have had a great popularity. His contribution to "The Popham Memorial Volume" (1864) is of historical authority. See his "Last Journal," with Introduction by Bishop A. Lee.

RIGHT REVEREND GEORGE UPFOLD, D.D., LL.D.

George Upfold.

THE original appointment of the apostolic Kemper as missionary bishop was to Missouri and Indiana. In the development of his work the surrender of Missouri to Hawks as the first diocesan of the Church in that State was shortly afterward followed by the separation of Indiana from Kemper's charge and the election for this new diocese of a bishop of its own.

Upfold was born at Shemly Green, near Guilford, Surrey, England, May 7, 1796. At the age of eight years his father brought him to this country, and the family settled in Albany. N. Y. Upfold was graduated at Union College, 1814, and received his degree in medicine at the College of Physicians and Surgeons in New York City, 1816. The following year he abandoned the practice of medicine and began the study of theology under the direction of Bishop Hobart. This prelate admitted him to deacon's orders in Trinity Church, New York, Oct. 21, 1818, and advanced him to the priesthood in Trinity Church, Lansingburg, July 13, 1820. He remained in Lansingburg for nearly two years, when he was called to New York, where he was successively rector of St. Luke's and St. Thomas's. In 1831 he became rector of Trinity Church, Pittsburg, in which charge he continued until his election to the episcopal office. He received the doctorate in divinity from Columbia College, 1831, and was made a doctor of laws by the Western University of Pennsylvania, 1856.

Upfold was consecrated, Dec. 16, 1849, by Bishops Bosworth Smith, McIlvaine, Kemper, and Hawks. He died in Indianapolis, Aug. 26, 1872.

WORKS.—1. "The Last Hundred Years" (1845); 2. "Manual of Devotions for Domestic and Private Use" (1863); 3. Episcopal addresses, occasional sermons, pastorals, and charges.

RIGHT REVEREND WILLIAM MERCER GREEN, D.D.

Photo by W. C. Babcock, from painting by Miss Helen Frances Colburn.

William Mercer Green.

THE first bishop of the American Church in Mississippi was born in Wilmington, N. C., May 2, 1798.

He was graduated at the University of North Carolina, Chapel Hill, 1818. He received deacon's orders from Bishop Channing Moore in Christ Church, Raleigh, April 29, 1821, and was advanced to the priesthood by the same prelate in St. James's Church, Wilmington, April 20, 1823. For four years Green was rector of St. John's Church, Williamsboro'. Removing to Hillsboro', he became rector of St. Matthew's Church, in which charge he remained until 1837, when his alma mater called him to the chair of belles-lettres and rhetoric, in which position he continued until his election to the episcopal office. In 1845 Green received the doctorate in divinity from he University of Pennsylvania.

He was consecrated to the episcopate of Mississippi, in St. Andrew's Church, Jackson, Miss., Feb. 24, 1850, by Bishops Otey, Polk, Cobbs, and Freeman. After a long and honored episcopate he "fell asleep," beloved and revered by all men, at his summer home at Sewanee, Tenn., Feb. 13, 1887. Few more saintly men have adorned the annals of the episcopate than Bishop Green. His life was a benediction and his memory lives in the hearts of his people.

WORKS.—1. "A Memoir of Bishop Ravenscroft"; 2. Occasional sermons, charges, addresses, pastorals.

RIGHT REVEREND JOHN PAYNE, D.D.

John Payne.

THE first missionary bishop of the American Church sent to Africa was a native of Virginia, where he was born, in Westmoreland County, Jan. 9, 1815.

He was graduated at the College of William and Mary, Williamsburg, Va., 1833, and in 1836 completed his theological course at the Theological Seminary of Virginia, near Alexandria. Having consecrated his life to the foreign missionary work, he was admitted to deacon's orders in Christ Church, Alexandria, July 17, 1836, by Bishop Channing Moore. He sailed directly for his chosen field, and prosecuted his missionary work for nearly five years ere returning to this country for ordination to the priesthood, and also for the restoration of his health, which had been undermined by the African climate. The bishop of Virginia, who had made him a deacon, conferred priest's orders upon him in St. George's Church, Fredericksburg, July 18, 1841. He returned at once to his mission field, where he remained until recalled by the Church for consecration to the missionary episcopate of Cape Palmas and parts adjacent. In 1851 his alma mater conferred upon him the degree of doctor of divinity.

Payne was consecrated in Christ Church, Alexandria, Va., July 11, 1851, by Bishops Meade, Eastburn, Lee, and Johns. Returning to Cape Palmas, he prosecuted his work with increased vigor until 1871, when, in failing health, he returned to the United States and resigned his missionary charge; which resignation was accepted with every recognition of the long and valued services rendered to the Church and in behalf of the race to whose service he had consecrated his life.

Payne died at his Virginia home in Westmoreland County (to which he had given the name of an African mission station very dear to his heart—Cavalla), after an honored and useful life, Oct. 23, 1874.

WORKS.—Missionary reports published from time to time in the "Spirit of Missions," and richly deserving of being collected and published in more permanent form.

RIGHT REVEREND FRANCIS HUGER RUTLEDGE, D.D.

Francis Huger Rutledge.

THE first bishop of the American Church in Florida was a native of Charleston, S. C., and was born April 11, 1799.

He was graduated at Yale, 1820, and completed his course of study for orders at the General Theological Seminary, New York. He was admitted to the diaconate in the parish church of Prince George, Winyaw, S. C., May 4, 1823, by Bishop Bowen, and received priest's orders from the hands of the same prelate in St. Paul's, Radcliffe, Nov. 20, 1825. The early years of his ministry were spent in Christ Church parish, in South Carolina. In 1827 he became incumbent of Grace Church, Sullivan's Island, having charge besides of St. Thomas's and St. Denis's. He remained in this arduous field of labor until 1839, when he removed to Florida to take charge of Trinity Church, St. Augustine. After six years' service in this cure, Rutledge, who had received his doctorate in divinity from Hobart College, 1844, removed to Tallahassee, where he became rector of St. John's Church. In this cure he continued until his election to the episcopate.

Rutledge was consecrated in St. Paul's, Augusta, Ga., Oct. 15, 1851, by Bishops Gadsden, Elliott, and Cobbs. After a laborious and self-denying episcopate he entered upon rest, Nov. 6, 1866, and was buried in the churchyard of Claremont parish, Stateburg, S. C.

WORKS.—Occasional sermons and episcopal addresses. The pastorals issued by Bishop Rutledge during the Civil War, and the prayers he set forth for use in his see, were so free from bitterness and so charitable in spirit as to be models of composition, most creditable to their author.

RIGHT REVEREND JOHN WILLIAMS, D.D., LL.D.

John Williams.

DESCENDED from a distinguished Puritan ancestry, John Williams was born in Deerfield, Mass., Aug. 30, 1817.

He was educated at Harvard, migrating before graduation to Trinity, where he took his degree, 1835. Of this institution he became tutor, professor, trustee, president, and chancellor.

He was admitted to deacon's orders in Christ Church, Middletown, Conn., Sept. 2, 1838, by Bishop Brownell, who advanced him to the priesthood in the same church, Sept. 26, 1841. His diaconate was spent at Christ Church. When priested he became rector of St. George's Church, Schenectady, N. Y. He received doctorates in divinity from Union, 1847, Trinity, 1849, Columbia, 1852, and Yale, 1883. Hobart conferred the doctorate of laws, 1870. His presidency of Trinity continued 1848–53.

Williams was consecrated to the coadjutor bishopric of Connecticut, Oct. 29, 1851, in St. John's Church, Hartford, by Bishops Brownell, Hopkins, Eastburn, Henshaw, Carlton Chase, Burgess, and De Lancey. He became bishop of Connecticut on the death of Brownell, and on the death of Alfred Lee became presiding bishop.

The administration of Bishop Williams has been marked by an almost unprecedented growth and development. With the purpose of providing a carefully trained and personally guided body of clergy representing the traditions of the see, he founded the Berkeley Divinity School at Middletown, of which he is still the honored head. He has not confined his labors to his see. By his writings, his scholarship, his culture, his gifts as an orator, his wise judgment and inflexible fairness, he is in every sense the most prominent prelate in the American Church. As a theologian he is conservative, and in full sympathy with the teachings of the post-Reformation Anglican doctors so far as they represent Catholic truth. He is a sympathetic counselor, and a judicious and experienced leader.

As the successor of Seabury, he visited England, 1884, assisting at the centennial observance of that bishop's consecration, and receiving many distinguished attentions.

WORKS.—He edited, in 1849, "Hawkstone," a tale in two volumes, "of and for England"; in 1851, with copious notes, Browne's "Exposition of the Thirty-nine Articles." His own writings are: 1. "A Translation of Ancient Hymns"; 2. "Thoughts on the Miracles"; 3. "Studies on the English Reformation" (the Paddock Lectures for 1881); 4. "The World's Testimony to Jesus Christ" (the Bedell Lectures for 1881); 5. "Studies in the Book of Acts" (1885); 6. "Syllabus for Ecclesiastical History" (1888); 7. Miscellaneous papers.

RIGHT REVEREND HENRY JOHN WHITEHOUSE, D.D., LL.D.

Henry John Whitehouse.

THE coadjutor to the aged Chase, and his successor in the see of Illinois, was born in New York, Aug. 19, 1803.

He was graduated at Columbia, 1821, and at the General Seminary, 1824. He was admitted to the diaconate in Grace Church, New York, Oct. 10, 1824, by Croes, acting for the bishop of New York, and was priested by White in Christ Church, Philadelphia, Aug. 26, 1827. He became rector of Christ Church, Reading, Pa., 1827, afterward holding the rectorship of St. Luke's, Rochester, N. Y., for fifteen years. He assumed charge of St. Thomas's, New York, 1844. He received his D.D. from Geneva, 1834, and an LL.D. from Columbia, 1865. Oxford conferred upon him the D.D., 1866, and on the occasion of the first Lambeth Conference, 1867, Cambridge gave him the LL.D.

Whitehouse was consecrated in St. George's Church, New York, Nov. 20, 1851, by Bishops Brownell, Alfred Lee, Eastburn, Hawks, A. Potter, G. Burgess, and J. Williams. On the death of Chase, 1852, he succeeded to the see of Illinois. He died Aug. 10, 1874.

Bishop Whitehouse was an excellent scholar, an eloquent preacher, and an inflexible administrator. He founded the Cathedral of SS. Peter and Paul, Chicago. It was largely due to him that the machinations of the disaffected section which finally resulted in the "Cummins' Schism" were in a measure rendered innocuous by the conviction and deposition of Cheney. The unpublished MSS. of this critical period prove that the full exposure and summary punishment of a leader in this intended disruption did much for the practical defeat of the conspirators.

Whitehouse took an active part in the preliminary measures attending the convening of the first Lambeth Conference, in recognition of which he was appointed preacher at the opening service.

At the General Convention at Baltimore, 1871, the last during his life, he made strenuous efforts to make the return of Cheney to the priesthood easy; the danger threatening the Church, which had occasioned the bishop's measures for upholding her discipline, having been averted.

WORKS.—Bishop Whitehouse's Convention addresses make up nearly a thousand octavo pages. Besides these, his occasional discourses, etc., are important contributions to the history of the times. The Lambeth sermon and another at the consecration of Bishop Pierce are noticeable productions.

RIGHT REVEREND JONATHAN MAYHEW WAINWRIGHT, D.D., D.C.L.

Jonathan Mayhew Wainwright.

WAINWRIGHT was born in Liverpool, England, Feb. 24, 1792.

He was graduated at Harvard, 1812, becoming a member of the faculty. He was admitted to deacon's orders by Griswold in Trinity Church, Boston, April 13, 1817, receiving the priesthood from Hobart in Christ Church, Hartford, May 29, 1818. After a brief service at Christ Church he became assistant minister of Trinity, New York, November, 1819. He was chosen rector of Grace, 1821, where he remained until 1834, when he accepted the rectorship of Trinity, Boston. He returned to New York, 1836, resuming his position at Trinity, being placed in charge of St. John's Chapel. He received his doctorate from Union, 1823, and from Harvard, 1835. He received, as secretary of the American House of Bishops, the honorary D.C.L. from Oxford, 1852.

Efforts to remit the sentence of Onderdonk having failed, special legislation to relieve the situation was taken in the General Convention of 1850, and on Nov. 10, 1852, in Trinity Church, New York, under the canon enacted for this purpose, Wainwright was consecrated provisional bishop of the diocese. The consecrators were Bishops Brownell, Doane, Kemper, De Lancey, Whittingham, C. Chase, A. Potter, Upfold, and J. Williams, and the Most Rev. Dr. Francis Fulford, bishop of Montreal and metropolitan. He died in New York, Sept. 21, 1854.

The first provisional bishop of New York was a critical scholar, a conservative and high-minded clergyman, a well-read theologian and canonist, and a polished gentleman. His life was devoted to his calling, and his sympathetic aid was ever extended to Church and individual needs.

WORKS.— 1. "Four Sermons on Religious Education and Filial Duty" (1829); 2. "Lessons on the Church"; 3. "Order of Family Prayer" (1845; reprinted frequently and still in use); 4. "Short Family Prayers" (1850); 5. "The Pathways and Abiding-places of our Lord" (4to, 1851); 6. "The Land of Bondage: Its Ancient Monuments and Present Condition" (4to, 1852).

Wainwright edited an illustrated *édition de luxe* of the Book of Common Prayer, used in the preparation of the critical "Standard" of 1844. He edited "A Book of Chants, Adapted to the Morning and Evening Service of the Church" (1819), and a volume entitled "The Music of the Church" (1828). In connection with Muhlenberg he edited "The Choir and Family Psalter" (1851). He was the editor of Bishop Ravenscroft's "Memoir and Sermons," and of an American reprint of the "Life of Bishop Heber." After his decease a memorial volume of sermons, thirty-four in number, was published by his widow, 1856.

RIGHT REVEREND THOMAS FREDERICK DAVIS, D.D.

Thomas Frederick Davis.

A NATIVE of North Carolina, born at Wilmington, Feb. 8, 1804, and graduated at the university of the State, at Chapel Hill, 1822, Davis was ordained to the diaconate in St. James's Church, of the city of his birth, Nov. 27, 1831, by Bishop Ives, and was priested by the same bishop in St. Bartholomew's Church, Pittsboro', Chatham County, Dec. 16, 1832.

His diaconate was spent at Pittsboro' and Wadesboro'. He was subsequently rector of St. James's, Wilmington, and of St. Luke's, Salisbury. In November, 1846, he became rector of Grace Church, Camden, S. C. On his election to the episcopate of South Carolina he received his doctorate in divinity from Columbia College, New York, and from the University of North Carolina.

His consecration took place in St. John's Chapel, New York, Oct. 17, 1853, by Bishops Brownell, Hopkins, Bosworth Smith, McIlvaine, and Doane, together with the bishop of Jamaica, W. I., Dr. Aubrey George Spencer, and the bishop of Fredericton, N. B., Dr. John Medley. Bishop Davis, after a faithful and laborious episcopate, died at Camden, S. C., Dec. 2, 1871.

WORKS.—Addresses, occasional sermons, and pastorals.

RIGHT REVEREND THOMAS ATKINSON, D.D., LL.D.

Thomas Atkinson.

BORN in Dinwiddie County, Va., Aug. 6, 1807, and educated in part at Yale, but graduating at Hampden Sidney College, Prince Edward County, Va., Atkinson, on leaving college, first studied law.

After nine years' practice in his profession he began a course of preparation for the ministry, and was admitted to the diaconate by Bishop Meade in Christ Church, Norfolk, Va., Nov. 18, 1836. He was advanced to the priesthood in St. Paul's, Norfolk, May 7, 1837, by Bishop Channing Moore. His ministerial service began at Norfolk, where he served for a short time as an assistant minister. For two years he was rector of St. Paul's, Norfolk. He then accepted the rectorship of St. Paul's, Lynchburg, where he continued in charge for nearly five years. In 1843 he became the rector of St. Peter's, Baltimore; and in 1852 he accepted the charge of Grace Church in the same city, where he remained until his election to the episcopate. In 1846 he received the doctorate in divinity from Trinity College, and in 1862 the University of North Carolina conferred upon him the doctorate of laws. He received the same degree from the University of Cambridge, England, on the occasion of his visit to England to attend the Lambeth Conference of 1867.

Dr. Atkinson's consecration to the see of North Carolina took place in St. John's Chapel, New York, Oct. 17, 1853. His consecrators were Bishops Brownell, McIlvaine, Doane, Otey, together with the Rt. Rev. Dr. George J. Trevor Spencer, some time bishop of Madras, and the bishop of Fredericton, Dr. Medley.

Bishop Atkinson died at Wilmington, N. C., Jan. 4, 1881. He had participated in the measures taken during the Civil War for the organization of the Church in the Confederate States; but at the close of the strife he was one of the first to return to the Union, and to find a hearty welcome from his brethren and friends. He was a preacher of unusual eloquence, a devout and holy man, one whose life was consecrated and whose end was peace.

WORKS.—1. Sermons on special occasions, lectures, charges, etc.; 2. A charge on "Sacramental Confession"; 3. A pamphlet in reply to criticism of the Roman Catholic bishop of Richmond, Va., of the above charge.

RIGHT REVEREND WILLIAM INGRAHAM KIP, D.D., LL.D.

William Ingraham Kip.

THE first bishop of the American Church consecrated for California was born in New York, Oct. 3, 1811.

He entered Rutgers College, New Brunswick, N. J., but shortly migrated to Yale, where he was graduated, 1831. After entering upon the study of law, he began his preparation for holy orders at the Virginia Theological Seminary, 1832. The following year he entered the General Theological Seminary, where he was graduated, 1835.

Kip received deacon's orders from Bishop B. T. Onderdonk, June 28, 1835, in St. John's Church, Brooklyn, N. Y., and was advanced to the priesthood by Bishop Doane in St. Peter's, Morristown, N. J., Oct. 20, 1835. His successive charges were Morristown, 1835–36; assistant at Grace Church, New York, 1836–37; and rector of St. Paul's Church, Albany, N. Y., 1837–53. He received the doctorate in divinity from Columbia, 1847, and was made a doctor of laws by Yale, 1872.

His consecration as missionary bishop of California took place in Trinity Church, New York, Oct. 28, 1853. His consecrators were Bishops Kemper, Boone, Alfred Lee, Freeman, George Burgess, Upfold, Whitehouse, and Wainwright. Proceeding to his distant see, Kip gave himself so successfully to his labors that, 1857, he was chosen by the Convention of the diocese to the episcopate of the see, which now took its place among the confederation of dioceses.

He was a polished writer, an eloquent speaker, a man of wide culture, a careful historian, a skilful polemic. His life was largely a sacrifice, for his tastes were not specially fitting for pioneer work among "gold-diggers." But having put his hand to the plow he never looked back; and a noble diocese is the full proof of his faithful episcopate. He died in San Francisco, April 7, 1893, full of years and honors.

WORKS.—1. "The History, Object, and Proper Observance of the Holy Season of Lent" (1843); 2. "Early Jesuit Missions in North America" (1846); 3. "Christmas Holidays at Rome" (1860); 4. "The Unnoticed Things of Scripture" (1865); 5. "The Catacombs of Rome"; 6. "The Double Witness of the Church"; 7. "The Early Conflicts of Christianity"; 8. "New York in the Olden Time"; 9. "Historical Scenes in the Old Jesuit Missions" (1875); 10. "The Church of the Apostles" (1877); 11. "The Early Days of My Episcopate" (1892); 12. Charges: (1) "Lay Coöperation"; (2) "The Characteristics of the Age"; 13. Addresses, pastorals, etc. Nearly all these have passed through numerous editions and are still read.

RIGHT REVEREND THOMAS FIELDING SCOTT, D.D.

Thomas Fielding Scott.

THE first missionary bishop sent to the northern Pacific coast, with jurisdiction including Oregon and Washington Territories, was a native of North Carolina, where he was born in Iredel County, March 12, 1807.

He was graduated at Franklin College (subsequently the University of Georgia), Athens, 1829.

Scott received the diaconate at the age of thirty-six, in St. Paul's Church, Augusta, March 12, 1843, from Bishop Stephen Elliott. The same bishop advanced him to the priesthood, Feb. 24, 1844, in Christ Church, Macon. His rectorates were successively St. James's, Marietta, Ga., and Trinity, Columbus. His alma mater conferred upon him the doctorate in divinity, 1853.

He was consecrated missionary bishop of the Territories of Oregon and Washington in Christ Church, Savannah, Jan. 8, 1854, by Bishops Elliott, Cobbs, and Davis. After a laborious and exhausting service at the remote frontier, Bishop Scott, while on a visit to the Atlantic coast, died in the city of New York, July 14, 1867, and was interred in Trinity cemetery. He was a man of great holiness of life and singular devotion to his work.

WORKS.—The annual reports to the Board of Missions, with a few occasional discourses and episcopal addresses, pastorals, etc.

RIGHT REVEREND HENRY WASHINGTON LEE, D.D., LL.D.

Henry Washington Lee.

THE diocese of Iowa formed a part of the vast jurisdiction of the apostolic Kemper for only a few years. It had received three visitations from him, when its few clergy organized a diocese.

The first bishop of Iowa was born in Hamden, Conn., July 29, 1815. After completing a course of study at the Episcopal Academy of Connecticut, at Cheshire, Lee removed to Taunton, Mass., where he opened a private school, which he kept up until ready for ordination. He was admitted to the diaconate in Grace Church, New Bedford, Mass., May 27, 1838, by Griswold, who advanced him to the priesthood in St. Anne's Church, Lowell, Oct. 9. 1839. He served, during his diaconate, at New Bedford; then became rector of Christ Church, Springfield, Mass., April 2, 1840. He entered upon the charge of St. Luke's, Rochester, N. Y., 1843. He received the doctorate in divinity from Hobart, 1850, and from the University of Rochester, 1852. At the first Lambeth Conference, 1867, Cambridge gave him the LL.D.

Lee was raised to the episcopate in St. Luke's, Rochester, Oct. 18, 1854, by Bishops Hopkins, McCoskry, George Burgess, De Lancey, Eastburn, and Whitehouse. After an episcopate of nearly twenty years, he died at Davenport, Ia., Sept. 26, 1874.

The first bishop of Iowa laid broad and deep foundations. He founded Griswold College, opened in 1859; secured the Episcopate Fund of upward of fifty thousand dollars; built the Bishops' House and Cathedral; obtained endowments for the diocesan college and theological school, and traversed the vast extent of a territory larger than all of England, doing the work of an evangelist and of an apostle. He saw the diocese he had found in utter feebleness take its stand among the leading sees of the middle West, and he died in the midst of plans and purposes for its further development. His theological views were "Evangelical," but he was broad and tolerant. He spared neither himself nor his own for his people's good.

WORKS.—1. Several Sunday-school books, which attained great popularity; 2. "Family Prayers" (frequently reprinted); 3. "Convention Addresses," detailing the progress of the Church in Iowa and Kansas, of which latter he held for a time the provisional oversight. His charges were thoughtful contributions to the theological literature of the day. An ardent "patriot" during the Civil War, his pastorals breathe a spirit of devotion to his country.

RIGHT REVEREND HORATIO POTTER, D.D., LL.D., D.C.L.

Horatio Potter.

A YOUNGER brother of the distinguished bishop of Pennsylvania, ᐧratio Potter was born in Beekman, Dutchess County, N. Y., Feb. 9, 1802.

He was graduated at Union College, 1826. He was ordered d. acon by Bishop Hobart, July 15, 1827, in Christ Church, Poughkeepsie, N. Y., and was priested by Bishop Brownell in Christ Church, Hartford, Conn., Dec. 14, 1828. His diaconate was spent at Trinity Church, Saco, Me. The following year he was appointed to tł e chair of mathematics and natural philosophy in Washington College (now Trinity). In 1833 he became rector of St. Peter's, Albany, N. Y., where he remained until chosen to the provisional episcopate of his native State. He received the doctorate in divinity from Trinity, 1838; the doctorate of laws from Hobart, 1856; and the D.C.L. from the University of Oxford, 1860.

Acting under the permissive legislation of the Church assembled in General Convention, and in succession to the lamented Wainwright, whose administration had been terminated all too soon, Potter was consecrated provisional bishop of New York in Trinity Church, Nov. 22, 1854. His consecrators were Bishops Brownell, Hopkins, Doane, McCoskry, Whittingham, Eastburn, Alonzo Potter, Williams, Whitehouse, H. W. Lee, and the bishop of Montreal, Dr. Fulford. On the decease of Onderdonk, in 1861, Potter became the diocesan bishop of New York. He died Jan. 2, 1887, his nephew, Dr. Henry Codman Potter, having been for some years his coadjutor in the episcopal office. His administration had been impartial, vigorous, and successful. In the midst of controversy, and with the environment of much of partizan feeling and strife, the Church grew and converts were multiplied.

WORKS.—1. "Introductory Sermon at St. Peter's, Albany" (1833); 2. "Intellectual Liberty: A Discourse" (1837); 3. "Lecture before the Young Men's Association of Troy" (1837); 4. "Sermon on the Death of President W. H. Harrison" (1841); 5. "Religious Tendencies of the Age" (1844); 6. "Rules for Fasting" (1846); 7. "Submission to Government the Christian's Duty" (1848); 8. "Stability of the Church as Seen in her History and Principles" (1848); 9. "Sermon on the Death of Hon. Jesse A. Spencer" (1849); 10. "Sermon on the Death of President Taylor" (1850); 11. "Duties of Justice" (1852); 12. Charges, addresses, pastorals, and pamphlets of various kinds.

RIGHT REVEREND THOMAS MARCH CLARK, D.D., LL.D.

Thomas March Clark.

THE successor of the amiable and devoted Henshaw in the see of Rhode Island was born in Newburyport, Mass., July 4, 1812.

He was graduated at Yale, 1831. He studied theology at Princeton, 1833–35, and on the completion of his course was licensed to preach by the Presbytery of his native place. Turning his attention to the Church, he applied to the apostolic Griswold for orders, and was made a deacon in Grace Church, Boston, Feb. 3, 1836, and was advanced to the priesthood in the same church and by the same bishop, Nov. 6, 1836. The first years of his ministry (1836–43) were spent at Grace Church, Boston, where he remained until his removal to Philadelphia to become the rector of St. Andrew's Church in that city. After a few years' service in that important charge (1843–47) he returned to Boston, and was for a time (1847–50) assistant minister of Trinity Church. Removing to Hartford, Conn., to take the rectorate of Christ Church, Clark remained in this cure (1850–54) until his election to the episcopal office. He received the doctorate in divinity from Union, 1851, and from Brown, 1860. At the Lambeth Conference of 1867 the University of Cambridge conferred upon him the doctorate of laws.

Clark was consecrated in Grace Church, Providence, Dec. 6, 1854, by Bishops Brownell, Hopkins, Doane, Eastburn, Southgate, Burgess, Williams, H. W. Lee, and H. Potter. On entering upon his see he became rector of Grace Church, Providence (1854–66), holding that cure for twelve years. The fortieth anniversary of his consecration was celebrated by the clergy and laity of the diocese and by the community at large, 1894. It attested the grateful sense of an attached people of the privileges and blessings of a successful episcopate. Bishop Clark's administration has been a period of growth and development. Tolerant, faithful, earnest, eloquent, a charming writer, a well-read scholar, an able administrator of affairs, his episcopate will ever be a memorable one in the annals of the Rhode Island Church.

WORKS.—1. "Lectures to Young Men on the Formation of Character" (1852); 2. "The Efficient Sunday-school Teacher" (1869); 3. "Primary Truths of Religion" (1869); 4. "Readings and Prayers for Aid in Private Devotion" (1888); 5. "Reminiscences" (1895); 6. Four episcopal charges, occasional sermons, addresses, pastoral letters, etc.

RIGHT REVEREND SAMUEL BOWMAN, D.D.

Samuel Bowman.

SAMUEL BOWMAN was born at Wilkesbarre, Pa., May 21, 1800. His early education was carried on under private instructors, while his theological studies were pursued under the direction of the venerable Bishop White. He received the diaconate and priesthood at the hands of this prelate, the first in Christ Church, Philadelphia, Aug. 14, 1823, and the latter in St. James's Church, in the same city, Dec. 19, 1824. His first ministrations were in Lancaster County, where he had charge of two congregations. In 1825 he became rector of Trinity Church, Easton, Pa. Returning to his former field of labor in 1827, he became the assistant to the venerable Rev. Joseph Clarkson, the first on whom Bishop White laid hands in ordination; and on the death of this excellent man, in 1830, he became rector of St. James's parish, Lancaster, continuing in this charge till his death. He received the doctorate in divinity from Geneva College in 1843. In 1847 he was elected bishop of Indiana, but declined the appointment.

Bowman received consecration as coadjutor bishop of Pennsylvania in Christ Church, Philadelphia, Aug. 25, 1858. His consecrators were Bishops Kemper, De Lancey, Alfred Lee, John Williams, and Horatio Potter. The new coadjutor threw himself heartily and with all his physical strength into the work of the see. His episcopate was brief, but fruitful in every good work. While on a series of visitations in the western portion of the State the destruction of a railroad-bridge by a land-slide (Aug. 3, 1861) compelled the bishop and other travelers by the train to take a walk of several miles. Lingering behind the rest of the passengers, he "fell asleep" by the way, "wearied with the march of life." Found lying on his face by the roadside, his body was tenderly cared for by kind hands, and was laid to rest in the churchyard at Lancaster, among the graves of his parishioners and friends.

WORKS.—A single occasional sermon, with the annual addresses to the Convention, are all of the literary remains of Bishop Bowman which have come to our knowledge.

RIGHT REVEREND ALEXANDER GREGG, D.D.

Alexander Gregg.

BORN at Society Hill, Darlington District, S. C., Oct. 8, 1819. Gregg was graduated at South Carolina College, 1838, and studied law, securing a wide practice in the northeastern circuit of the State.

He was baptized and confirmed in St. David's Church, Cheraw, S. C., 1843, and entered upon a course of study for holy orders. He was admitted to the diaconate in the church of his baptism, June 10, 1846, by Bishop Gadsden, who advanced him to the priesthood in St. Philip's Church, Charleston, Dec. 19, 1847. His sole ministerial charge was that of St. David's, Cheraw. His alma mater conferred upon him the doctorate in divinity, 1859.

Gregg was consecrated first bishop of Texas in the Monumental Church, Richmond, Va., Oct. 13, 1859, during the session of the General Convention. His consecrators were Bishops Hopkins, Bosworth Smith, Otey, Polk, Elliott, Green, Davis, and Atkinson. In 1874 his vast see, territorially sufficient for a college of apostles, was divided by the setting off of two missionary jurisdictions, which were committed to the care of bishops of their own. He continued in the full exercise of his apostolic work until July 11, 1893, when, after a long and trying illness, he fell asleep. His administration had been judicious, devoted, and abounding in self-denying labors. He was a man of strong intellectual powers, a graceful writer, a careful and accurate historian, and of unusual energy and force. He has left his impress on the great State which received him as her first bishop and remembers in love and gratitude his devout and devoted life.

WORKS.—1. "Relations of Master and Slave" (a convocation essay, 1852); 2. "The Scarcity of Clergymen, the Causes and Remedy" (a Convention sermon, 1856); 3. "An Account of the First Meeting of the University of the South" (1857); 4. "Perils and Duties of a Time of War" (1861); 5. "Proper Improvement of Victory in War" (1862); 6. "The Sin of Extortion" (1862); 7. "Eulogy on Hemphill and McLeod," (delivered in the House of Representatives, Austin, 1862); 8. Triennial charge on the "Relations of Church and State" (1862); 9. Second triennial charge, "Relations of the Church to the Church of Rome" (1865); 10. (With Rev. C. Gillette) "A Few Historic Records of the Church in the Diocese of Texas during the Rebellion" (1865); 11. "History of the Old Cheraws" (8vo, 1867).

RIGHT REVEREND WILLIAM HENRY ODENHEIMER, D.D., D.C.L.

William Henry Odenheimer.

THE third bishop of the Church in New Jersey was a native of Philadelphia, and was born Aug. 11, 1817.

He was graduated at the University of Pennsylvania, 1835. He was admitted to the diaconate by Bishop H. U. Onderdonk, Sept. 2, 1838, in St. Paul's Church, Philadelphia, and was ordained to the priesthood by the same bishop in St. Peter's Church, Oct. 3, 1841. His sole ministerial charge was St. Peter's Church. The University of Pennsylvania conferred upon him the doctorate in divinity, 1856.

Odenheimer was consecrated bishop of New Jersey in St. Paul's Church, Richmond, Va., Oct. 13, 1859, by Bishops Meade, McCoskry, Whittingham, Alfred Lee, Carlton Chase, Hawks, Alonzo Potter, and John Williams. His episcopate was eminently successful. He carried on with great vigor the many Church activities set in motion by his great predecessor, and had the satisfaction of seeing the see of New Jersey divided into two dioceses, of which he chose that of Northern New Jersey. He was an excellent scholar, energetic, active, and tireless in his episcopal work, as he had been during his rectorship; and he lived and died beloved of all men. He entered into rest at "Riverside," Burlington, N. J., Aug. 14, 1879, and his remains lie in the historic churchyard of St. Mary's in that town.

WORKS.—"Origin and Compilation of the Prayer-book"; 2. "The True Catholic no Romanist" (1842); 3. "Thoughts on Immersion"; 4. "The Young Churchman Catechized" (two parts); 5. "The Devout Churchman's Companion"; 6. "The Private Prayer-book"; 7. "Bishop White's Opinions"; 8. "The Clergyman's Assistant"; 9. Three charges: (1) "The Sacred Scriptures, the Inspired Record of the Glory of the Holy Trinity"; (2) "The Church's Power in her Controversy with Antichrist"; (3) "Canon Law," (1847) a volume of his sermons, with an introductory memoir by his widow, appeared in 1881.

Bishop Odenheimer's essay on canon law, prepared for the alumni of the General Theological Seminary, was the first contribution to this important subject published in the American Church. He also edited, with prefatory matter, Ringelbergius on "Study," and prepared, with F. M. Bird, "Songs of the Spirit" (1871).

RIGHT REVEREND GREGORY THURSTON BEDELL, D.D.

Gregory Thurston Bedell.

BEDELL was born in Hudson, N. Y., Aug. 27, 1817.

He was graduated at Bristol College, Pennsylvania, 1836, and, after a year spent in teaching, entered the Theological Seminary of Virginia, where he completed his course, 1840. He was admitted to the diaconate by his great-uncle, Bishop Channing Moore, in his father's church, St. Andrew's, Philadelphia, July 19, 1840. The same bishop advanced him to the priesthood in Holy Trinity Church, West Chester, Pa., Aug. 29, 1841. His first charge was that of the latter church, from which, 1843, he removed to the Church of the Ascension, New York. He received the doctorate in divinity from Norwich University, Vermont, 1856.

His consecration as coadjutor bishop of Ohio took place in St. Paul's Church, Richmond, Va., Oct. 13, 1859. The consecrators were Bishops Meade, McIlvaine, Johns, Eastburn, Upfold, Rutledge, Horatio Potter, and Payne. Upon the death of McIlvaine his coadjutor became the diocesan of Ohio. The see was divided, 1875, and the diocese of Southern Ohio created, Bedell retaining the northern part.

In October, 1889, he resigned his jurisdiction, in consequence of physical infirmities. This resignation was accepted with great reluctance. He died in New York, March 11, 1892.

Bedell was an "Evangelical" by inheritance and choice. His father, the celebrated rector of St. Andrew's, Philadelphia, was a distinguished representative of that party, and throughout his life the bishop was a consistent exponent of the principles he had adopted. His episcopate was abundant in labors and successful in results.

WORKS.—1. "The Divinity of Christ" (1848); 2. "Individual Responsibility for Missions to the Heathen" (1848); 3. "The Baptismal Renunciation" (1848); 4 "The Present Profit of Godliness" (1852); 5. "The Sacredness of the Grave" (1854); 6. "The Adaptation of Christianity to Man" (1854); 7. "Funeral Sermon on the Death of the Rev. David Moore, D.D." (1856); 8. "Fellow-workers" (1858); 9. Two sermons: "The Elements" and "The Basis of Parochial Strength" (1859); 10. "The Trusteeship of the Gospel" (1864); 11. "The Victories of the Reformation," etc. (1869); 12. "The Age of Indifference" (1871); 13. "Episcopacy, a Fact and a Law" (1872); 14. "Memorial Sermon on Bishop Auer" (1874); 15. "Woman's Work and Foreign Missions" (1877); 16. "The Church a Teacher" (1877); 17. "Canterbury Pilgrimage" (1878); 18. "The Pastor" (1878).

Besides these sermons he edited several tracts written by his father, and issued numerous parochial tractates. His pastoral on "Ritual Uniformity" (1874), his primary charge on "The Personal Presence of the Holy Spirit" (1874), and his "Notes on the Oriental Churches" (1875), were among his later contributions to Church literature. This list is not exhaustive. (See "Memoirs.")

RIGHT REVEREND HENRY BENJAMIN WHIPPLE, D.D.

Henry Benjamin Whipple.

BORN at Adams, Jefferson County, N. Y., Feb. 15, 1822, and in early life engaged in business and politics, Henry Benjamin Whipple, on turning his attention to consider the claims of personal religion, "forsook all, and followed Christ."

Acting in accordance with the advice of Bishop De Lancey, he became a candidate for holy orders, and was ordered deacon in Trinity Church, Geneva, N. Y., Aug. 17, 1849. The same bishop advanced him to the priesthood in Christ Church, Sackett's Harbor, N. Y., July 16, 1850. After a rectorate of seven years at Zion Church, Rome, N. Y., in the spring of 1857 he became rector of the Church of the Holy Communion, Chicago, where he remained until elected to the episcopate.

He was consecrated first bishop of Minnesota in St. James's Church, Richmond, Va., Oct. 13, 1859, by Bishops Kemper, De Lancey, Cobbs, George Burgess, Whitehouse, Scott, H. W. Lee, Clark, and Bowman. At the third Lambeth Conference, in 1888, he received from the University of Cambridge the degree of LL.D. At this gathering of the bishops he preached the opening sermon in Lambeth Chapel, and as the senior American bishop in attendance, and in view of his distinguished reputation, was the recipient of every attention.

Bishop Whipple's administration has been marked by the successful work he has undertaken among the Indians, which has won for him the title of the "Apostle to the Red Men." He has made Faribault, the seat of the diocesan institutions, a center of culture and Churchly training renowned throughout the Church. St. Mary's Hall for girls, Shattuck Hall for boys, Seabury Hall, the theological school for the trans-Mississippi bishops and sees, have been founded by this great-hearted bishop, and owe much of their extraordinary success to his fostering care. The diocese has grown and prospered under his administration, and his episcopate will ever be regarded as the golden age of the Minnesota Church.

WORKS.—1. Convention sermon (Illinois); 2. Episcopal addresses; 3. "Indian Papers and Reports"; 4. Consecration sermons (first bishop of Nebraska and third bishop of Wisconsin); 5. Sermon in Lambeth Chapel. A volume of his sermons has been published, comprising some of the above.

RIGHT REVEREND HENRY CHAMPLIN LAY, D.D., LL.D.

Henry Champlin Lay.

BORN in Richmond, Va., Dec. 6, 1823, Henry Champlin Lay was graduated at the University of Virginia, 1842, and completed his preparatory course for holy orders at the Theological Seminary of Virginia, 1846.

He was admitted to deacon's orders in Christ Church, Alexandria, July 10, 1846, by Bishop Meade. After serving as deacon for half a year at Lynnhaven parish, he removed to Alabama and entered upon the charge of the Church of the Nativity, Huntsville. In this church Bishop Cobbs advanced him to priest's orders, July 12, 1848. He received the doctorate in divinity from Hobart College, 1857, and from the College of William and Mary, 1873. Cambridge conferred upon him the degree of LL.D., 1867.

He was consecrated to the missionary episcopate of Arkansas and the Indian Territory in St. Paul's Church, Richmond, Va., Oct. 23, 1859, by Bishops Meade, McIlvaine, Polk, De Lancey, Whittingham, Elliott, Cobbs, and Atkinson. During the Civil War Lay became the diocesan of Arkansas, but on the return of peace the old order was reëstablished. In 1868 the see of Easton was created out of that portion of Maryland lying east of the Chesapeake Bay and the Susquehanna River, and Lay was translated to its charge, April 1, 1869. He died in Baltimore, Sept. 17, 1885, and was buried at Spring Hill Cemetery, in his own diocese.

Lay was deeply interested in the revision movement out of which grew the "Standard of 1892." He was a most faithful and acceptable missionary bishop, and in his diocesan work showed no abatement of zeal. A well-read theologian, a logical controversialist, an earnest and acceptable preacher, and a devout man of God, he was beloved and respected of all men.

WORKS.—1. "Letters to a Man Bewildered among Many Counselors"; 2. "Tracts for Missionary Use" (2 vols.); 3. "Studies in the Church" (1872); 4. "The Lord and His Basket" (a missionary address); 5. "Church in the Nation" (Bishop Paddock Lectures, 1885). To these titles should be added missionary reports, occasional sermons, and papers on "Social Science," published from time to time. His sermons of special note were: 1. "Fidelity to Truth" (1860); 2. "Missionary Success" (1866); 3. "Our Lord a Pattern to Bishops" (1868); 4. "The Man of Business" (1870); 5. "Longings after Unity" (1873).

RIGHT REVEREND JOSEPH CRUIKSHANK TALBOT, D.D., LL.D.

Joseph Cruikshank Talbot.

THE successor of Kemper and Upfold in the episcopal oversight of Indiana was a native of Virginia, and was born at Alexandria, Sept. 5, 1816.

Educated at the Pierpont Academy of his native city, he removed to Kentucky in 1835, and spent several years in business life in Louisville. In 1837 he received baptism in Christ Church, and was confirmed by Bishop Smith the same year. In 1841 he began his course of preparation for holy orders, and Sept. 5, 1846, he was made a deacon in Christ Church, Louisville, by Bishop Bosworth Smith. Sept. 6, 1848, the same bishop gave him priest's orders in St. John's Church in the same city. He had organized St. John's Church during his diaconate, and on his receiving the priesthood he continued in its charge for about seven years. In 1853 he removed to Indiana, and continued in charge of Christ Church, Indianapolis, until set apart for the work of a missionary bishop. The Western University of Pennsylvania, Pittsburg, Pa., conferred upon him the doctorate in divinity in 1854, and the University of Cambridge, England, gave him an LL.D. on occasion of the Lambeth Conference in 1867.

In 1859 the Church in General Convention elected Talbot to the missionary episcopate of the Northwest, a jurisdiction of almost limitless extent, embracing the present States and Territories of Nebraska, the Dakotas, Wyoming, Colorado, New Mexico, Arizona, Utah, Montana, and Idaho. He was consecrated in Christ Church, Indianapolis, Feb. 15, 1860, by Bishops Kemper, Bosworth Smith, Hawks, Upfold, and Bedell. In 1865, after faithful service in the Northwest, Talbot was elected coadjutor to the diocesan of Indiana, and his translation took place the same year. On Upfold's decease he became bishop of the see. He died at Indianapolis, Jan. 15, 1883.

Bishop Talbot was a man of great energy, of pleasing address, of marked executive ability, and of unusual devotion to work. He is lovingly remembered throughout the vast extent of territory to which he ministered in holy things; and his works follow him.

WORKS.—Occasional sermons, addresses, missionary reports, pastorals, and other official papers.

RIGHT REVEREND WILLIAM BACON STEVENS, D.D., LL.D.

William Bacon Stevens.

THE son of a United States officer in the War of 1812, and the grandson of a Revolutionary veteran, William Bacon Stevens was born in Bath, Me., July 13, 1815.

After completing his classical studies in Phillips Academy, Andover, in preparation for entering college, failure of health compelled him to travel abroad for two years, during which time he circumnavigated the globe, spending six months in the Sandwich Islands, where he devoted himself to a thorough investigation of the customs and religious beliefs of the people. He then spent six months in China, where he gave his services in connection with Sir Peter Parker's hospital work among the people of Canton. Returning with a measure of health, he pursued a course in medicine, and received his degree from Dartmouth College, Hanover, N. H., and on deciding to make his home at the South, repeated his course of study with special reference to the needs of Southern practice, receiving an *ad eundem* M.D. degree from the Medical College of South Carolina.

It was while in Charleston and engaged in his medical study that he formed the acquaintance with the first bishop of China, Dr. W. J. Boone, which resulted in a lifelong friendship, and which was among the earliest influences drawing him to the Church. Entering upon practice in Savannah, Ga., he pursued his calling with distinguished success for nearly five years, taking special interest in many matters outside of his profession, and receiving in 1841 the appointment of historian of the State of Georgia. Shortly after this recognition of his historical tastes and scholarly attainments he relinquished a lucrative practice and began a course of study for the sacred ministry under the direction of his friend and bishop, Dr. Stephen Elliott. On Feb. 26, 1843, he was admitted to the diaconate in Christ Church, Savannah, by Bishop Elliott, who advanced him to the "higher degree," Jan. 7, 1844, in the same historic church. Elected professor of belles-lettres, oratory, and moral philosophy in the University of Georgia, at Athens, in 1844, he organized Emmanuel Church in that collegiate town, and continued in the exercise of his professorial and rectoral duties until his election to St. Andrew's, Philadelphia, in 1848. He had been a deputy from Georgia to the General Convention the preceding year (1847), and received from the University of Pennsylvania the doctorate in divinity the year of his removal to the North (1848). In 1862 Union College conferred upon him the degree of LL.D. While in Italy in 1866–67 on account of his health, he was informed by his friend, the Rev. Thomas Bosworth, D.D., the distinguished Anglo-Saxon scholar and writer, that the University of Oxford had passed the "act" granting him the degree of D.D.; but his state of health prevented his presence at the encænia.

It was on the sudden demise of Dr. Bowman, the coadjutor of Bishop Alonzo Potter, that Dr. Stevens was chosen to the assistant bishopric of the diocese of Pennsylvania. His consecration took place in St. Andrew's Church, Philadelphia, Jan. 2, 1862. His consecrators were Bishops Hopkins, Alonzo Potter, Horatio Potter, Alfred Lee, Clark, H. W. Lee, and Odenheimer. In 1865 Bishop Stevens, on the death of Bishop Alonzo Potter, became diocesan of Pennsylvania.

During Bishop Stevens's episcopate the see of Pennsylvania was twice divided, the diocese of Pittsburg having been formed in 1865, and the diocese of Central Pennsylvania in 1871. In 1868 Bishop Stevens was appointed by the presiding bishop to take charge of the foreign churches connected with the American Church established on the continent of Europe, which position he held for six years, making extensive visitations throughout his charge, and rendering an exhaustive and most interesting report of the work which had been already done and the prospective openings awaiting the further efforts of the Church in the United States in this important field. Bishop Stevens's connection with the temporary chapel and church work at the first Paris Exposition, and his founding of the American Episcopal Church in Paris, as well as his efforts in behalf of the various reform movements on the Continent, are noteworthy events in an episcopate of almost invariable success. Alive to the needs and opportunities of the Church on the continent of Europe, Bishop Stevens also displayed a fervent zeal for the foreign missionary work, which made him a leader in all the general missionary operations of the Church abroad.

In the Church's educational work the bishop was equally interested and successful. The noble foundation of Lehigh University, by the Hon. Robert Packer, was made through him, and the institution was shaped in accordance with his advice. The Divinity School at West Philadelphia received large gifts through his influence, and was an object of his fostering care. The Episcopal Hospital had in him an intelligent adviser, an enthusiastic friend, and a hearty supporter; while numerous other charitable organizations and institutions claim him as founder and friend. He was an eloquent speaker, an impressive preacher, a charming writer, a man of courtly manners and of great affability. He was a careful student, a well-read theologian, deeply interested in all humanitarian measures, and preëminently a man of God. His more than a quarter-century of episcopal service will ever be remembered as a period of unprecedented Church growth, of which he was largely the inspirer, and ever the competent and interested director. His devotion to the study of God's Word, his habits of private prayer, his consecration of every moment of life to his Master's service, made him an apostle indeed, full of the Holy Ghost, the "angel" of the Church under his charge.

Bishop Stevens died in Philadelphia, June 11, 1887, and was buried in the churchyard of St. James the Less, in that city.

WORKS.—1. "Discourse before the Georgia Historical Society" (1841); 2. "History of Silk-culture in Georgia" (1841); 3. "History of Georgia" (2 vols., 1847, 1861); 4. "Parables of the New Testament Practically Unfolded" (1855); 5. "Consolation: The Bow in the Cloud" (1855); 6. "Home Service" (1856); 7. "The Lord's Day: Its Obligations and Blessings"; 8. "Past and Present of St. Andrew's, Philadelphia"; 9. "The Sabbaths of our Lord" (1872); 10. A volume of sermons (1879); 11. Discourses printed abroad and at home; 12. Charges, pastoral letters, episcopal addresses, funeral, patriotic, and occasional sermons, tracts, reviews, pamphlets, etc.

He edited the first and second volumes of the "Georgia Historical Society Collections," and wrote the preface to the same. The bishop's sermon at St. Paul's Cathedral, London, at the close of the Lambeth Conference of 1878, and published in London and in this country, elicited the fullest commendations of all who heard it, and is a discourse of lasting value. The Memorial edition of his "Parables" (1887) contains a sketch of the author's life.

Richd H. Wilmer

Richard Hooker Wilmer.

THE second bishop of Alabama was born at Alexandria, Va., March 15, 1816.

He was graduated at Yale, 1836, and completed the course of study preparatory to ordination at the Virginia Theological Seminary, 1839. He was admitted to deacon's orders in the Monumental Church, Richmond, Va., on Easter day, March 31, 1839, by Bishop Channing Moore, who advanced him to the priesthood, Easter day, April 19, 1840, in the same church. His ministry was spent (1839–43) at St. Paul's, Goochland County, and St. John's, Fluvanna County, Va.; 1843–44 he was rector of St. James's Church, Wilmington, N. C.; 1844–49 he was in charge of Grace and Wickliffe churches, in Clarke County, Va.; 1850–53 he officiated at Emmanuel Church, Loudon County, and at Trinity, Fauquier County, Va.; and from 1853 to October, 1858, he had charge of St. Stephen's and Trinity, Bedford County, Va. In 1858 he became rector of Emmanuel Church, Henrico County. He received the doctorate in divinity from William and Mary College, 1859, and from the University of the South, 1883. The University of Cambridge conferred upon him the LL.D., 1867.

He was consecrated bishop of Alabama in St. Paul's Church, Richmond, Va., March 6, 1862, by Bishops Meade, Elliott, and Johns.

At the close of the Civil War the bishop of Alabama resisted the order of the military authority of the United States requiring prayers for the *de facto* government. This action of the bishop, resulting in the temporary closing of the churches throughout the see and the restriction of episcopal ministrations to private houses or to churches without the limits of the military rule, established for all time to come, in this land at least, the principle that in spiritualities the Church's rule is supreme. The offensive action of the department commander was shortly reversed by higher authority.

Wilmer's episcopate has been able, vigorous, and abundant in results. He is a sound theologian, a delightful writer, a wise and impartial administrator, an earnest preacher, and a brave and fearless prelate. Beloved by his people, revered by his brethren, respected by all classes and conditions, a wise counselor, an impartial judge, a capable and clever man of affairs, his administration is historic, and will ever be held in remembrance.

WORKS.—1. "Recent Past from a Southern Standpoint" (a delightful volume of reminiscences: 1887); 2. "Guide-books for Young Churchmen" (1889); 3. Convention addresses, pastorals, sermons, etc.

RIGHT REVEREND THOMAS HUBBARD VAIL, D.D., LL.D.

Thomas Hubbard Vail.

BORN in Richmond, Va., but of New England parentage, Oct. 21, 1812, the first bishop of Kansas was baptized by the Rev. Dr. Buchanan at the Monumental Church of his native city.

On the death of his father the family returned to the North. Vail was graduated at Washington (now Trinity) College, 1831, and completed his studies for orders at the General Theological Seminary, 1835. He was made a deacon by Bishop Brownell, June 29, 1835, and was priested by Bishop Griswold, Jan. 6, 1837.

During his diaconate Vail officiated for a time as assistant to Dr. Wainwright, rector of St. Paul's, Boston, and while serving in this capacity organized All Saints' Church, Worcester, Mass. In 1837 he became rector of Christ Church, Cambridge, where he remained till his removal to Connecticut in 1839, to take charge of St. John's Church, Essex. In 1844 he became rector of Christ Church, Westerly, R. I., where he remained for fourteen years. In 1857 he became rector of St. Thomas's Church, Taunton, Mass., and in November, 1863, entered upon the rectorship of Trinity Church, Muscatine, Ia. He was a deputy from Rhode Island to the General Convention while at Westerly. He received the doctorate in divinity from Brown University, 1858. In 1875 the University of Kansas gave him the doctorate of laws.

He was consecrated bishop of Kansas in Trinity Church, Muscatine, Ia., Dec. 15, 1864, by Bishops Kemper, Whitehouse, H. W. Lee, and Bedell. He died at Bryn Mawr, Pa., Oct. 6, 1889, and was buried at Topeka, Kan. His administration was earnest and effective. He was a man of courtly manners, agreeable in his bearing, gracious to all men. He founded Bethany College, a school of the higher culture for girls, at Topeka, Kan., and by his devoted labors and earnestness in the pursuit of his high calling endeared himself to all hearts and secured universal respect.

WORKS.—1. "Plan and Outline, with Selection of Books, of a Public Library in Rhode Island" (1838); 2. "Hannah" (1839); 3. "The Comprehensive Church" (1841); 4. "Sermon at the Consecration of the Chapel of Griswold College" (1863); 5. Addresses, pastorals, reports, and occasional discourses.

A volume of charges has been published since his death. He edited Rev. H. F. Lyte's "Buds of Spring," with preface and memoir (1838).

RIGHT REVEREND ARTHUR CLEVELAND COXE, D.D., LL.D.

Arthur Cleveland Coxe.

THE coadjutor to the noble De Lancey, and his successor after a few months of assistantship, Arthur Cleveland Coxe, poet, preacher, author, prelate, was born at Mendham, N. J., May 10, 1818.

The son of a distinguished Presbyterian divine, and a descendant of a missionary in colonial days of the Society for the Propagation of the Gospel, Coxe, having become an earnest Churchman, passed, directly on graduating at the University of New York, in the class of 1838, to the General Theological Seminary, where he completed his studies for holy orders in 1841. He was made a deacon by Bishop B. T. Onderdonk in St. Paul's Chapel, New York, June 27, 1841, and was priested in St. John's, Hartford, Conn., Sept. 25, 1842, by Bishop Brownell.

His diaconate was mostly spent at St. Ann's, Morrisania, New York. Removing to Hartford, Conn., he became rector of St. John's Church, where he continued until 1854, when he entered upon the charge of Grace Church, Baltimore. In 1863 he removed to New York, and was rector of Calvary Church until his consecration. While in Baltimore he was elected bishop of Texas, which office he declined. He received the doctorate in divinity from St. James's College, Hagerstown, Md., in 1856, and from Trinity, Hartford, Conn., in 1868, and again from the University of Durham, England, in 1888. He received the doctorate of laws from Kenyon College, Gambier, O., in 1868.

Dr. Coxe was consecrated bishop coadjutor to the first bishop of Western New York in Trinity Church, Geneva, N. Y., Jan. 4, 1865, by Bishops De Lancey, Hopkins, McCoskry, H. Potter, Odenheimer, and J. C. Talbot. On April 5th of the same year Bishop De Lancey died, and Bishop Coxe became the diocesan of the see.

In 1872 the missions of the Church in Hayti were placed under the episcopal care of the bishop of Western New York. Late in the year, at no little personal sacrifice, he made a visitation of the island, consecrating the Church of the Holy Trinity, a memorial of Bishop George Burgess, ordaining six priests and five deacons, meeting the clergy of the mission in convocation, and administering confirmation to large numbers of candidates. Bishop Coxe retained the charge of the Haytian Church until the consecration of its own bishop, Dr. J. T. Holly, in 1874.

Bishop Coxe stands preëminent among the American bishops. In college and seminary days he produced many of his "Christian Ballads," which have won for him the hearts of Churchfolk all over the world. His first visit to England and the continent of Europe awoke the sympathy of English and American Churchmen in the efforts for reform in the Roman communion; while his "Impressions of England" is a loving tribute to the charms of the "old home" as recognized by all Americans with Churchly tastes. The Anglo-Continental Society, which has done so much to disseminate on the Continent a knowledge of Anglican catholicity, is largely an outgrowth of the publication in Oxford of his "Sympathies of the Continent." Ever prominent in his advocacy of the Church's home and foreign mission work, a determined opponent of all changes in the text of our English Bible, a fearless advocate of social reform and Christian purity, a liturgiologist, a critical patristic scholar, a polished writer, an eloquent preacher, with most winning manners and most agreeable in society, Coxe's quarter-century and more of the episcopate has been an epoch in the annals of his diocese. He is to-day a leader of religious thought, a molder of men, a lover and bishop of souls.

WORKS.—1. "Advent: A Mystery" (1837); 2. "Athwold" (three cantos, 1838); 3. "Christian Ballads" (1840; republished in England 1849, and again and again at home and abroad); 4. "Athanasion" (1840); 5. "Athanasion, and Other Poems" (1842); 6. "Hallowe'en" (privately printed 1842; published 1844); 7. "Saul: A Mystery" (1845); 8. "The Bible Rhyme" (1873); 9. "The Ladye Chace" (1877, improved and enlarged edition of "Athwold"); 10. "The Paschal" (1889; new edition 1893). The above are poems.

11. "Absolution and Confession" (1850); 12. "Sermons on Doctrine and Duty" (1855); 13. "Thoughts on the Services" (1859; enlarged edition 1860; republished in England; sixteen American editions); 14. "The Criterion" (1866; republished in England); 15. "Moral Reforms" (1869); 16. "Apollos; or, The Way of God" (1871; English edition 1874); 17. "L'Épiscopat de l'Occident" (Paris, 1874); 18. "Elements of Ecclesiology" (1874); 19. "Covenant Prayers" (1875); 20. "Institutes of Christian History" (Baldwin Lectures for 1886).

Of sermons the bishop has printed the following: 1. "The Household of Faith" (1846); 2. "Seventy Years Since" (1848); 3. "A City not Forsaken" (1849); 4. "The Priesthood and the People" (Oxford, 1851); 5. "The Faithful Witness" (1852); 6. "The New Dogma" (1855); 7. "Counsels of Unity" (1856); 8. "Truth and the Times" (1863); 9. "The Mocking of Ishmael" (1863); 10. "The Liturgy of Heaven" (1864); 11. "The Ministry" (1864); 12. "Restoration of Unity" (1865); 13. "A Father in Christ" (1865); 14. "Scriptural Bishoprics" (1866); 15. "Choice of a Bishop" (1868); 16. "Practical Wisdom" (1868); 17. "Death of Bishop Burgess" (1869); 18. "The Corporate Witness" (1874); 19. "The Anglican Cathedral" (Canada, 1875); 20. "The Russian War" (1877).

Translations and edited works: 1. Wilberforce's "Eucharistica" (1842); 2. "Sympathies of the Continent; or, Proposals for a New Reformation," by John Baptist von Hirscher, D.D. (Oxford, 1852); 3. Laborde on "The Immaculate Conception" (1855); 4. "Morals of Liguori" (1856); 5. Croswell's "Poems, with Biography" (1860); 6. Mrs. Sherwood's "Stories," with emendations (1860); 7. "The Churchman's Calendar" (annually, 1861–66); 8. Guettée's "Papacy" (1866); 9. Archbishop Leighton's "Moderate Episcopacy" (1868); 10. Bishop Burgess's "Poems, with Critical Review" (1869); 11. "The Ante-Nicene Fathers" (8 vols., 1884–87).

Pamphlets, lectures, etc.: 1. "Revivalism in the Church" (1843); 2. Tracts xiv., xv., xvi., of Parker's series (Oxford, 1850); 3. "Letter to the Bishop of Arras" (Oxford, 1856); 4. "Letter on Dr. Muhlenberg's Memorial" (1856); 5. "Apology for the English Bible" (1857); 6. "Mixed Societies" (1857); 7. "Memorial of Carey and Patterson" (1858); 8. "Fixed Principles" (1859); 9. Three tracts (1859); 10. "Address of Christian Unity Society" (1864); 11. "Letter to Father Nestor" (1865); 12. "Exposition of the General Convention of 1865" (1865); 13. "The Moravian Episcopate"; 14. "Signs of the Times" (1869); 15. "Letter to Pius IX." (1869); 16. "Lectures on Prophecy" (1871); 17. "Catholics and Roman Catholics" (1874); 18. Addresses, charges, etc.

RIGHT REVEREND CHARLES TODD QUINTARD, D.D., LL.D.

Charles Todd Quintard.

THE successor of the apostolic Otey in the episcopate of Tennessee was born at Stamford, Conn., Dec. 22, 1824.

He was graduated in medicine at the University of New York, receiving his M.D., 1846. In 1851 he was appointed professor of physiology and anatomy in the Medical College at Memphis, Tenn. Relinquishing his practice, he completed a course of study for orders, and was admitted to the diaconate in Calvary Church, Memphis, Jan. 1, 1855, by Bishop Otey, who priested him in the same church, Jan. 6, 1856. His first and only parish was the Church of the Advent, Nashville. During the Civil War he was a chaplain in the Confederate army, and by his devoted labors won the respect and regard of officers and men.

At the close of the war he was chosen to the vacant episcopate of Tennessee. His consecration took place in St. Luke's Church, Philadelphia, Oct. 11, 1865, during the session of the General Convention. His consecrators were Bishops Hopkins, Burgess, Atkinson, Bedell, Odenheimer, Stevens, and Coxe, together with the Most Rev. Francis Fulford, bishop of Montreal and metropolitan. Columbia conferred upon him the doctorate in divinity, 1866, and the following year he received, at the time of the Lambeth Conference, the degree of doctor of laws from Cambridge.

Quintard's administration has been marked by the revival and development of the Church in Tennessee. He will be held in everlasting memory as the second founder and father of the University of the South. The measures undertaken by him for the university began on the very day of his consecration. Not a vestige of buildings had escaped the desolations of war. Weaving together a rude, rustic cross, the bishop planted the symbol of our redemption where a noble theological hall now stands, and thereupon set about the plans he had adopted, which, after a little more than a quarter-century, attest the foresight, the judgment, the devotion of Sewanee's great-hearted founder and friend.

WORKS.—Prior to his ordination Quintard was a frequent contributor to the medical journals. In his active career as a bishop and a builder of churches and college halls he has published little, though at present engaged on an historical work. "A Plain Tract on Confirmation" and "Preparation for Confirmation," reprinted again and again, with addresses, etc., comprise the list of his printed works.

RIGHT REVEREND ROBERT HARPER CLARKSON, D.D., LL.D.

Robert Harper Clarkson.

THE first bishop of Nebraska was a grandson of the Rev. Joseph Clarkson, the first deacon upon whom White laid hands in ordination on his return from England as a bishop. He was born in Gettysburg, Pa., Nov. 19, 1826.

Graduating at Pennsylvania College, Gettysburg, 1844, he pursued his studies for orders at St. James's College, Hagerstown, Md., and was ordained to the diaconate in the college chapel, June 18, 1848, by Bishop Whittingham. Called to the charge of St. James's Church, Chicago, 1849, he was, on reaching the canonical age, advanced to the priesthood in the chapel of Jubilee College, by Bishop Philander Chase, Jan. 5, 1851. He remained in charge of St. James's Church for twenty years. During the most of this time he was a deputy to the General Convention from Illinois, and when elected to the missionary episcopate of Nebraska and Dakota was an assistant secretary of the House of Deputies. He received the doctorate in divinity from Racine College, 1857, and the doctorate of laws from the University of Nebraska, 1872.

His consecration took place in his parish church, Nov. 15, 1865. The consecrators were Bishops Hopkins, Kemper, McCoskry, H. W. Lee, Whipple, and Talbot. In 1868 the Church in Nebraska organized as a diocese and was received into union with the General Convention. Clarkson was chosen as the diocesan of the new see. He accepted the election, 1870, retaining the missionary jurisdiction of Dakota until late in 1883. He died March 10, 1884, and was buried beside the walls of the cathedral in Omaha.

Clarkson possessed every quality needed for a successful episcopate. Winning in his address, lovable in character, considerate of all men, conservative in his judgments, impartial, devoted to his duty, and not sparing himself, he was preëminently a man of God; and as a faithful priest, or as a bishop whose work was that of a pioneer, he was a builder on foundations he had himself laid, and was faithful to every trust, while his reward is above.

WORKS.—1. "Shall this House Lie Waste?" (1850); 2. "Consider the Years" (1859); 3. "What am I that I Should Withstand God?" (1865); 4. "Sketch of the Life of Bishop White" (1876); 5. "In Memoriam, W. B. Ogden," a paper read before the Chicago Historical Society (1877); 6. Missionary reports, etc.

RIGHT REVEREND GEORGE MAXWELL RANDALL, D.D.

George Maxwell Randall.

BORN in Warren, R. I., Nov. 23, 1810, and graduated at Brown University, in 1835, George Maxwell Randall pursued his theological studies in New York at the General Theological Seminary, completing his course in 1838.

He was ordered deacon in St. Mark's Church in his native town, July 17, 1838, by Bishop Griswold, who advanced him to the priesthood, Nov. 2, 1839. His first cure was the Church of the Ascension, Fall River, Mass. In 1844 he became rector of the Church of the Messiah, Boston, where he remained until elected to the missionary episcopate. He received his doctorate in divinity from his alma mater in 1856; was a deputy to the General Conventions, 1850–65; and was secretary of the House of Deputies, 1862–65.

He was consecrated missionary bishop of Colorado in Trinity Church, Boston, Dec. 28, 1865, by Bishops Hopkins, Bosworth Smith, Eastburn, Carlton Chase, Clark, and Vail, together with the bishop of Honolulu, Sandwich Islands, Dr. Thomas Nettleship Staley. Entering upon his work with the activity and enthusiasm which had characterized his entire ministerial career, Bishop Randall laid foundations, educational, parochial, and spiritual, on which he was not permitted to build. After nearly eight years of unremitting toil, he died in Denver, Colo., Sept. 28, 1873.

WORKS.—1. "Why I am a Churchman" (upward of 150,000 of this tract have been issued); 2. "Observations on Confirmation"; 3. Occasional discourses, episcopal addresses, missionary reports, pastorals, etc. Dr. Randall was editor of the "Christian Witness and Church Advocate," Boston, for many years.

RIGHT REVEREND JOHN BARRETT KERFOOT, D.D., LL.D.

John Barrett Kerfoot.

In 1865 the western portion of the diocese of Pennsylvania was set apart as a new see, and received its name from its chief city. The first bishop of the diocese of Pittsburg was born in Dublin, Ireland, March 1, 1816.

Brought to the United States at the age of three years, he grew up at Lancaster, Pa., and was graduated at Dr. Muhlenberg's institute at Flushing, L. I., known subsequently as St. Paul's College. He was admitted to the diaconate in St. George's Church, Flushing, March 1, 1837, and was priested March 1, 1840, in the same place, in each case by Bishop B. T. Onderdonk. He was the chaplain and an assistant professor of Latin and Greek at St. Paul's College, 1837–42. In the latter year he became the head of St. James's College, Hagerstown, Md. He occupied this position until 1864, when he accepted the presidency of Trinity College, Hartford, Conn. After two years' incumbency as the head of this institution, he was chosen bishop of Pittsburg. He received the doctorate in divinity from Columbia in 1850, and again from Trinity in 1865. He was made a doctor of laws by the University of Cambridge, England, at the Lambeth Conference of 1867.

His consecration took place in Trinity Church, Pittsburg, Jan. 25, 1866. His consecrators were Bishops Hopkins, McIlvaine, Whittingham, John Williams, J. C. Talbot, Coxe, and Clarkson. The bishop of Pennsylvania, Dr. Stevens, who had done so much to bring about the creation of the see and its successful organization, was prevented by sudden and extreme illness from participating in the consecration. Bishop Kerfoot was a man of strong intellect, wide scholarship, varied accomplishments, judicially impartial in his decisions, and laborious in the exercise of his vocation. He died at Myersville, Somerset County, Pa., July 10, 1881. His remains were interred at Homewood Cemetery, Pittsburg.

WORKS.—1. Inauguration address as president of Trinity College (1864); 2. Sermon at the consecration of Bishop Armitage (1866); 3. Semi-centennial sermon before the Board of Missions (1871); 4. Sermon preached at the consecration of Bishop Pinkney; 5. College and convocational sermons; 6. Convention addresses, pastorals, etc. Bishop Kerfoot contributed a lecture on "Inspiration" to the Philadelphia Lectures on the Evidences (1853–54). See "Life, with Selections from his Diaries and Correspondence," by Hall Harrison (2 vols., 1886).

RIGHT REVEREND CHANNING MOORE WILLIAMS, D.D.

Channing Moore Williams.

THE successor to the elder Boone as missionary bishop of the American Church in China, and the first bishop of Yedo, having jurisdiction in Japan, was a native of Virginia, and was born in Richmond, July 18, 1849.

He was graduated at William and Mary College, 1853, and two years later completed his course of study for orders at the Virginia Theological Seminary. His ordination to the diaconate by Bishop Meade took place in St. Paul's, Alexandria, July 1, 1855. In November of the same year he sailed for China. He received priest's orders from Bishop Boone in the Mission Chapel, Shanghai, Jan. 11, 1857. By request of the Foreign Committee he was transferred, shortly after his ordination to the priesthood, to Japan.

Chosen to succeed the excellent Boone (with the added care of Japan) by the Church in General Convention, October, 1865, he was consecrated in St. John's Chapel, New York, Oct. 3, 1866, by Bishops Hopkins, Alfred Lee, Johns, Payne, Horatio Potter, and Whipple. He received the degree of doctor of divinity from Columbia in 1867. The Church in General Convention in 1874 divided the see of Bishop Williams, assigning to him the oversight of Japan, and giving him the title of bishop of Yedo.

After long, faithful, self-denying, and successful service the bishop resigned his jurisdiction, in October, 1889, and after a brief interval of rest has resumed work in the field to which his life has been consecrated, under the episcopal oversight of his successor, Bishop McKim.

WORKS.—Missionary reports, translations of portions of the Scriptures and Book of Common Prayer, Manuals, and catechetical works, etc.

RIGHT REVEREND JOSEPH PÉRE BELL WILMER, D.D.

Joseph Pére Bell Wilmer.

BORN in Swedesborough, N. J., Feb. 11, 1812; graduated first at the University of Virginia, in 1831, and at Kenyon College, Gambier, O., in 1833; and completing his theological course at the Virginia Seminary the following year, Wilmer was ordained to the diaconate by Bishop Channing Moore, in St. Paul's, Alexandria, Va., July 10, 1834, and received priest's orders from the hands of the same bishop in St. Paul's Church, Petersburg, May, 1838.

His ministry was spent from 1834 to 1838 at St. Anne's, Albemarle, Va. For nearly a year he was the chaplain of the University of Virginia, at Charlottesville. In 1839 he became a chaplain in the United States army. In 1843 he resigned his military charge and accepted the cure of Hungar's parish, Northampton County, Va., after which he was for several years in charge of St. Paul's, Goochland County. In 1848 he accepted the rectorship of St. Mark's, Philadelphia, where he remained until the breaking out of the Civil War. Returning to Virginia, he remained on his estate until his election to the episcopate. In 1857 Union College conferred upon him the doctorate in divinity.

He was consecrated bishop of Louisiana in Christ Church, New Orleans, Nov. 7, 1866, by Bishops Hopkins, Green, R. H. Wilmer, and Quintard. He died suddenly in New Orleans, Dec. 2, 1878. His remains rest in Greenmount Cemetery, Baltimore, Md.

Bishop Wilmer was universally beloved. His episcopal ministrations were sought for and highly valued outside of the limits of his own branch of the Catholic Church of Christ. His soundness in the faith, his devotion to the work of the ministry, his varied talents and holy example, will ever be remembered, not alone in his see, but throughout the Church in the United States.

WORKS.—A few occasional discourses, episcopal addresses, pastoral letters.

RIGHT REVEREND GEORGE DAVID CUMMINS, D.D.

George David Cummins.

THE founder of what is popularly known as the "Cummins Schism" was born in Kent County, Del., Dec. 11, 1822.

He was graduated at Dickinson College, Carlisle, Pa., 1841. He received deacon's orders in St. Andrew's Church, Wilmington, Del., Oct. 26, 1845, from Bishop Alfred Lee, who advanced him to the priesthood in the same church, July 6, 1847. His ministry was spent at Christ Church, Norfolk, and St. James's, Richmond, Va.; Trinity, Washington, D. C.; St. Peter's, Baltimore; and Trinity, Chicago. He received the doctorate in divinity from Princeton, 1857.

He was consecrated assistant bishop of Kentucky in Christ Church, Louisville, Nov. 15, 1866, by Bishops Hopkins, Bosworth Smith, H. W. Lee, J. C. Talbot, Quintard, and Clarkson. In November, 1873, he communicated to the presiding bishop, his own diocesan, his resignation of his episcopal office and his withdrawal from the Church in the United States. In the following month he presided at the primary organization of what is commonly known as the Reformed Episcopal Church. He was formally deposed from his office and ministry as a bishop of the Church of God by the presiding bishop, June 24, 1874.

He died at Lutherville, Baltimore County, Md., June 20, 1876.

WORKS.—1. "Sketch of Life of Rev. William M. Jackson" (1856); 2. "Life of Mrs. Virginia Hale Hoffman, late of the P. E. Mission to Western Africa" (1859); 3. Occasional sermons; 4. Numerous publications respecting the organization, the objects, and the claims of the Reformed Episcopalians. See "Memoir" by his wife (1879).

RIGHT REVEREND WILLIAM EDMOND ARMITAGE, D.D.

William Edmond Armitage.

BORN in the city of New York, Sept. 6, 1830, and graduated at Columbia College, 1849, and at the General Theological Seminary, 1852, the coadjutor and successor of the apostolic Kemper in the see of Wisconsin received the diaconate in the Church of the Transfiguration, New York, June 27, 1852, from Bishop Carlton Chase, and was ordained priest in St. Mark's, Augusta, Me., Sept. 27, 1854, by Bishop George Burgess.

His first position was that of assistant minister at St. John's, Portsmouth, N. H., from which he was called to St. Mark's, Augusta, Me. Here he remained until called to the rectorship of St. John's, Detroit, which he held when elected to the episcopate. He received his doctorate in divinity from Columbia College in 1866.

He was consecrated coadjutor bishop of Wisconsin in St. John's, Detroit, Dec. 6, 1866, by Bishops Kemper, McCoskry, H. W. Lee, Whipple, J. C. Talbot, Coxe, Clarkson, Kerfoot, and Cummins, together with the bishop of Huron, Canada, Dr. Cronyn. On the death of Bishop Kemper he became the diocesan of Wisconsin.

He died in St. Luke's Hospital, New York, Dec. 7, 1873. His remains were interred in Detroit, Mich. He was a scholar, a polished writer, an earnest preacher, a wise administrator. His early death deprived the Church in the United States of the efficient services of a most promising and holy bishop.

WORKS.—Episcopal addresses and official papers. He edited "Hymns for Sunday-schools."

RIGHT REVEREND HENRY ADAMS NEELY, D.D.

Henry Adams Neely.

THE successor of the devout and gifted George Burgess in the frontier see of Maine was born in Fayetteville, Onondaga County, N. Y., May 14, 1830.

Following his graduation at Geneva College, 1849, he was appointed a tutor in his alma mater, which post he retained until 1852. He was made a deacon in Trinity Church, Geneva, N. Y., Dec. 19, 1852, by Bishop De Lancey, who priested him in Trinity, Utica, June 18, 1854. His ministry was spent at Calvary Church, Utica, 1853–55; Christ Church, Rochester, 1855–62; and as chaplain of Hobart College, 1862–64. In the autumn of 1864 he became an assistant minister of Trinity, New York, where he remained until his consecration. He received the doctorate in divinity from his alma mater, 1866.

He was consecrated bishop of Maine in Trinity Chapel, New York, Jan. 25, 1867, by Bishops Hopkins, John Williams, Horatio Potter, Odenheimer, Clarkson, and Randall. On his removal to his see he became rector of St. Luke's Church, Portland, which was made the cathedral of the diocese. Later a noble cathedral church was erected. This fine structure was consecrated St. Luke's day, Oct. 18, 1877. Bishop Neely has served for a number of years as chairman of the House of Bishops. He is an earnest and able worker, conservative in his views, a well-read and sound theologian, and a scholar of wide culture.

WORKS.—Occasional sermons, episcopal addresses, and other official papers.

RIGHT REVEREND DANIEL SYLVESTER TUTTLE, D.D.

Daniel Sylvester Tuttle.

BORN at Windham, Greene County, N. Y., Jan. 26, 1837, and graduated at Columbia in 1857, and at the General Theological Seminary, New York, in 1862, Tuttle was ordained a deacon in the Church of the Transfiguration, New York, June 29, 1862, by Bishop Horatio Potter, who advanced him to the priesthood in Zion Church, Morris, Otsego County, N. Y., July 19, 1863. His only charge was at Morris, first as an assistant minister, and then, on the decease of the rector, as incumbent of the cure. He received the doctorate in divinity from Columbia College, 1867, and from Sewanee, 1886.

When elected by the Church in General Convention to the missionary episcopate of Montana, Idaho, and Utah, Tuttle had not attained the canonical age for consecration. It was not until May 1, 1867, that he was set apart for his work. The service took place in Trinity Chapel, New York. The consecrators were Bishops Hopkins, Horatio Potter, Odenheimer, Randall, Kerfoot, and Neely.

After nearly twenty years of pioneer work, in which he was busied in laying foundations and in setting in order the Church in the vast territories committed to his care, Tuttle, whose "praise was in all the churches," was elected to the see of Missouri on the death of the lamented Robertson. He had refused prior offers of translation, but, after due consideration of the circumstances of this "call," he resigned the mission work intrusted to his care and entered upon the duties of the diocesan of Missouri, the third in succession from the missionary episcopate of the apostolic Kemper.

WORKS.—Missionary reports and papers, Convention addresses, pastorals, and official communications tc his mission and diocesan clergy.

RIGHT REVEREND JOHN FREEMAN YOUNG, D.D.

John Freeman Young.

THE successor of Rutledge, the first diocesan of the see of Florida, was born in Pittston, Kennebec County, Me., Oct. 30, 1820.

Educated at the Wesleyan Seminary at Readfield in his native State, and entering the Wesleyan University at Middletown, Conn., he became a convert to the Church, and, removing to Virginia, was graduated at the Theological Seminary at Alexandria in 1845. He was admitted to the diaconate by Bishop Henshaw in St. Michael's Church, Bristol, R. I., April 20, 1845, and was ordained priest by Bishop Stephen Elliott in St. John's Church, Tallahassee, Fla., Jan. 11, 1846. His ministry was spent in Florida, at St. John's, Jacksonville; in Texas, as a missionary in Brazoria County; in Mississippi at Livingston, Madison County; and in Louisiana at Napoleonville, Assumption Parish. After these Southern experiences he became an assistant minister of Trinity Church, New York, where he served until he was chosen to the episcopal office. He received the degree of doctor of divinity from Columbia College in 1865.

Young was the secretary of the primary Convention held in 1848 for the organization of the diocese of Texas. He was the secretary of the Russo-Greek Committee of the General Convention, and edited the papers issued by that committee in furtherance of the intercommunion of the Eastern, Anglican, and American Churches. In 1864 he visited Russia in the interest of this movement.

He was consecrated in Trinity Church, New York, July 25, 1867, by Bishops Hopkins, Payne, Gregg, Odenheimer, R. H. Wilmer, and Cummins. After a busy episcopate, in which the varied abilities of the bishop were called into abundant exercise, he died in New York, Nov. 15, 1885, and his remains were buried at Jacksonville, Fla.

WORKS.—1. "Devotional Manual for Candidates for Confirmation"; 2. "Hymns and Music for the Young" (2 vols.); 3. Occasional discourses, Convention addresses, pastorals, reports, etc.

RIGHT REVEREND JOHN WATRUS BECKWITH, D.D.

John Watrus Beckwith.

THE successor of the eloquent Elliott in the see of Georgia was born in Raleigh, N. C., Feb. 9, 1831, and was graduated at Trinity College, Hartford, 1852.

He received deacon's orders in St. James's, Wilmington, N. C., May 24, 1854, from Bishop Atkinson, who advanced him to the priesthood in Emmanuel Church, Warrenton, May 20, 1855. After service in his native State at Calvary Church, Wadesboro', Beckwith removed to Maryland, where he took charge of All-hallows' parish, Washington County. He continued in this charge until the breaking out of the Civil War, when he removed to Alabama, where he became rector of Trinity Church, Demopolis. At the return of peace he accepted the rectorship of Trinity Church, New Orleans, where he remained until his advancement to the episcopate. He received the doctorate in divinity from Trinity College, Hartford, and from the University of Georgia, 1868.

His consecration took place in St. John's Church, Savannah, April 2, 1868. His consecrators were Bishops Green, Atkinson, R. H. Wilmer, J. P. B. Wilmer, and Young. After an episcopate marked by material and spiritual prosperity and development he died at Atlanta, Ga., Nov. 23, 1890.

The second bishop of Georgia was eloquent, scholarly, devout. He was a leader of men, and both in his see and in the general councils of the Church he wielded a decided influence. As the founder of Church institutions, as a furtherer of the Church's advance, as a wise, conservative master builder, he was a model bishop of the church of God.

WORKS.—Episcopal addresses, Lenten charges, occasional Convention and controversial discourses. Bishop Beckwith contributed to "The History of the American Episcopal Church," by the bishop of Iowa, an interesting monograph on Bethesda College, founded near Savannah by George Whitefield.

RIGHT REVEREND FRANCIS McNEECE WHITTLE, D.D., LL.D.

Francis McNeece Whittle.

A NATIVE of the State over which he was in his maturity :
exercise spiritual jurisdiction, the fifth bishop of Virginia was boı
in Mecklenburg County, July 7, 1823, and was graduated at tl
Theological Seminary near Alexandria in 1847.

He was made a deacon in St. Paul's Church, Alexandria, Jul
16, 1847, and was advanced to the "higher degree" in St. John
Church, Charleston, Va., Oct. 8, 1848, by Bishop Meade. H
ministry was spent at Kanawha parish, Kanawha County; S
James's, Northam parish, Goochland County; and Grace Churcl
Berryville, Va. In 1857 he accepted the rectorship of St. Paul':
Louisville, Ky., where he remained until April, 1868. He receive
his doctorate in divinity from Kenyon, 1867, and his doctorate c
laws from William and Mary College, 1873.

May 17, 1867, he was elected coadjutor bishop of Virginia. Hi
consecration took place at St. Paul's, Alexandria, Va., April 30, 1868
His consecrators were Bishops Johns, Alfred Lee, and Bedell. Oı
the death of Bishop Johns, in 1876, he became the diocesan. Th
following year the western portion of the see was erected into a nev
diocese corresponding to the limits of the State of West Virginia
In 1893 the diocese of Southern Virginia was created out of th
remainder of the see, and Bishop Coadjutor Randolph became th
diocesan thereof.

Bishop Whittle's episcopate has been made noteworthy by a
remarkable development in material and spiritual matters. He ha:
witnessed the division of his see and its great growth in churches anc
communicants, and in the amount of its charitable contributions.

WORKS.—Episcopal addresses and occasional sermons.

RIGHT REVEREND WILLIAM CROSWELL DOANE, D.D., LL.D.

RIGHT REVEREND WILLIAM PINKNEY, D.D., LL.D.

Photo by W. C. Babcock, from painting by Miss Helen Frances Colburn.

RIGHT REVEREND WILLIAM HOBART HARE, D.D.

[redacted] [redacted]

RIGHT REVEREND BENJAMIN HENRY PADDOCK, D.D.

John Franklin Spalding.

THE successor of the devoted Randall in the missionary episcopate of Colorado and Wyoming was born at Belgrade, Me., Aug. 25, 1828.

He was graduated at Bowdoin College in the class of 1853, and at the General Theological Seminary in 1857. Returning to his native State for ordination, he was made a deacon in St. Stephen's, Portland, Me., July 8, 1857, and was priested in Christ Church, Gardiner, Me., July 14, 1858, by Bishop George Burgess. He served in the sacred ministry at St. James's, Old Town, Me., St. George's, Lee, Mass., Grace Church, Providence, R. I., as assistant; and in 1862 took charge of St. Paul's, Erie, Pa., where he continued in the rectorate till his election to the episcopate.

He was consecrated in his parish church at Erie, Dec. 31, 1873, by Bishops McCoskry, Bedell, J. C. Talbot, Coxe, and Kerfoot. His administration has been fruitful in all good works. Educational and charitable institutions have been founded and fostered; the missionary see has become a diocese; and the new see has itself been created by the setting off of Western Colorado as a missionary jurisdiction. The cathedral, and the College of St. John the Evangelist, with its various departments, at Denver, and the endowments secured and increased by the bishop's tireless energy and personal effort, make his episcopate noteworthy.

WORKS.—1. "A Manual for Mothers' Meetings"; 2. "The Church and its Apostolic Ministry" (1887); 3. "The Threefold Ministry of the Church of Christ"; 4. "The Pastoral Office"; 5. "The Best Mode of Working a Parish" (1888); 6. "Jesus Christ the Proof of Christianity" (1891); 7. Episcopal addresses, missionary reports and papers, etc.

RIGHT REVEREND EDWARD RANDOLPH WELLES, D.D.

RIGHT REVEREND JOHN HENRY DUCACHET WINGFIELD, D.D., LL.D.

John Henry Ducachet Wingfield.

A NATIVE of Portsmouth, Va., where he was born Sept. 24, 1833, and educated at first privately and then at St. Timothy's, Maryland, at which institution he was for two years an instructor, Wingfield was graduated at William and Mary College in 1853.

He pursued the vocation of a teacher until 1855, when he spent a year at the Theological Seminary of Virginia, and then resumed his professorial work as the head of the Ashley Institute in Little Rock, Ark. He was ordered deacon in Christ Church, Little Rock, Jan. 17, 1858, by Bishop Freeman, and was priested by Bishop Johns in the chapel of the Virginia Seminary, July 1, 1859.

After serving as a curate to the rector of Christ Church, Little Rock, he assisted his venerable father, the Rev. John H. Wingfield, in Trinity Church, Portsmouth, Va., and subsequently served in Maryland at Christ Church, Rock Spring, returning to Trinity, Portsmouth, 1866. He served at St. Paul's, Petersburg, Va., 1868, where, in 1871, he founded St. Paul's School for girls; and in 1874 became rector of Trinity Church, San Francisco, Cal. His doctorate in divinity was conferred on him in 1869, by the College of William and Mary. The same institution gave him the doctorate of laws in 1874, and St. Augustine College honored him with a D.C.L., 1888.

The missionary jurisdiction of Northern California having been created at the General Convention in 1874, Wingfield was chosen as the first bishop, and was consecrated in St. Paul's, Petersburg, Va., Dec. 2d of the same year, by Bishops Johns, Atkinson, Lay, Pinkney, and Lyman.

On removing to his missionary see he became president of the Missionary College of St. Augustine at Benicia. Later he assumed the headship of St. Mary's-of-the-Pacific, in Benicia, and also became rector of St. Paul's Church, Benicia. During a laborious and devoted administration Bishop Wingfield has declined four opportunities for translation: in 1879 the bishopric of Louisiana; in 1882 the assistant bishopric of Mississippi; and in 1886 and 1887 the see of Easton.

His administration, under many untoward circumstances impeding his work and with a tragic episode in which all hearts were won to him in sympathy and marked respect, has been earnest, acceptable, and successful. His eloquence, zeal, devotion, and unflagging energy commend the bishop and his work to all men.

WORKS.—1. "The Sacrament of Warriors"; 2. "Answers to the Charge of Uncharitableness"; 3. "The Churchman's Gratitude"; 4. Sermons, Pastorals, etc.

RIGHT REVEREND ALEXANDER CHARLES GARRETT, D.D., LL.D.

RIGHT REVEREND WILLIAM FORBES ADAMS, D.C.L.

RIGHT REVEREND THOMAS UNDERWOOD DUDLEY, D.D., LL.D., D.C.L.

Thomas Underwood Dudley.

THE successor of Benjamin Bosworth Smith in the see of Kentucky was born in Richmond, Va., Sept. 26, 1837.

He was graduated at the University of Virginia in 1858. After taking his M.A. degree he was professor of Latin and Greek at his alma mater, and during the Civil War was an officer in the army of the Confederate States. On determining to take holy orders he pursued the course of theological study at the Virginia Seminary, completing his work in 1867. On June 28th of the same year he was made a deacon by Bishop Johns in the chapel of the Theological Seminary, and received priest's orders in the same place, June 26, 1868, from Bishop Whittle. His ministry was spent at Harrisonburg, Va., and from 1869 to 1875 he was assistant minister and then rector of Christ Church, Baltimore. He received the doctorate in divinity from St. John's College, Annapolis, 1874, and later from the University of the South. The University of King's College, Windsor, N. S., made him a D.C.L., and Griswold College conferred upon him the degree of LL.D.

He was consecrated bishop coadjutor of Kentucky in his parish church in Baltimore, Jan. 27, 1875, by Bishops Bosworth Smith, Johns, Stevens, and Pinkney, together with the bishop of Huron, Dr. Helmuth. In 1884, on the death of Bishop B. B. Smith, he became the diocesan of Kentucky. He was made chancellor of the University of the South, 1893. His administration has been conservative and abounding in all good works. His sympathies and labors have been especially given to the interests of the colored people. He is a leader among men, a workman for Christ and His Church who needeth not to be ashamed.

WORKS.—1. "A Sunday-school Question Book on the Christian Year"; 2. "The Bohlen Lectures for 1868"; 3. "A Wise Discrimination, The Church's View" (1881); 4. "The Baldwin Lectures" (1891); 5. "Address on the Historic Christ" (1894); 6. "Reasons why I am a Churchman" (1894); 7. Occasional sermons, addresses, pastorals, etc.

RIGHT REVEREND JOHN SCARBOROUGH, D.D.

John Scarborough.

ON the north coast of England, in Yorkshire, stands a bold headland jutting out into the sea. Here still remain the ruins of a castle whose feudal lord took his name from the place. In the Saxon tongue "scar" means "rock," and "borough" a "stronghold." Thence came the name of the place and of the leading family there. The ancient keep was destroyed by Cromwell's men, but was rebuilt, and is again a partial ruin. The branch of the family to which the fourth bishop of New Jersey belongs lived near the town of the same name, on the Ouse River, and close to the North Sea. The bishop's father, however, held an appointment in the revenue service, and made his home in the north of Ireland, at Castlewellan, County Down, where the future bishop was born, April 25, 1831.

While yet a lad he crossed the ocean with two elder brothers. He was graduated at Trinity, Hartford, 1854. Three years later he completed his course at the General Theological Seminary, and was ordained to the diaconate in Trinity, New York, June 28, 1857, and priested in St. Paul's, Troy, N. Y., Aug. 14, 1858, by Bishop H. Potter. His first charge was the curacy of St. Paul's, Troy. In 1860 he became the first rector of the Church of the Holy Comforter, Poughkeepsie, N. Y. After seven years spent in this charge he became rector of Trinity, Pittsburg, where he remained until his elevation to the episcopate. His alma mater conferred upon him the doctorate in divinity in 1872. He was a deputy to the General Convention in 1871 and again in 1874.

His consecration took place in St. Mary's, Burlington, N. J., Feb. 2, 1875. His consecrators were Bishops H. Potter, Stevens, Kerfoot, Littlejohn, Doane, M. A. De Wolfe Howe, and Paddock. Bishop Scarborough's episcopate has witnessed the division of the original see of New Jersey and a marked advance in material and spiritual prosperity. Untiring in his devotion to every detail of his work, judicious and impartial in his administration, conservative, scholarly, and wielding a powerful influence, the fourth bishop of New Jersey is beloved by all classes and conditions of men, who recognize in him a man of God and a true-hearted bishop of souls.

WORKS.—Episcopal addresses, pastoral letters, occasional sermons, etc.

RIGHT REVEREND GEORGE DE NORMANDIE GILLESPIE, D.D.

RIGHT REVEREND WILLIAM EDWARD McLAREN, D.D., D.C.L.

RIGHT REVEREND WILLIAM STEVENS PERRY, D.D., LL.D., D.C.L.

Bishop Perry is an hereditary member of the Society of the Cincinnati and chaplain general of the order, and is a member of the various patriotic hereditary societies of the country. In 1887 he was unanimously elected by the Synod of the see bishop of Nova Scotia, which appointment he declined.

In his diocesan work the present Bishop of Iowa has seen a threefold increase of congregations of churches and of communicants. He has consecrated between fifty and sixty churches, and has ordained upward of one hundred to the ministry. He has reopened Griswold College in its several departments, academic, theological, and preparatory; has founded St. Katharine's Hall for girls, Kemper Hall for boys, and Lee Hall for training candidates for orders. Wolfe Hall, the collegiate department, is at the earliest possible moment to be affiliated with the State University, and thus renew and exceed the promise of its foundation. The Bishop has also founded St. Luke Hospital in the see city.

WORKS.—1. "Historical Sketch of the Church Missionary Association of the Eastern District of Massachusetts" (1859); 2. "Bishop Seabury and Bishop Provoost: An Historical Fragment" (1862); 3. "Documentary History of the Protestant Episcopal Church in South Carolina" (edited in conjunction with Hawks) (1862); 4. "The Connection of the Church of England with Early American Colonization" (1863); 5. "Bishop Seabury and the 'Episcopal Recorder'" (1863); 6. "A Century of Episcopacy in Portland: A Sketch of the History of the Episcopal Church in Portland, Me., from the Organization of St. Paul's, Falmouth, November 4, 1763, to the Present Time" (1863); 7. "Documentary History of the Protestant Episcopal Church in the United States of America," containing numerous unpublished documents concerning the Church in Connecticut (edited, in conjunction with Hawks, 1863–64); 8. "The Collects of the Church" (1864); 9. "A Memorial of the Rev. Thomas Mather Smith, D.D." (1866); 10. "Questions on the Life and Labors of the Great Apostle" (1869); 11. "Historical Collections of the American Colonial Church" (vol. i., Virginia, 1871; vol. ii., Pennsylvania, 1872; vol. iii., Massachusetts, 1873; vol. iv., Maryland, 1878; vol. v., Delaware, 1878); 12. "Life Lessons from the Book of Proverbs" (1872); 13. "Handbook of General Conventions of the Protestant Episcopal Church, giving History and Constitution, 1785–1874" (1874; later editions); 14. "Journals of the General Convention, 1785–1835" (3 vols., 8vo, 1874); 15. "A Sunday-school Experiment" (1874; later editions); 16. "Historical Notes and Documents Illustrating the Organization of the Protestant Episcopal Church in the United States of America" (1874); 17. "The Reunion Conference at Bonn" (1876); 18. "The American Cathedral" (1877); 19. "Some Summer Days Abroad" (1881); 20. "Historical Sketch of the Protestant Episcopal Church, 1784–1884" (1884); 21. "The Centenary of the Consecration of Bishop Seabury" (1884); 22. "History of the American Episcopal Church, 1587–1883" (2 vols., 1885); 23. "The Election of the First Bishop of Connecticut" (1885); 24. "Men and Measures of the Massachusetts Convention of 1785–89" (1885); 25. "Centenary of the Consecration of Bishop White" (1887); 26. "Centenary of the British Colonial Episcopate" (discourse delivered in St. Paul's Cathedral, London, and printed in London and in the United States, 1887); 27. "A Missionary Apostle: Centenary of the Consecration of Bishop Charles Inglis, of Nova Scotia" (delivered in Westminster Abbey, London, 1887); 28. "The Church's Centennial Thanksgiving" (1889); 29. "The General Ecclesiastical Constitution of the American Church" (Bohlen Lectures, 1890); 30. "Proofs of the Historic Episcopate: An Essay" (1891); 31. "Christian Character of George Washington" (address before New York Society of Sons of the Revolution, in St. Bartholomew's Church, Sunday, Feb. 22, 1891; several editions); 32. "The Influence of the Clergy in the War of the Revolution" (1891); 33. "Relations of the Clergy to their Vestries and Congregations: An Essay on Canon Law" (1892); 34. "Christ Church, Philadelphia, in the Revolution" (1892); 35. "The Christian Patriotism of our Fathers" (1892); 36. "Relations of the

RIGHT REVEREND CHARLES CLIFTON PENICK, D.D.

RIGHT REVEREND ALEXANDER BURGESS, D.D., LL.D.

RIGHT REVEREND GEORGE WILLIAM PETERKIN, D.D., LL.D.

RIGHT REVEREND GEORGE FRANKLIN SEYMOUR, D.D., LL.D.

RIGHT REVEREND SAMUEL SMITH HARRIS, D.D., LL.D.

Samuel Smith Harris.

THE successor to the see made vacant by the deposition of the aged and infirm McCoskry was born in Antauga County, Ga., Sept. 14, 1841.

He was graduated from the University of Alabama in 1859, and after a course of special study was admitted to the bar the following year. After several years of successful practice he became a candidate for holy orders, and was admitted to the diaconate in St. John's, Montgomery, Ala., Feb. 10, 1869, by Bishop R. H. Wilmer, who advanced him to the priesthood in the same church, June 30th of the same year. His successive charges were St. John's, Montgomery, Ala; Trinity, Columbus, Ga.; Trinity, New Orleans; and St. James's, Chicago, where he remained until his consecration.

He was a deputy to the General Convention of 1874 from Georgia, and in 1877 from Illinois. In December, 1878, he was unanimously elected on the first ballot to the episcopate of Quincy, which appointment he declined. He received his doctorate in divinity from William and Mary College in 1874, and was made a doctor of laws by the University of Alabama in 1879.

He was consecrated bishop of Michigan in St. Paul's, Detroit, Sept. 17, 1879, by Bishops R. H. Wilmer, J. C. Talbot, Clarkson, Welles, Gillespie, McLaren, Perry, and Burgess. After a prosperous episcopate, in which he showed his great intellectual abilities, his skill and impartiality as an administrator, his magnetic influence over men, and his oratorical and rhetorical powers, this devout bishop of souls died in London at the close of the third Lambeth Conference, Aug. 28, 1888. His remains were interred in Detroit.

WORKS.—1. "The Relation of Christianity to Civil Society" (Bohlen Lectures for 1882); 2. "Dignity of Man" (sermons, with memorial address by Bishop H. C. Potter, 1889); 3. "Thoughts on Life, Death, and Immortality" (selected from his unpublished writings by Charlotte W. Slocum, 1891); 4. Sermons, addresses, lectures, pastorals, etc.

RIGHT REVEREND THOMAS ALFRED STARKEY, D.D.

Thomas Alfred Starkey.

BORN in Philadelphia, and entering into active life as a civil engineer, the successor of Odenheimer as bishop of Northern New Jersey was ordered deacon in the Church of the Ascension, Philadelphia, Feb. 21, 1847, by Bishop A. Potter, who priested him in Trinity, Pottsville, Pa., May 21, 1848.

His ministry was spent in Schuylkill County, Pa., where he founded the Church of the Holy Apostles at St. Clair; in Troy, N. Y., as rector of Christ Church; in Albany, as rector of St. Paul's; in Cleveland, O., as rector of Trinity Church; in Washington, D. C., as rector of the Epiphany; and, after an interval of rest and recuperation from severe physical suffering, in Paterson, N. J., as rector of St. Paul's Church, in which position he remained until his consecration. He received the doctorate in divinity from Hobart College in 1864.

His consecration took place in Grace Church, Newark, Jan. 8, 1880. His consecrators were Bishops Clark, Vail, Littlejohn, M. A. De Wolfe Howe, Scarborough, and Seymour. Starkey's administration has been judicious, careful, and successful. He is a preacher of rare gifts, a thinker, and is deeply interested in all Church activities. He is sagacious, conservative, and devout. His influence is felt not alone at home, but abroad, where in the Lambeth Conference of 1888 he took a most useful and creditable part in making more sure and certain the relations between the mother Church of England and our own.

WORKS.—Convention addresses, reports and papers on Immigration, sermons, etc.

RIGHT REVEREND JOHN NICHOLAS GALLEHER, D.D.

John Nicholas Galleher.

BORN in Washington, Ky., Feb. 17, 1839, and educated at University of Virginia, Galleher made choice of the law for vocation, but, after taking a partial course in preparation for adn sion to the bar, turned his attention to the sacred ministry, and came a candidate for holy orders. After pursuing his studies at General Theological Seminary for a time, he was made a deacoı Christ Church, Louisville, June 17, 1868, by Bishop Cummins. was priested in Trinity Church, New Orleans, La., May 30, 18 by Bishop J. P. B. Wilmer. His successive cures were at Loı ville, Ky., as assistant in Christ Church; as rector of Trinity, N Orleans; at the Memorial Church in Baltimore; and at Zion Chur New York, where he remained until his election to the episcopa He received the doctorate in divinity from Columbia in 1875.

He was consecrated the third bishop of Louisiana in Trin Church, New Orleans, Feb. 5, 1880, by Bishops Green, R. H. W mer, Robertson, and Dudley. He died, after a successful and w administration of his see, in which his varied gifts and abilities w fully recognized and admired, in New Orleans, Dec. 7, 1891.

WORKS.—Episcopal addresses and sermons.

RIGHT REVEREND GEORGE KELLY DUNLOP, D.D.

George Kelly Dunlop.

A NATIVE of County Tyrone, Ireland, where he was born
10, 1830, and educated at the Royal College of Dungannon a
the Queen's University, Galway, where he was graduated in
taking the second classical scholarship, Dunlop emigrated t
United States in October, 1852.

After a course of private study in preparation for holy o
he was made a deacon in Palmyra, Mo., Dec. 3, 1854, by B
Hawks, who advanced him to priest's orders, Aug. 7, 1856.
ministry was spent in Missouri, at St. Charles; as rector of C
Church, Lexington; and at Grace Church, Kirkwood, where h
mained until chosen to the missionary episcopate of New M
and Arizona. During his rectorate at Lexington he was prof
of the Greek and Latin languages in a local college. In 185
declined a similar chair at Racine. In 1880 that institution
ferred upon him the degree of doctor of divinity.

He was consecrated in Christ Church, St. Louis, Nov. 21, 1
by Bishops Whipple, Robertson, Spalding, Perry, A. Burgess,
Seymour.

After a laborious episcopate in a field at once lacking in pro
and in opportunity for development, Bishop Dunlop died at
Cruces, N. M., March 12, 1888, and his remains were interred u
the altar of St. Paul's Church, Las Vegas. He was a godly
learned man, full of the Holy Ghost.

WORKS.—Missionary reports and appeals.

RIGHT REVEREND LEIGH RICHMOND BREWER, D.D.

Leigh Richmond Brewer.

BORN in Berkshire, Vt., Jan. 20, 1839, Brewer was grad from Hobart College in 1863, and from the General Theol Seminary in 1866.

He was admitted to the diaconate in the Church of the Annu tion, New York, July 1, 1866, by Bishop H. Potter. His adv ment to the priesthood took place in Christ Church, Oswego, June 16, 1867, by Bishop Coxe. After spending six years i charge of Grace Church, Carthage, N. Y., he became rect Trinity Church, Watertown, N. Y., in which position he conti until his election to the missionary episcopate of Montana. alma mater conferred upon him the doctorate in divinity in 1

He was consecrated in his parish church, Dec. 8, 1880, by Bis Huntington, Tuttle, Bissell, and B. H. Paddock. Bishop Bre episcopate has been full of labors and is not wanting in suc He brought to his work every intellectual and physical qualific for a sagacious and conservative administration. In a frontier j diction and amid a population difficult to reach and influen spiritual things, he has made a record of success of which the Ch has no reason to be ashamed. On the foundations he has lai is now witnessing the uprising of the fair and stately " City of G

WORKS.—Missionary reports, addresses, and appeals.

RIGHT REVEREND JOHN ADAMS PADDOCK, D.D.

John Adams Paddock.

THE son of a clergyman honored and remembered in his field of work, the brother of the godly and able bishop of Massachusetts, John Adams Paddock, missionary bishop of Washington Territory, and the first bishop of the see of Olympia, in the State of Washington, was born in Norwich, Conn., Jan. 19, 1825.

He was graduated at Trinity College in the class of 1845, and at the General Theological Seminary in 1849. He was ordered deacon in St. Peter's, Cheshire, Conn., July 22, 1849, by Bishop Brownell, who priested him in Christ Church, Stratford, April 30, 1850. He held but two pastoral charges. For five years and a half he served at the historic Christ Church, Stratford. In 1855 he became rector of St. Peter's, Brooklyn, N. Y., in which position he remained until raised to the episcopate. He was a member of the standing committee of Long Island from the time of the organization of the diocese until his consecration. His zeal for missions was shown by his faithful and long-continued service on the foreign committee of the Board of Missions. Trinity College conferred upon him his divinity doctorate in 1860.

He was consecrated missionary bishop of Washington Territory in his parish church in Brooklyn, Dec. 15, 1880, by Bishops Bosworth Smith, A. Lee, H. Potter, Stevens, Tuttle, B. H. Paddock, Scarborough, Penick, and Seymour. His missionary episcopate was marked by a phenomenal development in the material prosperity of the see, as well as by abundant spiritual gains. He founded the Annie C. Wright School for girls, a school for boys, a college, a hospital, and other Church and charitable institutions. He was a wise and active master-builder, and his work, now that he has passed away, will be had in everlasting remembrance. He died, after a long and painful illness, in Tacoma, Wash., March 4, 1894.

WORKS.—1. "History of Christ Church, Hartford, Conn."; 2. Tenth anniversary sermon at St. Peter's Church, Brooklyn; 3. Address before the House of Convocation, Trinity College, Hartford; 4. Occasional sermons, missionary reports and papers, episcopal addresses, pastorals, etc.

RIGHT REVEREND CORTLANDT WHITEHEAD, D.D.

Cortlandt Whitehead.

THE successor of the erudite and accomplished Kerfoot was in New York, Oct. 30, 1842.

Prepared for college at Phillips Academy, Andover, whe was graduated in 1859, he entered Yale the same year, and his A.B. in 1863. His theological course was taken at the I delphia Divinity School, where he was graduated in 1867. received deacon's orders in Trinity Church, Newark, N. J., Jun 1867, and was ordained priest in St. Mark's Chapel, Black H Colo., Aug. 8, 1868, by Bishop Randall. Devoting his early mir to the western mission field, he served for three years in Colo Returning to the East, he became rector of the Church o Nativity, South Bethlehem, Pa., which position he held unti election to the episcopate. He was one of the secretaries o Diocesan Convention of Central Pennsylvania, 1871–82, and v deputy to the General Convention from the same diocese in 1871 in 1880. He received his doctorate in divinity from Union in 1 from Hobart in 1887, and from St. Stephen's in 1890.

He was consecrated bishop of Pittsburg in Trinity Church, F burg, Jan. 25, 1882, by Bishops Stevens, Bedell, M. A. De W Howe, Scarborough, Peterkin, and the bishop of Huron, Ont., Helmuth.

Of distinguished Revolutionary and colonial ancestry, a gra writer, a scholar of the highest culture, a sound theologian, a servative Churchman, and a genial, impartial, great-hearted bi of souls, Whitehead's episcopate has been from the first spec blessed of God. He is beloved by all men, and the successes o past give promise of a brilliant future.

WORKS.—Sermons and addresses, missionary reports and papers.

RIGHT REVEREND HUGH MILLER THOMPSON, D.D., LL.D.

Hugh Miller Thompson.

THE successor to the apostolic Green, in Mississippi, was born in the county of Londonderry, Ireland, June 5, 1830.

His parents emigrated to the United States during his childhood, and he was fitted for college by private instructors at Cleveland, O. He studied for orders at Nashotah House, Wisconsin, and was admitted to the diaconate in Nashotah Chapel, June 6, 1852, by Bishop Kemper, who advanced him to the priesthood in St. John's Church, Portage, Wis., Aug. 31, 1856. His successive cures were Grace Church, Madison, Wis.; the Nativity, Maysville, Ky.; the missions at Portage and Baraboo, Wis.; St. John's, Elkhorn, Wis.; the Atonement, Milwaukee; St. Matthew's, Kenosha, Wis.; Grace, Galena, Ill.; St. James's, Chicago; Christ, New York; and Trinity, New Orleans. In 1860 he became professor of ecclesiastical history at Nashotah House, which position he held together with his rectorship in Kenosha. Here he founded Kemper Hall, a seminary for girls, still maintained with success. At the same time he became editor of the "American Churchman," which during the decade of its existence wielded a great influence. He was editor of the "Church Journal," New York (which had been consolidated with the "Gospel Messenger" of Syracuse, N. Y.), 1872–75. He received the doctorate in divinity from Hobart, 1863, and the doctorate of laws from the University of Mississippi.

He was consecrated bishop-coadjutor in his parish church, New Orleans, Feb. 24, 1883, by Bishops Green, R. H. Wilmer, Harris, and Galleher. In 1887, he became the Diocesan. His episcopate has been successful in the revival of a measure of the ante-bellum prosperity and in the fostering of new ventures. His rare ability and varied gifts, his powers as a metaphysician, a theologian, a scholar of wide attainments, and a reasoner, have been recognized at home and abroad. He is an impressive and original preacher, and a writer of taste and strength.

WORKS.—1. "Unity and its Restoration"; 2. "Sin and Penalty"; 3. "First Principles"; 4. "The Kingdom of God"; 5. "Absolution" (second edition, 1894); 6. "Is Romanism the Best Religion for the Republic?"; 7. "Copy: Essays from an Editor's Drawer" (1872, many editions); 8. "The World and the Logos" (Bedell Lectures, No. 3, 1886); 9. "The World and the Kingdom" (Bishop Paddock Lectures, 1888); 10. "The World and the Man" (Baldwin Lectures, 1890); 11. "The World and the Wrestlers: Personality and Responsibility" (Bohlen Lectures, 1895); 12. Sermons, addresses, lectures, pastorals, etc.

RIGHT REVEREND DAVID BUEL KNICKERBACKER, D.D.

David Buel Knickerbacker.

THE third incumbent of the see which, held jointly with Missouri by Kemper as a missionary jurisdiction, had numbered Upfold and Talbot as its diocesans, was born at Schaghticoke, N. Y., Feb. 24, 1833.

He was graduated at Trinity College, 1853, and at the General Theological Seminary, 1856. He received deacon's orders in Trinity Church, New York, June 29, 1856, from Bishop H. Potter, and was advanced to the priesthood in Gethsemane Church, Minneapolis, July 12, 1857, by Bishop Kemper. His sole rectorate was that of Gethsemane Church, in which he was priested, and from which he was called, after a quarter-century's work, to the office and administration of a bishop in the Church of God. He was a deputy to succcessive General Conventions, and a member of the standing committee of Minnesota, for more than twenty years. He was the founder of St. Barnabas's Hospital and of the Orphans' Home in Minneapolis, and was active in the development of the Church in and about Minneapolis, which during his rectorate grew from a village of five hundred souls into a city with nearly one hundred thousand inhabitants. Trinity College conferred upon him the doctorate in divinity in 1873.

He was consecrated bishop of Indiana in St. Mark's Church, Philadelphia, Oct. 14, 1883, by Bishops Coxe, Whipple, Robertson, Niles, Lyman, Scarborough, Gillespie, and Seymour, together with the Most Rev. Dr. Medley, bishop of Fredericton and metropolitan. Knickerbacker threw himself into the work of the diocese with the activity and earnestness which had marked his rectorate. He founded educational and charitable institutions, secured endowments, and gave himself in tireless labor to the work of the Church under his charge. Spared to see great results of his exertions, and winning the regard and love of all men, he died suddenly, at Indianapolis, Dec. 31, 1894, and the laments of all good men followed his body to its burial.

WORKS.—1. Parish reports and papers; 2. Episcopal addresses, pastorals, and sermons.

RIGHT REVEREND HENRY CODMAN POTTER, D.D., LL.D., D.C.L.

Henry Codman Potter.

THE son of the great bishop of Pennsylvania, and the coadjutor and successor of his venerable uncle, the fifth bishop of New York, Henry Codman Potter was born in Schenectady, N. Y., May 25, 1835.

Educated in the Episcopal Academy, Philadelphia, he entered upon a business career, which after a few months he abandoned for a course of preparation for holy orders. He was graduated at the Virginia Theological Seminary, 1857. He was admitted to the diaconate in St. Luke's Church, Philadelphia, May 27, 1857, by his father, Bishop Alonzo Potter. He received priest's orders in Trinity Church, Pittsburg, Oct., 15, 1858, from the bishop-coadjutor, Dr. Samuel Bowman. His successive pastorates were at Christ Church, Greensburg, Pa., 1857, 1858; St. John's, Troy, N. Y., 1859–66; Trinity, Boston, as assistant on the Greene Foundation; and 1866–68, rector of Grace Church, New York, in which position he remained until his election to the coadjutor episcopate. He was the secretary of the House of Bishops from 1865 to 1883. He refused the presidency of Kenyon in 1863, and the bishopric of Iowa in 1875. He received from Union College the degrees of A.M. in 1863, D.D. in 1865, and LL.D. in 1878. He has also the D.D. from Harvard and the University of Oxford, England, and an LL.D. from the University of Cambridge, England.

Dr. Potter was consecrated October 20, 1883, in his parish church in New York, by Bishops Bosworth Smith, J. Williams, Clark, Whipple, Stevens, Littlejohn, Doane, and Huntington. He became diocesan in 1887. He has specially signalized his episcopate by the establishment of the Cathedral of St. John the Divine, and the founding and furthering of institutions and Church charities of the widest possible influence for good. Indefatigable in labor, cultured, tolerant, and sagacious, the bishop's efforts have been fairly divided among all classes and conditions of men. Even the "slums" of the great city over which he has the spiritual rule have received his personal attention; and his residence for a time in "darkest" New York will be remembered even when his shining abilities and his abundant services to the Church and State have passed from mind.

WORKS.—1. "Thirty Years Reviewed"; 2. "Our Threefold Victory"; 3. "Young Men's Christian Associations and their Work"; 4. "The Church and her Children"; 5. "The Religion for To-day"; 6. "Sisterhoods and Deaconesses" (1871); 7. "The Gates of the East" (1876); 8. "Sermons of the City" (1881); 9. Charge on "The Offices of Wardens and Vestrymen"; 10. "Waymarks" (1891); 11. Addresses, etc.

RIGHT REVEREND ALFRED MAGILL RANDOLPH, D.D.

Alfred Magill Randolph.

THE bishop-coadjutor of his native State, and the first bishop of Southern Virginia, was born in Winchester, Frederick County, Va., Aug. 31, 1836, and was graduated from William and Mary College in 1855, and from the Theological Seminary of Virginia in 1858.

He was made a deacon by Bishop Meade in the seminary chapel, July 2, 1858, and was advanced to the priesthood, Nov. 18, 1860, in St. George's, Fredericksburg, by Bishop Johns. His first rectorate was at Fredericksburg, in St. George's Church. His second and only other charge was Emmanuel Church, Baltimore, of which he was rector when called to the episcopal office. He received the doctorate in divinity from his alma mater in 1875.

He was consecrated in his parish church in Baltimore, Oct. 21, 1883, by Bishops Alfred Lee, W. B. W. Howe, Dudley, Perry, Burgess, and Peterkin.

In 1894 the diocese of Virginia was divided, and Bishop Randolph chose the new see of Southern Virginia as his charge. Bishop Randolph's rectorates were notably successful in spiritual results and in material prosperity. In his episcopal work he has displayed the same energy, ability, and tolerant catholicity which marked his earlier ministry. In his conscientious and active following of the traditions of the original see of Virginia he has endeared himself to an attached and grateful people.

WORKS.—Episcopal addresses, pastorals, sermons, and tracts.

RIGHT REVEREND WILLIAM DAVID WALKER, D.D., LL.D., D.C.L.

William David Walker.

A NATIVE of New York City, where he was born June 29, 1839, Walker was graduated from Columbia College, 1859, and from the General Theological Seminary, 1862.

He was admitted to deacon's orders in the Church of the Transfiguration, New York, June 29, 1862, by Bishop Horatio Potter, who advanced him to the priesthood in Calvary Church, New York, June 29, 1863. His ministry was spent as an assistant at Calvary, having special oversight of the parish chapel, in which his fostering care developed a large congregation, with all the activities of an independent city parish. It was in his masterful management of this important charge that he displayed that ability as a man of affairs, that wise judgment, and that conservative Churchmanship which, added to his powers as a preacher and sermonizer, and his large-hearted sympathies for all classes, led the House of Bishops to nominate him for the missionary episcopate of North Dakota. He received his doctorate in divinity from Racine, 1884, and from the University of Oxford, 1894. In 1886 Griswold College gave him the LL.D., which he also received from Trinity College, Dublin, 1894. He is a D.C.L. of the University of King's College, Windsor, N. S.

He was consecrated in Calvary Church, New York, Dec. 20, 1883, by Bishops Clark, Coxe, Clarkson, Morris, Littlejohn, B. H. Paddock, J. A. Paddock, and H. C. Potter.

He has for a number of years served as one of the government commissioners to whom the charge of the Indians is committed. In his abundant and successful labors he makes use of the "cathedral car," by means of which he preaches and officiates in a hundred and more hamlets and villages to which the Word and the Sacraments can come in no other way. He is widely known and beloved at home and abroad. His devotion to the Indians within the limits of his see has resulted in the evangelization of numbers of the red men. His work, which abounds in requirements of self-denial, tedious and comfortless journeyings, and exposure to dangers seen and unseen, has endeared him to Churchmen everywhere; and his ingenious expedient for bringing the Church's ministrations to the scattered and isolated people of his charge has been adopted elsewhere.

WORKS.—Occasional sermons, missionary reports, etc.

RIGHT REVEREND ALFRED AUGUSTIN WATSON, D.D.

Alfred Augustin Watson.

IN 1883 the diocese of East Carolina was created out of the ern portion of the original see. The first bishop of the new dic was born in the city of New York, Aug. 21, 1818.

He was graduated at the University of New York in 1837. voting himself to the study of law, he was admitted in 1841 to tice in the Supreme Court of his native State. After a year's cessful effort he turned his attention to the sacred ministry, having taken a full course of study, he was admitted to the d nate in St. Ann's Church, Brooklyn, Nov. 3, 1844, by Bishop Onderdonk. He was priested by Bishop Ives in St. John's, Fay ville, N. C., May 25, 1845. The first fourteen years of his min were spent at Grace Church, Plymouth, and St. Luke's, Washin County, N. C. In 1858 he accepted the rectorship of Christ Ch Newbern, N. C. At the breaking out of the Civil War he came chaplain to the Second Regiment of the State troops. A close of the strife he accepted the position of assistant to Bi Atkinson, who was the rector of St. James's Church, Wilmin In 1864 he succeeded to the rectorship, and continued in this until elected to the episcopate. He received the doctorate in d ity from the University of North Carolina in 1868. He was a n ber of the standing committee of the diocese and a deputy t General Conventions for many years.

He was consecrated in his parish church at Wilmington, Apr 1884, by Bishops Green, Neely, W. B. W. Howe, Lyman, Seyn and Randolph. Bishop Watson is a well-read theologian, a sc of rare ability, probably the most accomplished and capable ca ist in the Church, and a man of the highest culture. He is at revered and beloved, and his administration has been attended a marked development of the spiritualities and temporalities o Church under his care.

WORKS.—Occasional sermons, episcopal addresses, essays, tracts, etc.

RIGHT REVEREND WILLIAM JONES BOONE, D.D.

William Jones Boone.

THE son of the first bishop of the American Church in China (a nephew of the first bishop of Georgia and a cousin of the first bishop of Western Texas; born at Shanghai, May 17, 1846, and, familiar from his earliest years with mission life and work) was chosen by the Church in the United States as the fourth bishop to China.

Sent to the United States for his education, he was graduated at Princeton in the class of 1865, and pursued his studies for orders at the Philadelphia and Virginia schools. He was admitted to deacon's orders in St. Paul's Church, Petersburg, Va., July 26, 1868, by Bishop Beckwith, and was ordained to the priesthood Oct. 28, 1870, in the Church of St. John the Evangelist, Hankow, China, by Bishop C. M. Williams.

While in this country Boone served as an assistant minister at Emmanuel Church, Athens, Ga., and as rector of St. James's, Eufala, Ala. Appointed to the mission at Wuchang, China, he remained at this post for ten years, after which he became the head and chaplain of the theological department of St. John's College. He was a member and for a time the president of the standing committee of the mission. Kenyon gave him the doctorate in divinity at the time of his consecration.

Chosen to succeed the scholarly Schereschewsky at a special meeting of the House of Bishops in April, 1884, he was consecrated in the English Cathedral of the Holy Trinity, Shanghai, Oct. 28, 1884, by Bishop C. M. Williams and the Rt. Rev. Dr. George Evans Moule and the Rt. Rev. Dr. Charles Perry Scott, of the English Church. After a brief episcopate Bishop Boone died at his post. He was faithful, self-denying, and devout. His life was consecrated to the missionary work, and his works follow him.

WORKS.—Missionary reports and papers, translations and pastorals.

RIGHT REVEREND NELSON SOMERVILLE RULISON, D.D.

Nelson Somerville Rulison.

BORN in Carthage, N. Y., April 24, 1842, Rulison received his education at the Gouverneur Academy of his native place, and at the General Theological Seminary, from which he was graduated in the class of 1866.

He was made a deacon in Grace Church, Utica, N. Y., May 27, 1866, by Bishop Coxe, and received the priesthood from Bishop Horatio Potter in the Church of the Annunciation, New York, Nov. 30, 1866. His ministry was spent at the Annunciation, New York, as assistant minister; at Zion Church, Morris, N. Y.; St. John's, Jersey City, N. J.; and St. Paul's, Cleveland, O. He was a deputy to the General Convention from the diocese of Ohio, and was a member of the standing committee. He received the doctorate in divinity from Kenyon in 1879.

He was consecrated bishop coadjutor of Central Pennsylvania in St. Paul's, Cleveland, O., Oct. 28, 1884, by Bishops Bedell, Stevens, M. A. De Wolfe Howe, Jaggar, McLaren, Harris, Whitehead, and Knickerbacker. On the death of Bishop Howe, July 31, 1895, Bishop Rulison became the diocesan in fact, although Bishop Howe had in 1889 practically withdrawn from the episcopal oversight of the diocese, and had made his coadjutor the ecclesiastical authority of the see. Bishop Rulison has been specially interested in the educational and missionary work of the see, and by his zeal and earnestness has achieved marked successes.

WORKS.—1. "History of St. Paul's Church, Cleveland, O."; 2. Baldwin Lectures, (1895); 3. Occasional sermons, episcopal addresses, and essays.

RIGHT REVEREND WILLIAM PARET, D.D., LL.D.

Geo Worthington

RIGHT REVEREND SAMUEL DAVID FERGUSON, D.D.

RIGHT REVEREND EDWIN GARDNER WEED, D.D.

RIGHT REVEREND MAHLON NORRIS GILBERT, D.D.

RIGHT REVEREND ELISHA SMITH THOMAS, D.D.

RIGHT REVEREND ETHELBERT TALBOT, D.D., LL.D.

RIGHT REVEREND JAMES STEPTOE JOHNSTON, D.D.

RIGHT REVEREND ABIEL LEONARD, D.D.

RIGHT REVEREND LEIGHTON COLEMAN, D.D., LL.D.

RIGHT REVEREND JOHN MILLS KENDRICK, D.D.

RIGHT REVEREND CYRUS FREDERICK KNIGHT, D.D., LL.D.

RIGHT REVEREND CHARLES CHAPMAN GRAFTON, D.D.

RIGHT REVEREND WILLIAM ANDREW LEONARD, D.D.

RIGHT REVEREND THOMAS FREDERICK DAVIES, D.D., LL.D.

RIGHT REVEREND ANSON ROGERS GRAVES, D.D., LL.D.

RIGHT REVEREND WILLIAM FORD NICHOLS, D.D.

E. R. Atwill

RIGHT REVEREND HENRY MELVILLE JACKSON, D.D.

RIGHT REVEREND DAVIS SESSUMS, D.D.

[redacted]

RIGHT REVEREND PHILLIPS BROOKS, D.D.

Oct. 14, 1891, by Bishops Williams, Clark, Whipple, Littlejohn, Doane, Niles, M. A. De Wolfe Howe, H. C. Potter, and Talbot. The administration of Bishop Brooks was but brief. He died, deeply lamented, Jan. 23, 1893.

There were those of his brethren who felt that he was not fitted for the routine work and the administrative labors of the episcopate. He was impatient of details; he disliked "functions"; he despised display. He was, besides, far from claiming to be an exact or widely read theologian. But when he had become the bishop of his native State—his beloved Massachusetts—he spared no pains to bring the ministrations of his high office to all men; and the brief episcopate of Phillips Brooks brought many thoughtful men into close relations with the Church who had long stood aloof, and who were drawn into the fold by the personal magnetism of this great man.

Phillips Brooks was a typical New Englander, proud of his ancestry, his birth-city, and his college. It was to Harvard that he felt that much of his developed intellectual powers were due; and as a student, an alumnus, a preacher, an overseer, the love of Harvard was a marked characteristic, giving him a power over the undergraduates and attaching to himself the regard and love of all the members, officers, and graduates of the university.

His fame as the "prince of preachers" had extended throughout the English-speaking world. His many great gifts were ever exercised in the service of man and to the glory of God. Crowds attended his ministrations in this country and abroad. His writings were read with avidity by all classes of men. His style manifested the tenderness and sympathy of a true poetic nature, the brilliancy of a rhetorician, the power of a close reasoner, and the full evidence of the love of God and of his fellow-men animating his soul. He was deeply interested in all humanitarian movements, and his successive charges were stepping-stones in his rapid advance to the position of a leader of Christian thought. His sudden death brought to an unlooked-for close the high hopes which had been formed of his future; but "he, being dead, yet speaketh" through his works and the abiding memories of his consecrated life.

WORKS.—1. "Our Mercies" (1863); 2. "Sermons" (1875); 3. "Lectures on Preaching" (1877); 4. "Influence of Jesus" (Bohlen Lectures, 1879); 5. "The Pulpit and Popular Skepticism" (1879); 6. "Alexander Hamilton Vinton: Memorial Sermon" (1881); 7. "Candle of the Lord, and Other Sermons" (1881); 8. "Sermons Preached in English Churches" (1883); 9. "Oldest School in America" (oration at celebration of the two hundred and fiftieth anniversary of the foundation of the Boston Latin School, 1885); 10. "Twenty Sermons" (1886); 11. "Tolerance" (1887); 12. "A Christmas Sermon" (1890); 13. "The Light of the World, and Other Sermons" (1890); 14. "The Spiritual Man, and Other Sermons" (1891); 15. "The Symmetry of Life" (reprinted from his second series of sermons, 1892); 16. "The Good Wine at the Feast's End" (sermon, 1893); 17. "The Living Christ, an Easter Sermon"; 18. "Baptism and Confirmation"; 19. "Sermons" (1893); 20. "Addresses" (with introduction by Julius H.

RIGHT REVEREND ISAAC LEA NICHOLSON, D.D.

RIGHT REVEREND CHARLES REUBEN HALE, D.D., LL.D.

RIGHT REVEREND GEORGE HERBERT KINSOLVING, D.D.

RIGHT REVEREND LEMUEL HENRY WELLS, D.D.

RIGHT REVEREND WILLIAM CRANE GRAY, D.D.

William Crane Gray.

THE first bishop of Southern Florida was born at Lambe N. J., Sept. 6, 1835.

While a lad of ten years his family removed to Tennessee, his education preparatory to his college course was pursued. uating at Kenyon in 1859, and taking his theological studies a ley Hall, Gambier, O., he was ordered deacon by Bishop O Christ Church, Nashville, June 26, 1859. The same bishop p him on Ascension day the following year, in St. Peter's, Col Tenn. After more than a year's missionary work, in 1860 came rector of St. James's, Bolivar, Tenn., where in twenty he built a new church and rectory, a Church school for girls, mission chapel for colored people. Accepting, after this lon successful rectorate, the charge of the Church of the Advent, ville, he remained as its rector until chosen to the episcopal In 1881 Kenyon conferred upon him the degree of D.D., and i the University of the South gave him the same honorary titl

He was consecrated Dec. 29, 1892, at the Church of the A Nashville, by Bishops Quintard, Dudley, Weed, Nelson, and His work as bishop has been singularly blessed. His labor in every section of his see, and new churches and Church act spring up in his pathway at every step.

WORKS.—Missionary reports, episcopal addresses, appeals, etc.

RIGHT REVEREND FRANCIS KEY BROOKE, D.D.

RIGHT REVEREND WILLIAM MORRIS BARKER, D.D.

RIGHT REVEREND JOHN McKIM, D.D.

RIGHT REVEREND FREDERICK ROGERS GRAVES, D.D.

Frederick Rogers Graves.

BORN of devoted Church parents at Auburn, N. Y., in 185[illegible] graduating from Hobart in 1878, and from the General [illegible] logical Seminary in 1881, Graves was made a deacon by B[illegible] Horatio Potter in St. Paul's Chapel, New York, June 12, 1881

He was priested in the Church of our Saviour, Hong[illegible] Shanghai, China, Oct. 28, 1882, by Bishop C. M. Williams. [illegible] whole ministry has been spent in China. After a short time [illegible] at St. John's College, Shanghai, he was appointed to Wuc[illegible] where with his native deacons and catechists he has labored fait[illegible] and well. He received the divinity doctorate from the Ge[illegible] Theological Seminary in 1893.

He was elected missionary bishop of Shanghai by the Chur[illegible] General Convention in 1892, the Ven. Samuel R. J. Hoyt, D.D., [illegible] deacon of Davenport, who had been for years in the foreign [illegible] having first been elected and declined. A number of the deputie[illegible] left for their homes when the testimonials of the missionary b[illegible] elect were received, leaving an insufficient number to confir[illegible] action of the upper house. At the special meeting in New [illegible] in March, 1893, at which McKim was chosen for Yedo, Grave[illegible] reëlected for Shanghai, and he was consecrated at the same [illegible] and place and by the same bishops as was Bishop McKim. H[illegible] in the midst of grievous trials and hindrances, accomplished [illegible] for the Master. He will yet do more, wisely and well, for the C[illegible] of God, to the service of which his life has been devoted.

WORKS.—Missionary reports and translations.

RIGHT REVEREND ELLISON CAPERS, D.D.

Ellison Capers.

THE coadjutor to the venerable William Bell White Howe i see of South Carolina is the son of an eminent bishop or s intendent of the Methodist communion. He was born in Ch ton, S. C., Oct. 14, 1837, and was graduated at the South Ca Military Academy in 1857.

Appointed assistant professor of mathematics in his alma m he resigned at the breaking out of the Civil War, 1861, servi the Confederate army till its close, and rising to the rank of briga general. Ordained to the diaconate, May 3, 1867, in St. L Church, Charleston, by Bishop W. B. W. Howe, he received pr orders, Sept. 13, 1868, in Trinity, Abbeville, from the same pr From 1867 to 1887 he was rector of Christ Church, Greenville, save a year's service at St. Paul's, Selma, Ala. From 1887 unt election to the episcopal office he was rector of Trinity Ch Columbia, S. C. He was secretary and treasurer of the dio board of missions, 1879–93, and was a deputy to the General vention, 1880, 1883, and 1886, declining the honor for the nex sessions. In 1888 he received the D.D. from South Carolina lege, and from the University of the South in 1893.

In 1893 he was elected bishop coadjutor of South Carolina was consecrated in his parish church at Columbia, July 20th o year, by Bishops Lyman, Watson, Weed, and Jackson. The supervision and administration of ecclesiastical affairs has al devolved upon him by the death of Bishop Howe, which occ Nov. 25, 1894. He is a man of commanding presence, l hearted, tolerant, and wise; and the see of South Carolina is happily filled.

WORKS.—Occasional sermons, episcopal addresses, pastorals, etc.

RIGHT REVEREND THOMAS FRANK GAILOR, D.D.

Thomas Frank Gailor.

THE bishop coadjutor chosen for the see of Tennessee ‹
request of the venerable and beloved Quintard for relief fr‹
excessive duties, is a native of Mississippi, where he was b
Jackson, Sept. 17, 1856.

He was graduated with the highest honors at Racine in
being the head of the College, the Edwards's Greek prizema
the Quintard medalist. He was Greek prizeman at the G
Theological Seminary, where he completed his preparati‹
orders, receiving in 1880 the graduating degree of S.T.B. H
ordered deacon May 15, 1879, and was priested the followin
both by Bishop Quintard. His whole ministry was spent i
nessee. He was rector of the Church of the Messiah, P
1879–82, when his connection with the University of the
began by his appointment to the chair of ecclesiastical histo
polity. In 1883 he became chaplain of the university, and i
vice-chancellor. His devotion to the interests of the educ
work at Sewanee constrained him to decline the wardens
Racine College, the rectorships of Trinity, Chicago, and T
New Orleans, and in 1891 the bishopric of Georgia. In 18
General Theological Seminary gave him the divinity degree,
was repeated from Columbia, Trinity, and the University
South.

He was unanimously elected bishop coadjutor of Tenne
the first ballot, in 1893, and was consecrated on the f‹
St. James, July 25th of that year, in the chapel of St. Aug
Sewanee, by Bishops Quintard, Dudley, Perry, Seymour, W
Johnston, Jackson, Nelson, Hale, and Kinsolving.

WORKS.—1. "Manual of Devotions" (six editions); 2. Sermon on "The U
Idea" (1887); 3. Sermon on "Apostolic Succession" (1890); 4. Sermon on "
Education" (1892); 5. Lectures before the New York Church Club (1886
6. Educational pamphlets, addresses, etc.

RIGHT REVEREND THOMAS FRANK GAILOR, D.D.

RIGHT REVEREND WILLIAM LAWRENCE, D.D.

RIGHT REVEREND JOSEPH BLOUNT CHESHIRE, JR., D.D.

Arthur Crawshay Alliston Hall.

THE successor of Bissell in the see of Vermont is a native of England, having been born at Binfield, Berkshire, April 12, 1847.

He was educated at Christ Church College, Oxford, taking his B.A. in 1869, and proceeding M.A., in course, in 1872. He was ordained deacon by the bishop of Oxford, December, 1870, and priest by the same prelate, Dec. 21, 1871, as a member of the Society of St. John the Evangelist, Cowley, Oxford. He was licensed preacher in the diocese of Oxford, 1870–73; came to the United States in 1873; was assistant minister of the Church of the Advent, Boston, 1874–82; was in charge of the Mission Church of St. John the Evangelist, Boston, 1883–91. He was naturalized and became a citizen of the United States while ministering in Boston. He was licensed preacher in the diocese of Oxford, 1892–93. He received an honorary D.D. from the University of Oxford, 1893. The same year he received the same degree from Trinity, Hartford, and from Bishop's College, Lennoxville, P. Q.

He was elected bishop of Vermont, Aug. 30, 1893, and was consecrated in St. Paul's Church, Burlington, Vt., on the festival of the Purification, Feb. 2, 1894, by Bishops Neely, Niles, Coleman, Grafton, and Lawrence, together with the Most Rev. Dr. Travers Lewis, archbishop of Ontario, Canada. He was released from all obligations to the Society of St. John the Evangelist prior to his consecration to the see.

Bishop Hall is a preacher of rare ability and eloquence. He is a well-read theologian, and a writer of taste and culture. He has in his brief episcopate won all hearts.

WORKS.—1. "Meditations on the Creed" (1876); 2. "Meditations on the Lord's Prayer" (1879); 3. "Confession and the Lambeth Conference" (1879); 4. "The Christian Law concerning Marriage and Divorce" (1881); 5. "Meditations on the Example of the Passion" (1882); 6. "Apostolical Succession" (1886); 7. "Concerning Christ and the Church: A Devotional Exposition of the Epistle to the Ephesians" (1886); 8. "Catholic not Protestant nor Roman Catholic" (1887); 9. "Exposition of the Gospel Canticles" (1887); 10. "Meditations on the Collects, for the Sundays and Holy Days" (1888); 11. "The Eucharistic Sacrifice and the Sacrifice of Masses" (1889); 12. "The Saintly Life: Notes for Meditation on the Epistle to the Philippians"; 13. "Reasonable Faith" (four sermons on: A Personal God, The Trinity, The Godhead of Christ, The Incarnation, 1889); 14. "The Inspiration of Holy Scripture" (1890); 15. "Self-discipline" (1890); 16. "The Words from and to the Cross" (1891); 17. "The Gospel Woes" (two volumes · (1) Holy Week and Good Friday Meditations; (2) Lenton sermons, 1891); 18. "The Virgin Mother: Retreat Addresses on the Life of the Blessed Virgin Mary" (1894); 19. "Reading the Bible," "Retreats," and other sermons, addresses, tracts, etc.

RIGHT REVEREND JOHN BROCKENBROUGH NEWTON, M.D.

[redacted]

John Brockenbrough Newton

THE son of distinguished parents and the representative Virginia families dating back to colonial days, John Brocken Newton was born in Westmoreland, Va., Feb. 7, 1839, and w cated at the Episcopal High School near Alexandria, in his State.

Determining upon the medical profession as his vocation, his M.D. at the Medical College of Virginia in 1860. Dur Civil War he was first an assistant and then a full surgeon Confederate forces, and served throughout the war. On the tion of hostilities he practised medicine for a time in Westm County. Abandoning his profession, he entered upon a co theological study, and was ordered deacon June 25, 1871, a vanced to the priesthood June 29th the following year, b Bishop Whittle. For nearly five years he was rector of Farnham parish, Essex County, Va.; for more than eight year of St. Luke's, Norfolk; and for nine years rector of the Monu Church, Richmond.

Elected bishop coadjutor of Virginia, Jan. 31, 1894, he w secrated in his parish church in Richmond, May 16th, by I Whittle, Dudley, Jackson, and Capers. Eloquent, able, and he has entered upon his life-work with enthusiasm and every p of success.

WORKS.—Occasional sermons and addresses.

RIGHT REVEREND JOHN HAZEN WHITE, D.D.

John Hazen White.

BORN in Cincinnati, O., March 10, 1849, of New England parentage, young White turned his attention, after a full course in the highest schools of the city, to business life.

Three years were thus occupied, when in 1869 he entered Kenyon College and was graduated in the class of 1872. Having determined upon the ministry as his life-work, he entered the Berkeley Divinity School at Middletown, Conn., graduating in 1875. He was ordered deacon, June 4, 1875, and was priested, May 28, 1876, both by Bishop Williams. His ministerial and other posts were as assistant at St. Andrew's, Meriden, Conn., 1875–77; vice-rector and instructor in Latin at St. Margaret's School, Waterbury, Conn., and curate at St. John's in that city, 1877–78; rector of Grace Church, Old Saybrook, Conn., 1878–81; rector of Christ Church, Joliet, Ill., 1881–86; rector of Christ Church, St. Paul, Minn., 1886–89; rector of St. John the Evangelist's, St. Paul, Minn., 1889–91; warden of Seabury Divinity School, Faribault, Minn., 1891 until his election to the episcopate. His D.D. was conferred by Kenyon and Seabury, 1895.

He was consecrated bishop of Indiana, May 1st, SS. Philip and James's day, 1895, in St. Paul's, Indianapolis, Ind., by Bishops Tuttle, McLaren, Leonard, Whitehead, Gilbert, Nicholson, and Hale.

Bishop White is scholarly, accomplished, earnest, and devout. He is well fitted to be a leader of men.

WORKS.—Sermons and addresses.

RIGHT REVEREND FRANK ROSEBROOK MILLSPAUGH, D.D.

RIGHT REVEREND PETER TRIMBLE ROWE, D.D.

Lewis William Burton

Joseph Horsfall Johnson.

BORN in Schenectady, N. Y., January 7, 1847, and educated at a private school in Albany and at Williams College, the first bishop of Los Angeles was graduated from the latter institution in 1870, and from the General Theological Seminary in 1873, being a classmate of Leonard, of Nevada and Utah, and of Talbot, of Wyoming and Idaho.

He was ordained deacon in the Church of the Transfiguration, New York, June 29, 1873, by Bishop Horatio Potter, who advanced him to the priesthood in the chapel of the House of Mercy, New York, June 29, 1874. His successive charges have been Holy Trinity Church, Highland, N. Y., 1873–79; Trinity Church, Bristol, R. I., 1879–81; St. Peter's Church, Westchester, N. Y., 1881–86; Christ Church, Detroit, Mich., 1886–96. He was a member of the Standing Committee of Michigan for five years, was dean of the Detroit Convocation, and represented his diocese in the General Convention of 1895. In 1892 he was elected missionary bishop of Northern Michigan, but declined. He received the degree of D.D. from Nashotah in 1894.

In 1895 the diocese of Los Angeles was formed from that of California, and on December 3d of that year Dr. Johnson was elected bishop. He was consecrated at Christ Church, Detroit, on St. Matthew's day, February 24, 1896, by Bishops Davies, Worthington, W. A. Leonard, Talbot, A. Leonard, Nicholson, and Gailor.

WORKS.—Sermons, addresses, etc.

RIGHT REVEREND HENRY YATES SATTERLEE, D.D.

Henry Yates Satterlee.

THE first bishop of Washington was born in New York City, January 11, 1843, a direct descendant from the Rev. William Satterlee, of Pembroke College, Oxford, and vicar of St. Ida's Ide, Devonshire, at the time of Charles I., whose son Benedict removed to America during the Commonwealth. He was graduated from Columbia College in 1863, and from the General Theological Seminary in 1866.

He was ordered deacon, November 21, 1865, in St. Paul's Church, Flatbush, Long Island, by Bishop Horatio Potter, who ordained him priest in St. Ann's Church, New York, January 11, 1867. He was assistant at Zion's Church, Wappinger's Falls, N. Y., from 1865 to 1875, his service dating from his seminary days, and he became rector of the parish in 1875. He succeeded Dr. Washburn in the rectorship of Calvary Church, New York, in 1882, remaining there until his elevation, at which time he was a member of the Standing Committee of his diocese. He declined the assistant bishopric of Ohio in 1888, and the Michigan see in 1889. Union College conferred upon him the D.D. degree in 1882, and Princeton the same honor in 1896. He received an LL.D. from Columbia in 1897.

Dr. Satterlee was elected bishop of the new diocese of Washington, December 4, 1895, and was consecrated in Calvary Church, New York, on the feast of the Annunciation, March 25, 1896, by Bishops Coxe, Huntington, Dudley, Scarborough, Penick, Whitehead, Potter, Rulison, Paret, Talbot, W. A. Leonard, Nelson, and Cheshire.

In his New York pastorate Dr. Satterlee successfully maintained an enormous burden of work, being especially helpful in his relations to the poor. Calvary Chapel, on the East Side, Galilee Mission, the men's lodging-house, coffee-houses, etc., are the result of his efficient energy, and about a thousand persons use these buildings daily. He has been a leader, also, in the Church Temperance Society.

A conservative Churchman, an earnest preacher, a wise administrator, an indefatigable worker, a courteous gentleman, and a loving bishop of souls, the diocese of the capital city has taken from its start the strong impress of its chief pastor.

WORKS.—(1) "Christ and His Church" (1878); (2) "Life Lessons from the Prayer-book" (1890); (3) "A Creedless Gospel and the Gospel Creed" (1895); (4) sermons, pastorals, etc.

RIGHT REVEREND HENRY YATES SATTERLEE, D.D.

RIGHT REVEREND GERSHOM MOTT WILLIAMS, D.D.

RIGHT REVEREND JAMES DOW MORRISON, D.D., LL.D.

James Dow Morrison.

THE first bishop of the missionary district of Duluth was born at Waddington, N. Y., October 16, 1844, and was graduated at McGill University, Montreal, in 1865, with first-class honors, winning the Logan gold medal for natural sciences. In 1868 he took his M.A. degree, in course.

He was ordered deacon in the diocese of Quebec in February, 1869, and ordained priest in the diocese of Montreal in February, 1870. He served as missionary at Hemmingford, Canada, from 1869 to 1871. He became rector of Christ Church, Herkimer, N. Y., in 1871, and was examining chaplain for the diocese of Albany, 1872–97. He was archdeacon of Ogdensburg, 1881–97, and a deputy to the General Convention since 1883. He received the doctorate in divinity from Union College in 1879, and an LL.D. in 1880 from his alma mater, from examinations.

He was elected missionary bishop of Duluth, October 21, 1896, and was consecrated on the feast of the Purification, February 2, 1897, in the Cathedral of All Saints, Albany, by Bishops Doane, Huntington, Scarborough, Starkey, Walker, Gilbert, Wells, Lawrence, Cheshire, and Hamilton, Lord Bishop of Niagara.

Bishop Morrison is a profound student, an authority on philology, a deep Hebraist, and a thorough Greek scholar. United to his intellectual gifts is that capacity for hard practical work which is essential to a successful episcopate in a new soil.

WORKS.—(1) Reconfirmation of Roman Converts (1895); (2) sermons, addresses, etc.

Chauncey B. Brewster

Chauncey Bunce Brewster.

CHAUNCEY BUNCE BREWSTER was born in Windham, Conn., September 5, 1848, the eldest son of the Rev. Joseph Brewster, and a lineal descendant of William Brewster, elder of the *Mayflower* company.

He was graduated at Yale in 1868, receiving his M.A. degree in 1871. Previous to that date he took a postgraduate course at his alma mater, and was a tutor of Latin and Greek there while pursuing his divinity course at Berkeley. He received deacon's orders from Bishop Williams at the Berkeley Divinity School ordination of 1872, and was priested at Meriden, Conn., by Bishop Williams, May 2, 1873. While deacon he served St. Andrew's parish, Meriden, Conn., and he became rector of Christ Church, Rye, N. Y., in 1873, remaining there until 1881, when he assumed charge of Christ Church, Detroit, Mich. In 1885 he was called to Grace Church, Baltimore, and in 1888 was transferred to Grace Church, Brooklyn. Among the notable results of his ministry at that church was the extinguishment of the mortgage on the parish property, held by Trinity Church, New York. He was a deputy to several General Conventions, and was president of the Standing Committee of the diocese of Long Island at the time of his election to the episcopate. He received the doctorate in divinity from Trinity College in 1897.

On May 5, 1897, the aged and infirm Williams appealed for a coadjutor, and on June 8th Dr. Brewster was elected. His consecration occurred October 28, 1897 (Sts. Simon and Jude's day), at Trinity Church, New Haven, and was an event of great interest to the diocese, the date marking the centenary of the consecration of Jarvis to the see of Connecticut. His consecrators were Bishops Littlejohn, Doane, Potter, Paret, Whitaker, Lawrence, Whitehead, Worthington, and Nichols, the beloved Williams being unable to attend.

Bishop Brewster gives every promise of furthering the distinguished work of his notable predecessors in the ancient see of Connecticut.

WORKS.—(1) "The Key of Life" (Good Friday addresses, 1895); (2) articles in reviews, sermons, etc.

RIGHT REVEREND WILLIAM NEILSON McVICKAR, D.D.

[illegible], F., [illegible]
[illegible], T., [illegible]
[illegible], M., [illegible]
[illegible], J. J., [illegible]
[illegible], T. F., [illegible]
British North America, [illegible] bishops, [illegible]; episcopate in, [illegible] sq.
Brondel, J. B., lx.
Brooklyn, R. C. diocese, lix.
Brownsville, R. C. vicariate, [illegible]
Bruté, S. G., lx[illegible]
Buffalo, R. C. diocese, lix.
Burgess, G., lxv.
Burke, M. F., lxi; lx[illegible]
Burke, T. M. A., lix.
Burlington, R. C. diocese, lix.
Burn, W. J., xliii.
Burns, F., liv.
Byrne, A., lxi.
Byrne, T. S., lxi.
Caillet, L. E., lviii.
Caledonia, Canadian diocese, xliii.
Calgary, Canadian diocese, xliii.
Canada, xliii. See British North America.
Cantwell, N., lviii.
Cardenas, L. P. y, lvii.
Carrell, G. A., lix.
Carroll, J., lv sq.
Chabrat, Guy I., lxi.
Chance, J. J., lxi.
Chandler, T. B., presents Memorial, xxxvi; named for bishop, xlv.
Chapelle, P. L., lviii.
Charleston, R. C. diocese, lix.
Chatard, F. S., lxiii.
Cheverus, John, lvii.
Cheyenne, R. C. diocese, lix.
Chicago, R. C. archdiocese, lvii.
Church, American, position in regard to episcopate, xxii sq.; separation from state, xxviii; creeds discussed in English papers, xxx. See White, Seabury, Act of Conformity, etc.
Church, Protestant Episcopal. See Church, American.
Church, "Protestant Episcopal, in the State of Pennsylvania," xxiii.
Cincinnati, R. C. archdiocese, lvii.
Claggett, N. J., unites Scottish and English lines, xlii.
Clancy, W., lix.
Clark, D. W., liv.
Clement, xx.
Cleveland, R. C. diocese, lix.
Coke, Thomas, made a Methodist superintendent, xlviii; urges Wesley to lay his hands on him, xlix sq.; letter to Seabury, l[illegible]; sermon at Baltimore Conference, [illegible]; letter to White, [illegible]; invited to Dr. West's, [illegible]; no decisive answer given to West's [illegible], too late for succession, [illegible]
Columbia, Canadian diocese, xliii.
Columbus, R. C. diocese, lx.
Concanen, R. L., lvii.
Concordia, R. C. diocese, lx.
Conn[illegible], J., lv[illegible]
Conroy, J. J., lviii.
Consecration, canonical, xx–xxi; Roman, variations from, xxi; of American bishops, act of Parliament, xxxvi.
Convention, Philadelphia, May 24, 1784, xxiii; 1785, xxvi; June, 1786, xxxii sq.
Convention, Wilmington, xxxvi sq.
Conwell, H., lviii.
Cooper, E., lii.
Corrigan, M. A., lviii; lxi.
Cosgrove, H., lix.
Cotter, J. B., lxiii.
Courtney, F., xliii.
Covington, R. C. diocese, lix.
Coxe, A. C., lxv; lxvi; lxviii.
Creeds, Nicene and Athanasian, position of English bishops on, xxxi; xxxvi sq.; final action, xxxviii.
Cretin, J., lviii.
Cronyn, B., xliii.
Curtis, A. A., lxiii.
Cushing, P., xlvi.
Dallas, R. C. diocese, lix.
Damas, xvii.
Davenport, R. C. diocese, lix.
David, J. B., lxi.
De Goesbriand, L., lix.
De Neckere, L., lvii.
Denver, R. C. diocese, lx.
Descent into hell, in creed, xxx–xxxi; position of archbishops, xxxvi sq.; final action, xxxviii.
Detroit, R. C. diocese, lx.
Diocese, unit of early Church, xix.
Domenec, M., lxii.
Drew, "Life of Dr. Coke," quoted, xlix sq.
Dubois, J., lviii.
Dubourg, W. V., lvii.
Dubuis, C. M., lx.
Dubuque, R. C. archdiocese, lvii.
Duché, J., xxx.
Dufal, P., lx.
Duggan, J., lvii.
Duluth, R. C. diocese, lx.
Dunn, A. H., xliii.
Dunne, E. J., lix.
Durier, A., lxi.
Dwenger, J., lx.
Eccleston, S., lvii.
Egan, M., lviii.
Elder, W. H., lvii; lxi.
Eleutherus, xx.
Emory, J., liv.
Emory, R., "The History of the Discipline," quoted, li.
England, J., lix.
English Conference, li.

Jerusalem, Church of, Episcopacy in, xiii–xv.
Jones, L., xliii.
Joos, E., lx.
Joyce, I. W., liv.
Juncker, H. D., lix.
Junger, A., lxi.
Junia, an apostle, xii.
Kain, J. J., lviii; lxiii.
Kansas City, Kan., R. C. diocese, lx.
Kansas City, Mo., R. C. diocese, lx.
Katzer, F. X., lvii; lx.
Keane, J. J., lxii; lxiii.
Kelly, J. B., xliii.
Kelly, P., lxii.
Kenrick, F. P., lvii; lviii.
Kenrick, P. R., lviii.
Kerfoot, J. B., lxviii.
Kingdon, H. T., xliii.
King's College, Windsor, N. S., xlvi.
Kingsley, C., liv.
Knox, A., condemns Wesley, li.
Krautbauer, F. X., lx.
La Crosse, R. C. diocese, lxi.
Lamy, J. B., lviii.
Lavialle, P. J., lxi.
Leaming, chosen as coadjutor to Seabury, xl.
Lee, A., lxv; lxvi; lxviii.
Lee, J., "History of the Methodists," quoted, xlvii *sq.*
Lefevre, P. P., lx.
Leray, F. X., lvii; lxi.
Lewis, J. T., xliii.
Lightfoot, Bishop, threefold ministry before middle of second century, xii; Episcopacy in Jerusalem, xii; "Epistle to the Galatians," quoted, xii; "Christian Ministry," quoted, xiii *sq.*; episcopate in first century, associated with St. John, xiii; Ignatian Epistles genuine, xv.
Lincoln, R. C. diocese, lxi.
Linus, xx.
Little Rock, R. C. diocese, lxi.
Littlejohn, A. N., lxviii.
Lookens, L., lix.
Loras, M., lvii.
Loughlin, J., lix.
Louisville, R. C. diocese, lxi.
Ludden, P. A., lxii.
Luers, J. H., lx.
Lullworth Castle, lv *sq.*
MacColl, Canon, "Christianity in Relation to Science and Morals," quoted, xix.
Machebeuf, J. P., lx.
Machray, R., xliii.
Mackenzie River, Canadian diocese, xliii.
Madison, sent to England for consecration, xlii.
Maes, C. P., lix.
Mallalieu, W. F., liv.
Manchester, R. C. diocese, lxi.
Manogue, P., lxii.
Mansfield, chosen as coadjutor to Seabury, xl.
Mansfield, Lord, views on Methodist ordination, l.
Manucy, D., lxi; lxxvi.
Marcus, first Gentile bishop of Jerusalem, xv.
Marechal, A., lvii.
Marquette, R. C. diocese, lxi.
Martin, A. M., lxi.
Marty, M., lxii.
Matthias, chosen by the Eleven, xi.
Matz, N. C., lx.
May, M., lix.
McCloskey, J., lviii.
McCloskey, W. G., lxi.
McColgan, E., lvii.
McDonnell, C. E., lix.
McFarland, F. P., lx.
McFaul, J. A., lxiii.
McGill, J., lxii.
McGovern, T., lx.
McKendree, W., liv.
McLean, J., xliii.
McMahon, L. S., lx.
McMullen, J., lix.
McNeirny, F., lix.
McQuaid, B. J., lxii.
Medley, J., xliii.
Meerschaert, T., lxiii.
Melcher, J., lx.
Merrill, S. M., liv.
Messmer, S. G., lx.
Methodist Episcopal Church superintendency, xlvi *sq.*; first services, *do.*; first American Conference, *do.*; preachers prohibited from administering sacraments, xlvii; Conference in Baltimore, 1780, denounces irregularities, *do.*; separation agreed to, lii; occupants of episcopal office, liv. See Wesley, Coke, etc.
Mexico, lxvii *sq.*
Michaud, J. S., lix.
Miége, J. B., lx.
Miles, R. P., lxi.
Milwaukee, R. C. archdiocese, lvii.
Mobile, R. C. diocese, lxi.
Monterey and Los Angeles, R. C. diocese, lxi.
Montgomery, G., lxi.
Montreal, Canadian diocese, xliii.
Moore, B., at Convocation in Middletown, xxv.
Moore, J., lxii.
Moore, "Life of Wesley," quoted, xlix.
Moosonee, Canadian diocese, xliii.
Mora, F., lxi.
Moreno, F. G. D., lviii.
Morris, T. A., liv.
Moss, Bishop, objection to omission of descent into hell in creed, xxxi.
Mountain, G. J., xliii.

Mountain, J., xliii.
Mrak, I., lxi.
Mullen, T., lx.
Murray, A., letter to White, xxx.
Narcissus, xv.
Nashville, R. C. diocese, lxi.
Natchez, R. C. diocese, lxi.
Natchitoches, R. C. diocese, lxi.
Neale, L., lvii.
Neras, J. C., lxii.
Nesqually, R. C. diocese, lxi.
Neumann, J. N., lviii.
New England, resentment against the South, xl.
New Orleans, R. C. archdiocese, lvii.
New Westminster, Canadian diocese, xliii.
New York, R. C. archdiocese, lvii.
Newark, R. C. diocese, lxi.
Newfoundland, Canadian diocese, xliii.
Newman, J. P., liv.
Newnham, J. A., xliii.
Niagara, Canadian diocese, xliii.
Ninde, W. X., liv.
North Carolina, R. C. vicariate, lxiii.
Northrop, H. P., lix; lxiii.
Nova Scotia, xliii. See British North America.
O'Connor, J., lxi.
O'Connor, M., lx; lxii.
O'Farrell, M. J., lxiii.
O'Gorman, J., lxi.
O'Hara, W., lxii.
O'Hare, James F., lxii.
O'Regan, A., lvii.
O'Reilly, B., lx.
O'Reilly, J., lxiii.
O'Reilly, P. T., lxii.
O'Sullivan, J., lxi.
Odin, J. M., lvii; lx.
Ogdensburg, R. C. diocese, lxi.
Omaha, R. C. diocese, lxi.
Onesimus, xv.
Ontario, Canadian diocese, xliii.
Oregon City, R. C. archdiocese, lviii.
Oxenden, A., xliii.
Parker, Samuel, xxiii; position respecting the episcopate, xxiv; at Convocation in Middletown, xxv; correspondence with White, xxvi; xxxi; in regard to Scotch succession, xxxiii; proposed for bishop, xl.
Peck, J. T., liv.
Pellicer, A. D., lxii.
Peoria, R. C. diocese, lxii.
Perché, N. J., lvii.
Perrin, W. W., xliii.
Perry, "Historical Notes and Documents," quoted, xxiii *sq.*
Persico, I., lxii.
Phelan, R., lxii.
Philadelphia, R. C. archdiocese, lviii.
Philadelphia Convention. See Convention, Philadelphia.
Pilmore, J., xxxiv; xlvi.
Pinkham, W. C., xlvii.
Pittsburg, R. C. diocese, lxii.
Pius I., xx.
Pius VI., lvi.
"Plan for Obtaining the Consecration of Bishops," etc., xxvi *sq.*
Polycarp, xv; bishop of Smyrna, xvi.
Porro, F., lvii.
Portier, M., lxi.
Portland, R. C. diocese, lxii.
Potter, H., lxv.
Potter, H. C., lxv.
"Proposed Book," xxx *sq.*
Providence, R. C. diocese, lxii.
Provoost, opposition to Seabury, xxxii *sq.*; xl *sq.*; bishop elect, xxxviii; sails for England, xxxix; consecration, *do.*; return to America, *do.*
Purcell, J. B., lvii.
Qu'Appelle, Canadian diocese, xliii.
Quarter, W., lvii.
Quebec, Canadian diocese, xliii.
Quigley, D. J., lix.
Quinlan, J., lxi.
Rademacher, J., lx; lxi.
Rankin, T., xlvi.
Rappe, A., lix.
Reeves, W. D., xliii.
Resé, F., lx.
Reynolds, I. A., lix.
Richmond, R. C. diocese, lxii.
Richter, H. J., lx.
Ridley, W., xliii.
Riley, H. C., lxviii.
Riordan, P. W., lviii.
Roberts, J. W., liv.
Roberts, R. R., liv.
Rochester, R. C. diocese, lxii.
Roman Catholic episcopate in U. S., lv *sq.*
Roman Catholic succession in America, lvii *sq.*
Roman Church, succession in, xx.
Rosati, J., lvii; lviii.
Rosecrans, S. H., lix.
Rupert's Land, Canadian province and diocese, xliii.
Ryan, J., lix.
Ryan, P. J., lviii.
Ryan, S. V., lix.
Sacramento, R. C. diocese, lxii.
St. Augustine, R. C. diocese, lxii.
St. Cloud, R. C. diocese, lxii.
St. Joseph, R. C. diocese, lxii.
St. Louis, R. C. archdiocese, lviii.
St. Palais, M. de, lxiii.
St. Paul, R. C. archdiocese, lviii.
Salpointe, J. B., lviii; lxiii.
Salt Lake, R. C. diocese, lxii.
San Antonio, R. C. diocese, lxii.
San Francisco, R. C. archdiocese, lviii.
Santa Fé, R. C. archdiocese, lviii.

Saskatchewan, Canadian diocese, xliii.
Savannah, R. C. diocese, lxii.
Scanlan, L., lxii.
Scannell, R., lix; lxii.
Schwebach, J., lxi.
Scott, L., liv.
Scranton, R. C. diocese, lxii.
Seabury, Samuel, consecrated, xxv; declines invitation to Philadelphia Convention, *do.*; offers services for ordination, *do.*; objects to radical Southern views, *do.*; congratulates White and Provoost on their consecration, xxxix; proposes meeting to bring about uniformity, *do.*; independence of position, xl; his self-abnegation, xli; presiding bishop, *do.*
Seghers, C. J., lviii.
Selkirk, Canadian diocese, xliii.
Serapion, xv.
Shanahan, J. F., lx.
Shanley, J., lx.
Sharp, Granville, appeals for needs of American Church, xxx.
Sillitoe, A. W., xliii.
Silvanus, probably an apostle, xii.
Simpson, M., liv.
Sioux Falls, R. C. diocese, lxii.
Smith, B. B., lxviii.
Smith, Robert, opposition to Scotch succession, xxxiv *sq.*
Smith, William, attempt to obtain episcopate in Maryland, xxxii; Wilmington Convention refuses to sign papers for consecration, xxxix; liii.
Smith, William (compiler of Institution Office), xxxiv.
Smyth, C., lvii.
Soter, xx.
Sotion, xvii.
Soule, J., liv.
South Carolina, radical view as to bishops, xxiv; xxxii.
Spalding, J. L., lxii.
Spalding, M. J., lvii; lxi.
Spencer, A. G., xliii.
Springfield, R. C. diocese, lxii.
Stanser, R., xliii.
Stevens, W. B., lxviii.
Stewart, C. J., xliii.
Strachan, J., xliii.
Strawbridge, R., xlvi; irregular proceedings, xlvii.
Sullivan, E., xliii.
Sweatman, A., xliii.
Symeon, succeeds James at Jerusalem, xv.
Syracuse, R. C. diocese, lxii.
Taylor, W., liv.
Telesephorus, xx.
Theophilus, xv.
Thoburn, J. M., liv.
Thomson, E., liv.
Tierny, M., lx.
Timon, J., lix.
Timothy and Titus, charge of churches committed to, xii.
Toebbe, A. M., lix.
Toronto, Canadian diocese, xliii.
Tosi, P., lxiii.
Trenton, R. C. diocese, lxiii.
Tuigg, J., lxii.
Tyler, W., lx.
Urlin, R. D., "John Wesley's Place in History," quoted, li.
Van De Velde, J. O., lvii; lxi.
Van De Vyver, A., lxii.
Vasey, appointed by Wesley for America, xlviii; l.
Verdaguer, P., lxiii.
Verot, A., lxii.
Vertin, J., lxi.
Victor, xx.
Vincennes, R. C. diocese, lxiii.
Vincent, J. H., liv.
Virginia, anticipatory canons circumscribing bishop, xxiv; growing indifference, xxxii; laxity in doctrine and morals, xlii.
Wadhams, E. P., lxi.
Walden, J. M., liv.
Wallingford Convocation, xl.
Walmesley, C., lv.
Warren, H. W., liv.
Watterson, J. A., lix.
Waugh, B., liv.
Weld, Thomas, lv *sq.*
Wesley, Charles, disapproves of his brother's ordinations, l *sq.*
Wesley, John, sends over Boardman and Pilmore, xlvi; erroneous ideas in regard to American Methodists, xlviii; holds that presbyters have right to ordain, *do.*; refuses to ordain, *do.*; finally consents, *do.*; ordains Whatcoat and Vasey, *do.*; action in regard to Coke, *do.*; rebukes Asbury for assuming title of bishop, xlix; defines his position, *do.*; his ordination of Whatcoat, etc., secret, l; accepts position forced on him by action of Coke, *do.*; weakness of mind, l *sq.*; deprecates separation from Church, li.
West, Rev. Dr., lii *sq.*
Whatcoat, appointed by Wesley for America, xlviii; li; liv.
Wheeling, R. C. diocese, lxiii.
Whelan, J., lxi.
Whelan, R. V., lxii; lxiii.
White, William, "The Case of the Episcopal Churches Considered," xxii *sq.*; "Fundamental Principles," xxiii; letter to Parker on succession, *do.*; statesmanship, xxv; wishes bishop to preside in councils, xxvi; "Memoirs of the Church," quoted, xxvii *sq.*; author of "Plan and Address," *do.*; view of effect of aban-

	PAGE
Jackson, H. M.	327
Jaggar, T. A.	239
Jarvis, A.	19
Johns, J.	87
Johnson, J. H.	375
Johnston, J. S.	303
Kemp, J.	35
Kemper, J.	71
Kendrick, J. M.	309
Kerfoot, J. B.	169
Kinsolving, G. H.	341
Kip, W. I.	127
Knickerbacker, D. B.	275
Knight, C. F.	313
Lawrence, W.	359
Lay, H. C.	147
Lee, A.	85
Lee, H. W.	131
Leonard, A.	305
Leonard, W. A.	317
Littlejohn, A. N.	195
Lyman, T. B.	219
Madison, J.	11
McCoskry, S. A.	73
McIlvaine, C. P.	65
McKim, J.	351
McLaren, W. E.	241
McVickar, W. N.	387
Meade, W.	51
Millspaugh, F. R.	369
Moore, B.	21
Moore, R. C.	33
Morris, B. W.	193
Morrison, J. D.	381
Neely, H. A.	179
Nelson, C. K.	337
Newton, J. B.	365
Nichols, W. F.	323
Nicholson, I. L.	335
Niles, W. W.	205
Odenheimer, W. H.	141
Onderdonk, B. T.	55
Onderdonk, H. U.	49
Otey, J. H.	60
Paddock, B. H.	217
Paddock, J. A.	260
Paret, W.	280
Parker, S.	23
Payne, J.	113
Penick, C. C.	240
Perry, W. S.	245
Peterkin, G. W.	255
Pierce, H. N.	203
Pinkney, W.	207
Polk, L.	75
Potter, A.	105
Potter, H.	133
Potter, H. C.	277
Provoost, S.	9
Quintard, C. T.	163
Randall, G. M.	167
Randolph, A. M.	279
Ravenscroft, J. S.	47
Robertson, C. F.	191
Rowe, P. T.	371
Rulison, N. S.	287
Rutledge, F. H.	115
Satterlee, H. Y.	377
Scarborough, J.	235
Schereschewsky, S. I. J.	251
Scott, T. F.	129
Seabury, S.	1
Sessums, D.	329
Seymour, G. F.	257
Smith, B. B.	63
Smith, R.	15
Southgate, H.	103
Spalding, J. F.	221
Starkey, T. A.	261
Stevens, W. B.	151
Stone, W. M.	53
Talbot, E.	301
Talbot, J. C.	149
Thomas, E. S.	299
Thompson, H. M.	273
Tuttle, D. S.	181
Upfold, G.	109
Vail, T. H.	157
Vincent, B.	311
Wainwright, J. M.	121
Walker, W. D.	281
Watson, A. A.	283
Weed, E. G.	295
Welles, E. R.	223
Wells, L. H.	343
Whipple, H. B.	145
Whitaker, O. W.	201
White, J. H.	367
White, W.	5
Whitehead, C.	271
Whitehouse, H. J.	119
Whittingham, W. R.	81
Whittle, F. M.	187
Williams, C. M.	171
Williams, G. M.	379
Williams, J.	117
Wilmer, J. P. B.	173
Wilmer, R. H.	155
Wingfield, J. H. D.	227
Worthington, G.	291
Young, J. F.	183

[To insu
be i
the
then

p. xlvi., lin
"I
p. 19, lin
p. 145 (n
"
W
lin
of
lin
re
Ju
In
mi
Co
na
U
re
of
p. 163, lin
lin
p. 181, lin
sp
O
p. 187, lin
p. 193, lin
se
lin
p. 201, lin
m
p. 213, lin
lin
h
p. 227, lin
U
m
p. 231, lir
"
p. 233, lir
U
ar
Cl
p. 253, lir
lir
p. 267, ac
p. 271, lir
p. 273, lir
A
re
w

Coxe, 1
Cli

Newto
Ric

Rulisc
hei

	Page
[illegible], H. M.	327
Jaggar, T. A.	239
Jarvis, A.	11
Johns, J.	45
Johnson, J. H.	375
Johnston, J. S.	323
Kemp, J.	35
Kemper, J.	71
Kendrick, J. M.	326
Kerfoot, J. B.	256
Kinsolving, G. H.	341
Kip, W. I.	127
Knickerbacker, D. B.	275
Knight, C. F.	333
Lawrence, W.	339
Lay, H. C.	247
Lee, A.	85
Lee, H. W.	131
Leonard, A.	305
Leonard, W. A.	317
Littlejohn, A. N.	195
Lyman, T. B.	215
Madison, J.	11
McCoskry, S. A.	73
McIlvaine, C. P.	65
McKim, J.	351
McLaren, W. E.	241
McVickar, W. N.	357
Meade, W.	51
Millspaugh, F. R.	360
Moore, B.	21
Moore, R. C.	33
Morris, B. W.	193
Morrison, J. D.	381
Neely, H. A.	170
Nelson, C. K.	337
Newton, J. B.	365
Nichols, W. F.	323
Nicholson, I. L.	335
Niles, W. W.	205
Odenheimer, W. H.	141
Onderdonk, B. T.	55
Onderdonk, H. U.	49
Otey, J. H.	69
Paddock, B. H.	217
Paddock, J. A.	269
Paret, W.	289
Parker, S.	23
Payne, J.	113
Penick, C. C.	249
Perry, W. S.	245
Peterkin, G. W.	255
Pierce, H. N.	203
Pinkney, W.	207
Polk, L.	75
Potter, A.	105
Potter, H.	133
Potter, H. C.	277
Provoost, S.	3
Quintard, C. T.	193
Randall, G. M.	197
Randolph, A. M.	279
Ravenscroft, J. S.	47
Robertson, C. F.	141
Rowe, P. T.	371
Rulison, N. S.	257
Rutledge, F. H.	115
Satterlee, H. Y.	377
Scarborough, J.	235
Schereschewsky, S. I. J.	251
Scott, T. F.	129
Seabury, S.	1
Sessums, D.	329
Seymour, G. F.	257
Smith, B. B.	63
Smith, R.	15
Southgate, H.	103
Spalding, J. F.	221
Starkey, T. A.	261
Stevens, W. B.	151
Stone, W. M.	53
Talbot, E.	301
Talbot, J. C.	149
Thomas, E. S.	299
Thompson, H. M.	273
Tuttle, D. S.	181
Upfold, G.	109
Vail, T. H.	157
Vincent, B.	311
Wainwright, J. M.	121
Walker, W. D.	281
Watson, A. A.	283
Weed, E. G.	295
Welles, E. R.	223
Wells, L. H.	343
Whipple, H. B.	145
Whitaker, O. W.	201
White, J. H.	367
White, W.	5
Whitehead, C.	271
Whitehouse, H. J.	119
Whittingham, W. R.	81
Whittle, F. M.	187
Williams, C. M.	171
Williams, G. M.	379
Williams, J.	117
Wilmer, J. P. B.	173
Wilmer, R. H.	155
Wingfield, J. H. D.	227
Worthington, G.	291
Young, J. F.	183

CPSIA information can be obtained at www.ICGtesting.com
234568LV00003B/18/P

9 781141 979967